D0149459

Culturematic

How
Reality TV
John Cheever
a Pie Lab
Julia Child
Fantasy Football
Burning Man
the Ford Fiesta Movement
Rube Goldberg
NFL Films
Wordle
Two and a Half Men
a 10,000-Year Symphony
and ROFLCon Memes
Will Help You Create and
Execute Breakthrough Ideas

Culturematic

GRANT McCRACKEN

HARVARD BUSINESS REVIEW PRESS • Boston, Massachusetts

Library of Congress Cataloging-in-Publication Data

McCracken, Grant David, 1951-
    Culturematic : how reality TV, John Cheever, a Pie Lab, Julia Child, fantasy
football, Burning man, the Ford Fiesta movement, Rube Goldberg, NFL films,
Wordle, Two and a half men, a 10,000-year symphony, and ROFLcon memes will
help you create and execute breakthrough ideas / [Grant McCracken].
        p. cm.
    ISBN 978-1-4221-4329-2 (alk. paper) *4861 4928   05/12*
    1. Management—Social aspects. 2. Popular culture—Economic aspects.
3. Technological innovations. 4. Creative thinking. 5. New products.
6. Diffusion of innovations. I. Title.
    HD30.19.M34 2012
    658.4—dc23

                                                            2011046401

For my mother and father

Contents

All life is an experiment.

The more experiments

you make, the better.

—Ralph Waldo Emerson

Introduction

It's the oddities that get your attention.

Item: Andy Samberg makes his own sketches for *Saturday Night Live.*

"Interesting," I think to myself. "This could be something."

Item: Gatorade replays a football game from 1993.

Really interesting. Nobody outside the Delaware River region cared about this game in the first place. Why replay it?

Item: People handing out pie in Greensboro, Alabama. To change this city, they have decided on pie.

"Pie!" I say to myself. "Really!"

I am sitting in my kitchen in Rowayton, Connecticut. I am monitoring American culture as if listening to shipping lanes on a shortwave radio. I've got the giant headphones on. I'm trying to dial out the noise and dial in a signal. What I'm getting is oddities.

As an anthropologist who studies American culture and business, I recognize some of what I hear out there. I have an idea of what marketers are doing, how capital markets work, the theater of politics, the logic of fashion, the economics of television. I get most of these. And, of course, I *like* having my preconceptions confirmed. But it's the things I don't understand that are useful. These send a message. These say, "Your models are broken."

In fact, the world is busting through my anthropological models as if they were made of balsa wood and tissue paper. The problem, of course, is change, the sheer propulsive force of change. What once took a century now takes a decade. What once took a decade can now happen in a year. The world sprints into the future. Models waddle. Always too little. Always too late.

Lately, the puzzles have been accumulating. Recall the Honda ad from a couple of years ago. It turns the pieces of an Accord into a Rube Goldberg machine. A cog hits a bolt . . . which hits a tire . . . which hits a muffler. It's a weird way to sell a car. Most ads give us the car as a perfect act of engineering, not a rickety, random chain of cause and effect. And then I start to see Goldberg machines all over the place. At the moment, there are seventy-six hundred of them on YouTube. Wait, what?

Laboratories without scientists? This is really weird. The new laboratory is everywhere, in subcultures like Steampunk, institutions like Harvard's Artscience Lab, commercial enterprises like IDEO, the Syyn Labs in Los Angeles, the Culture Lab in Mumbai, Le Laboratoire in Paris, the FreedomLab in Amsterdam, the Ars Electronica Futurelab in Austria, Gary Hamel's management lab, and the Pie Lab of Project M.[1] Weird. There are no beakers, test tubes, or lab coats, no chemists, pathologists, or technicians. No scientists. No science. Just labs. Go figure.

I came upon an oddity while interviewing Bud Caddell. He has a genius for making culture. (He managed to break into a TV show with nothing more than a Twitter account.) I wanted to see how he did it. Caddell is a planner and strategist by profession, but it didn't seem to me he was using planning or strategy to make culture. "It's like you're poking the world with a stick!" I finally said to him, my confusion and frustration showing. Very odd indeed.

I look at my cross-eyed cat and say, "So, Zsa Zsa, what idea would help me explain Andy Samberg, the Gatorade campaign, using pie for social good, science-free laboratories, Rube Goldberg machines, and the method of Bud Caddell?" She blinks at me sweetly and as usual gives not a word of advice. Apparently, it's for her to know and me to find out.

Eventually, I found an idea that helps explain these oddities. I call it Culturematic. A Culturematic is a little machine for making culture. It is designed to do three things: test the world, discover meaning, and unleash value. A Culturematic is what Caddell used to "break into" *Mad Men*. Posing as "Bud Melman," he starting tweeting as if from the *Mad Men* mailroom. Suddenly, the *Mad Men* story had a new character. *Mad Men* got a little more collaborative. TV got a little more participatory. Our culture changed. Caddell became an early Internet celebrity. Out of a cultural innovation that was cheap and easy came a torrent of value . . . for him and for us.

What Andy Samberg does for *Saturday Night Live* (*SNL*) is another good example. Samberg's "Digital Shorts" appear most weeks: "Dick in a Box" with Justin Timberlake, "Shy Ronnie" with Rihanna, "Jizz in My Pants" with Molly Sims. These came from a tiny production company called The Lonely Island, consisting of Samberg and two of his high school friends, Jorma Taccone and Akiva Schaffer.

The Lonely Island turns out to be a brilliant Culturematic. It's good at testing the world, discovering meaning, and unleashing value. Traditionally, the *SNL* show runner, Lorne Michaels, expects a new comedian like Samberg to become part of the cast at 30 Rockefeller Plaza. Even the likes of Bill Murray and Tina Fey were obliged to sign on. But Samberg was allowed to stay aloof. Why? It was to give *SNL* a little spaceship that could go places and do things out of the range of the *SNL* players. At 30 Rock, no one invests so much as a second in something that might not work. Because the clock is ticking. But The Lonely Island can try stuff until something works. Here, failure is acceptable, because, as Michaels puts it, it's the guys, not the cast, who "take the risk."[2]

The rewards are huge. Samberg, Taccone, and Schaffer got freedom. While the rest of the team fought for oxygen at 30 Rock, The Lonely Island folks got to investigate new comedic territory. They took the "digital short" to new levels. This was something we hadn't quite seen before, the music video meets sketch comedy meets frank disclosure meets celebrity appearance meets social commentary. And they used this short to go places *SNL* had never gone before, partnering with celebrities instead of merely jamming them into the skit. Michaels's rewards were greater still. Digital shorts revived *SNL* with digital and social media. "Jizz in My Pants" has been viewed more than 100 million times. Each viewing is an ad for *SNL* and its advertisers. This is a great torrent of value.

We are all Lorne Michaels now. Every organization needs a Culturematic like The Lonely Island. The senior manager navigates an increasingly inscrutable world. It is really useful to have a landing party standing by, a team who can search for navigable space and habitable worlds. Managers can wait for the future to happen to them. Or they can use Culturematics to examine their options. Culturematics are a new management tool.

A Culturematic can take the form of The Lonely Island. Or it can be a fictional character that lives on Twitter, a pie giveaway in

Alabama, or a meeting in the desert like Burning Man. In each case, we see three defining properties: test the world, create meaning, unleash value.

It's still a little vague, isn't it? Some of you are saying, "I'm not exactly sure what he means." Me neither. I am still working it out. The idea will get clearer as you read the rest of the book. (Wait until you hear about the three guys who created fantasy football.) The fact is that this little book about Culturematics is itself a Culturematic. It's an effort to provoke you, create meaning, and, well, yes, unleash value. This is how Culturematics work. They think things out as they go. There was a single clear question in all of this. Could I take all the oddities and find their center? Could I find the grammar, the algorithm from which they spring? And, no, I don't have it exactly right. And that's where you come in. Please make this idea better.

More pressingly, I hope you will investigate Culturematics by making some. Chapters 5 and 6 have lots of how-to advice. Create your own laboratory. Run your own experiments. Try stuff out. Keep a log. Learn from your mistakes. Keep on firing probes into the world. And phone home. If we can get this Culturematic thing right, we will have discovered one of the engines of cultural innovation.

I have a series of objectives. The first is to catch up with Boing Boing, the Web site that reports on the latest in science, technology, and gadgets. The technical side of innovation is exploding. *Make Magazine* flourishes. The attendance at Maker Faire doubles each year. Mark Frauenfelder, founder of Boing Boing, published *Made by Hand*. Matthew Crawford gave us a book called *Shop Class as Soulcraft*. Do-it-yourself enthusiasm is everywhere in the world of the tinkerer, the mechanically adroit, the digitally adept.[3]

The cultural side of innovation is less impressive. Some of the thousands of videos and updates uploaded to the Internet are good, but some are naive, artless, or jejune. Honestly, how many more kitten videos and LOL cats must we watch? Some cultural content is underdeveloped and anti-evolutionary. I'm hoping this book will encourage cultural creators as Boing Boing does the technically minded. DIY tech has taken off. DIY culture is just getting started.

Second, it is time to make innovation a little more practical and a lot less fashionable. In the old days, by which I mean eight years ago, we were still calling it *invention*. We weren't being creative; we were being clever. And we weren't thinking outside the box; we were simply solving problems. And then invention went all Hollywood. Now it was glamor and gurus. People started to posture about how *inspired* they were. The process became precious and self-worshipping.[4] A Culturematic approach asks us to return to something a little more practical and a lot more curious. I wanted to call the book *Ingenuity Makes a Comeback*. The publisher didn't like it. And Zsa Zsa just looked at me.

Third, we need to save innovation from mechanization. Once *Business Week* announced the "innovation economy," the corporation decided to "get serious." And that can be a scary thing. We tried to manage innovation in a way it had never been managed before. We tried to domesticate it. And that meant turning innovation into a system. And that meant the tyranny of close management. Designers, ethnographers, marketers, creatives of every kind were brought to heel, bound into the hierarchies and processes of the traditional corporation. The trouble is, new ideas don't like to be managed. They don't respect passport control. They come and go as they please. This makes close scrutiny a bad idea. The corporation has to learn to leave the creative alone. (Perhaps it's time to start wearing buttons to work: "Creativity. It's what you pay us for."[5])

Fourth, I wanted to document the dazzling activity going on out there. And I learned soon enough that you can't capture everything. You can only suggest some of the range, depth, and diversity of our new ingenuity. (Don't be surprised if I have missed your favorite Culturematic. And please come to Culturematic.com and describe it.) Our era is Elizabethan or Victorian. It flourishes with new ideas. Compared with the couch potato of the 1950s, we are all mad scientists. One of my inspirations was *The Whole Earth Catalog*, a book so fascinating I actually once took it into the bath with me. (I needed a bath and I didn't want to stop reading.) *The Whole Earth Catalog* gave me a glimpse of a world I wanted to live in. It changed my life. My own book can't hope to achieve that greatness. (But if you take it into the bath, let me know. That would be a good sign.)

Fifth, a new model of business creativity is called for. Clients have always turned to the agency for out-of-the-box thinking. But these days, they also need foundational work, an entirely new voice, for instance, or an unprecedented approach. This takes more than clever people in a room bouncing ideas off one another. In a Culturematic future, creatives will also run their own Culturematic investigations and experiments. The client will have to change as well, giving these creatives more time and more budget. We are no longer asking these creatives to work with known materials, the present periodical table. We are asking them to find the fundamental changes taking place in our culture and the opportunities these open up. And this will require new room for error and experiment. We need a line in the budget that reads "5 percent for Culturematics."[6]

Sixth, we have an opportunity to address a crisis brewing in the world of marketing. Agencies are beginning to doubt the efficacy of firing yet another ad into the world, especially one directed at a consumer target on behalf of big, immobile brand. Everyone, the marketer and the consumer, now finds this a little tedious. What we all want is a more genuine creativity. We want brands that are works in progress, engagements in and of the world. Brands need to be about *becoming*, not about *being*. They need to be great, sprawling experiments, driving half forms at full speed. "Keep it simple" branding is dead. Brands made up of Culturematics— brands that *are* Culturematics—what a glorious thing this would be! The brand would become a space station, launching and landing probes in constant succession.

Seventh, we can make ourselves useful to the world of the start-up. If the gods are kind, start-ups will find their capital, consumers, markets, and payday. In the meantime, there's a problem. Start-ups are inclined to put all their eggs in one basket, all their bets on a single idea. And this is wrong. If nothing else, it's an evolutionary error. What we want instead is a Culturematic cluster, a bundle of experiments, investigating the world in a variety of ways, defined with enough intellectual generosity that several outcomes—some of them quite different—are possible. Are there venture capitalists out there who understand the Culturematic proposition? Are there people looking to fund ingenuity bundles instead of this-one-idea-take-it-or-leave-it? I hope this book will encourage a new approach.

Eighth, I am hoping that some Culturematics will sustain their inventors. The people who invented fantasy football created a new professional sport, but they didn't see what their little Culturematic was going to do in the world. The torrent of value escaped them. Twitter cofounder Biz Stone, on the other hand, was the beneficiary of Twitter's success. In a perfect world, each of us would create a Culturematic that would fund a lifetime of invention and a great succession of Culturematics.

And now the moment comes. Time to build your own lab. Refit a garage, find a coffee shop with a particularly good view of the street, or set aside a corner of your desktop. Furnish it with workstations, video cameras, mockups, and data streams. Create experimental zones. And away you go. I am not saying you must have a Siamese cat available for emergency consultations. Some people have had good luck with Labradors. Feline or canine, some kind of advice is called for.

Time to build your first what-if. Get in touch with everyone with your name in the United States, and treat them as a record of what your life might have been. Imitate Bud Caddell, and take on a new identity on Twitter. (You could be the twin brother of *NCIS*'s Jethro Gibbs, for instance, the one who knows what Jethro is really thinking. Or give us a running commentary on Nurse Jackie from the point of view of a patient on *Nurse Jackie*.) Play Lorne Michaels. Create your own Lonely Island team, a group of smart people who use Culturematics in search of the blue oceans your organization needs. Create a Culturematic conference in the manner of an Evelyn Rodriguez (chapter 3). Do a two-part Culturematic, like the one created for Old Spice by the W+K agency, that begins with old media and follows up with a new media campaign (chapter 3). Create new subtitles for a film clip (chapter 7). Create a Dan Harmon lab for the collaborative creativity (chapter 3). Plan a restaurant that will do for American cuisine in the twenty-first century what Alice Waters's restaurant Chez Panisse did in the twentieth century. Or find another example in these pages. This book is your handbook, your Culturematic manual.

So go on. Start experimenting. Fire some Culturematics into the future. Provoke the world. Make a discovery. Make a fortune. Build a community of Culturematic-makers. And keep us posted. (At Culturematic.com, we have operators standing by.)

1 Welcome to Culturematics

Want to be a cultural innovator? Culturematic is our app for that. Culturematics are little, manageable, vivid, thought-provoking, and actual. They are cheap, cheerful, and multiple. We fire them into the world to see what phones home. A Culturematic is a probe of the possible. It's a way to investigate the future. Welcome to a new face of American ingenuity. Let's begin with the most elementary form. This Culturematic has three steps.

Step One: Test the World

Think of a way to provoke the world. This will often start with "What if I . . . " Here are a few examples. What if I . . .

> . . . ate all my meals at McDonald's for a month?

> . . . swam across my neighborhood using local swimming pools?

> . . . invented a professional sports league?

> . . . e-mailed from the *Mad Men* mailroom?

. . . went searching for myself in Italy, India, and Indonesia?

. . . put seven people in a house in Brooklyn and turned on the cameras?

. . . made my own content for *Saturday Night Live*?

. . . drove my car until it ran out of gas?

. . . prepared every recipe from a Julia Child cookbook in a year?

Good what-ifs are easy to spot. They make us tilt our heads and go "hmm." They speak to us because they go against the grain of expectation. They flirt with paradox. They provoke our curiosity. E-mailing from a fictional mailroom? What? Drive our cars until we run out of gas? Huh? Inventing a sports league? Dude!

That moment when we tilt our heads—that's the moment we can climb out of culture and into innovation. We are on the verge of making something new. As the phrase has it, we are "onto something." And, no, we can't quite say what. That's what it is to be on the verge of the new. We are not really sure. This may be a false positive, a bum lead. We have to launch lots of Culturematics to find the ones that work. It is impossible to say ahead of time. (If we could tell ahead of time, then we would not be on the verge of the new.) The only thing we can do is keep at it. Play out the what-if and see where it goes.

Step Two: Discover Culture

The successful Culturematics will phone home. They will play out. They will discover meaning. They will produce culture. Andy Samberg and The Lonely Island created new comedic ground for

Saturday Night Live and our culture. Bud Caddell helped make a TV show collaborative and participatory. When Elizabeth Gilbert, author of *Eat, Pray, Love*, went searching for herself in Italy, India, and Indonesia, she found something that appealed to millions of women, a way of seeing themselves. When Morgan Spurlock ate all his meals at McDonald's for a month, he helped millions of people rethink fast food. Of course, none of these people were working single-handedly. They were taking advantage of deeper cultural changes. But each Culturematic these people invented was so apt, so endearing, so engaging, they pushed these cultural changes, giving perhaps as much as they got.

Like Samberg and the people in the preceding examples, we use Culturematics to change culture. We make an innovation that enables us to see ourselves, or something in the world, differently. The Culturematic reframes the way we see the world. It reframes the way culture frames the world. Again, some Culturematics will turn out to be experiments that come to nothing. Others will scale up.

Step Three: Unleash Value

When Wilfred Winkenbach and friends hacked the National Football League to create fantasy football, they unleashed a great torrent of value. Thirty-two million people now play fantasy sports of one kind or another, generating a reported annual impact of between $3 billion and $4 billion across the sports industry. Videotaping seven amateurs living in a house revolutionized American TV, creating a new industry within the industry. Culturematics are value detection devices. Sometimes they phone home with data, sometimes with cash.[1]

Julie Powell's Culturematic became a blog and then a best-selling book called *Julie and Julia: My Year of Cooking Dangerously*, and these in turn became a film that starred Meryl Streep and took in $130 million worldwide. Morgan Spurlock's Culturematic became a documentary called *Super Size Me*. The film generated nearly $30 million on an investment of $65,000. Elizabeth Gilbert turned her Culturematic into a memoir called *Eat, Pray, Love*, a book that sold four million copies. The subsequent movie, starring Julia Roberts, took in more than $200 million worldwide.[2]

Many Culturematics return nothing. This is not to say they fail. They tell us that this is a tree up which we no longer wish to bark. They satisfy our curiosity. And they tell us that the thing that captivated our curiosity doesn't actually captivate anyone else's. Good to know! We have private enthusiasms. But if we want to hit a gusher, we have to look elsewhere. The search for the future is an exercise in *edge finding*. We don't know what we are looking for. We are not even sure what it is when we find it. We are working by instinct, by intuition. We are flying by the seat of our pants. To find the innovation that returns lots and lots of value, we will have to try many things that return next to nothing. It's the nature of the hunt.

In sum, Culturematics let us test the world, discover meaning, and unleash value. And this makes them an excellent way to innovate in a turbulent, inscrutable, confusing world. Think of them as little ingenuity machines.

Reality TV

Twenty years ago, a Culturematic transformed TV. Specifically, two people asked "What if we put a bunch of amateurs in a house and filmed what happens?" Thus spoke Mary-Ellis Bunim and Jonathan Murray in 1991, when they created a reality television program called *The Real World*. The original idea was to create a soap opera, but this was too expensive. (MTV was looking for something to supplant the music video, which had been free.)[3]

At this point, it wasn't clear what would work. You could put any number of things in front of the camera: grape harvests, boat races, kids playing soccer. Cheap, certainly. Entertaining? Who knew?

Seven people in a house? With no training, script, makeup, or direction? This could turn into an ugly chaos difficult to look at, let alone film or turn into a TV show.

At this point, Bunim and Murray were in effect playing the *Late Show* game called "Is This Anything?" where David Letterman and Paul Schaffer decide whether an act is "something or nothing."[4] Seven people stuck in a house could well be nothing. The only way was to try it and see. So Bunim and Murray set up a house in Brooklyn and turned on the cameras.

The cost was nothing; that much was clear. Or as close to nothing as this industry ever gets. The pilot for a prime-time TV show requires celebrity actors, a union crew, many months of development, and as much as $2 million.[5] *The Real World* pilot was shot with amateurs over three days on cheap Hi-8 cameras without the benefit of studio lighting or sound.[6] Cost? Compared with prime-time TV, this was free.

When Bunim and Murray looked at the early results, they were pleased. *The Real World* looked like something. The early numbers were gratifying. What no one anticipated was that this little show would change the very landscape of American television. *The Real World* wasn't merely something. It was revolutionary. *Vogue* editor Robert Sullivan heralded the birth of a new genre:

> In just one season, reality TV has gone from being the sideshow that the networks looked on as filler to being one of the main events, a scheduled highlight. Nearly 52 million people tuned in to the last night of *Survivor* . . . and when the second series aired, viewership for all four networks was up 22 percent for the entire evening.[7]

Over the last two decades, reality TV has proven the most productive idea in the history of television, turning out hundreds of
experiments, many of which survived to maturity: the *Real Housewives* series, *Project Runway, Wipeout, Ice Road Truckers, Jon & Kate
Plus 8, Jersey Shore, American Idol, Deadliest Catch, Hell's Kitchen,
Big Brother, Mob Wives, The Amazing Race, Man vs. Wild*, and the
latest experiment from Bunim-Murray Productions, *Keeping Up
with the Kardashians*. The viewership numbers can be astronomical.
The first episode of the fifth season of *American Idol* drew 35.5 million viewers. (These days, most prime-time TV is happy to get 12
million viewers.) For its part, *The Real World* is the little engine that
could. Now in its twenty-fourth season, it has proven a miracle of
resiliency. Reality TV began as a shot-in-the-dark experiment, but
now it dominates the cable channels and the broadcast networks.[8]

Some people like to sneer at reality TV. It's not artful or crafted.
Some shows have the subtlety of a peep show or a train wreck. But
Culturematics don't care. They are evolutionary experiments,
brute trials, happy to discover anything that works, something
that survives. And in any case, reality TV may yet have a virtue.
Television critic James Poniewozik offers this spirited defense:

> The new network shows of fall 2002 were a creatively
> timid mass of remakes, bland family comedies and
> derivative cop dramas. Network executives dubbed them
> "comfort"—i.e., familiar and boring—TV. Whereas
> reality TV — call it "discomfort TV"—lives to rattle
> viewers' cages. It provokes. It offends. But at least it's
> trying to do something besides help you get to sleep.[9]

Pie Lab

John Bielenberg had a problem: how to reach out to people and
move them to reach out to one another. Bielenberg wanted to
build community.

There were no easy answers. Americans are pretty good at rebuffing strangers. Years of door-to-door selling and telemarketing have seen to that. Plus, Americans are standoffish. Oh, they talk a good game. They wax lyrical about the importance of community, about wanting to know their neighbors, about building a "village." But when it comes down to it, they protect their privacy and keep to their own. To make matters worse, Americans watch a lot of shows like *Law and Order* and *CSI*—shows that feature scary strangers doing gruesome things. On balance, it feels like a good idea to keep one's distance.

What Bielenberg needed was a Culturematic. The idea of pie had come up when he was running Project M, an idea incubator in Belfast, Maine, that came out of the Design for Good Movement. But it wasn't until Bielenberg was trying to make himself welcome in Greensboro, Alabama, that the idea became a reality. The team had just finished a survey of the community. Clearly, there was lots to do. But how to get involved? One team member said she was good at making pies.[10] "Perfect," they thought. "Let's try pie."[11]

The skeptics couldn't believe their ears. Someone was going to try to solve social problems with pie? Surely, this was proof that Project M and the Greensboro team were softheaded do-gooders who couldn't grasp how desperate things were in this part of Alabama. One in three kids in Hale County is raised in poverty. One in four households has no connection to the municipal water system. The skeptics were adamant. Pie could not help Hale County, not even what Bielenberg and the team called "experimental pie."

But as a Culturematic, pie is deliberately, deceptively soft. It's gooey for good reason. With its reputation for indulgence, generosity, and sociality, it can change the way people feel about one another. The Pie Lab, as it came to be called, was betting that this staple of Thanksgiving could serve as an engine for social good. And indeed, pie turned out to work quite well. The residents of

Greensboro thought, "How dangerous can these people be? They're handing out free pie!" Soft and gooey helped break the ice. Conversation happened. Social distance collapsed. People began to see they shared interests. The stage for change was set.

Pie Lab started as a pop-up pie shop in 2009 and has since become a permanent eatery in a main street storefront in Greensboro.[12] What happens next? The team will have to wait and see. As long as anything happens, that's good. Any conversation, any collapsing of social distance in this world, is a small victory from which other victories can spring.

Bielenberg calls his approach Thinking Wrong. The idea is to use "random and serendipitous" events to push people out of traditional patterns of thought and action. And what's as random and serendipitous as free pie from a stranger? It forces people out of that habitual frame of mind, and that little script that runs, "Ok, that's the shopping done. Now I have to get to the library and pick up Betty at 4:00. Oh, what's this? Pie?" And before we know it, we're sharing a joke with the guy who coaches our daughter's best friend in soccer. And it turns out that the weird-looking guy we see at the Saturday market, he's actually a retired veterinarian and one of the people who *started* the market. Who knew? The Pie Lab recipient has been broken out of her routines, out of her inclination to ignore her neighbors. Change starts, as Bielenberg likes to say, one slice at a time. Pie Lab is a gentle intervention with a deeper purpose, a Culturematic operating on culture, a way of terraforming community.[13]

Fantasy Football

Fantasy football now entertains 27 million people. They play this game an average of nine hours a week. The fantasy football industry is valued at around $800 million.[14]

The game was invented by Wilfred Winkenbach, Bill Tunnel, and Scotty Starling in a Manhattan hotel room in the early 1960s. The idea was simple. Take the numbers generated by a professional sport, and use them to create outcomes in a fantasy league.

Professional football was throwing off a lot of numbers. At the end of any given Sunday, it was possible to determine not just the points scored by every team, but the yards gained by every running back, the number of interceptions made by every cornerback, the number of sacks recorded by every defensive end. (In American sports, almost everything gets counted.)

For most of us, these numbers are a record of events past. They tell us what happened as National Football League teams battle their way through a season. But for Winkenbach, Tunnel, and Starling, these numbers were not backward-looking. Potentially, they generated new events taking place in a new league. You could actually make these numbers the stuff of a new reality. For Winkenbach and company, what those exertions and heroics on the field were really doing was creating the foundation of an alternate world.

It's like the "discovery" of pineapple juice. There was a time when juice was treated as an extraneous accident of the canning process. Once the meat of the pineapple was in the can, the juice was thrown away.[15] It was left to an outsider to say, "Could I have that, please?" Mixed drinks and the International House of Pancakes would never be the same. The NFL was producing numbers with extraordinary but hidden value. Until Winkenbach and the guys came along, these numbers were being thrown away.

The economics are astounding. Winkenbach found a way to fund a new universe of professional sport for pennies on the dollar. The McCaskey family spends a couple of hundred million dollars to put its team, the Chicago Bears, on Soldier Field every year. Winkenbach created his universe for whatever it cost to gather, store, program, and deliver the data. Compare this with the cost of all NFL players, coaches, staff, equipment, and stadiums, and we end up with an extraordinary ratio, perhaps one fantasy dollar to one million NFL dollars. Or put it this way: the *whole* of a fantasy football league costs less to operate than the minimum salary of a single NFL player ($375,000).[16]

Of course, Winkenbach was "exploiting" someone else's resources for his own purposes and profit. But that's the point of a Culturematic. He had found a way to extract value from the world.

What Winkenbach wrought would become an industry. But when it was just three guys sitting in a Manhattan hotel room, none of this was obvious. Fantasy sport was a kooky idea, a shot into the future. Would it work? Would millions want to play? Sitting in that hotel room, the guys really didn't know. At best, they figured, fantasy football was going to be a minority enthusiasm, something for people in the sports business and in sports journalism. And at this point, they didn't really care. It could be fun. If it wasn't, well, no harm, no foul.

Like any Culturematic, fantasy football had no guarantee of success. If it was going to work, it would have to speak to the American sports fan. All Culturematics must satisfy this condition. They must make us go, "Hmm, that's interesting." They must speak to something in our culture. And fantasy football did. It proved to be an excellent way of engaging especially the new sports fan. Fans were getting smarter. Many of them had played the game at some level. Still more had been raised in a family that took the game seriously. Millions were listening to learned commentary on ESPN. This knowledge went deep. Many fans could describe the defensive formations that would work against Peyton Manning versus the ones that would work (God willing) against Michael Vick. Fans with this much knowledge were tiring of just sitting in the stands. (Even painting their faces purple and putting on Viking horns wasn't enough.) People with this much knowledge wanted more involvement. Fantasy football let them into the game.

Beneath the smarter fan was a still deeper trend. Americans as a group were moving from a passive, lean-back posture—couch potatoes waiting to be entertained—to something more active and engaged. They were beginning to embrace the so-called lean-forward posture that was distinctly post-coach-potato. In football, in sports, in popular culture, and in just about every other domain, Americans wanted more traction.[17]

But for three guys sitting in a New York hotel room, fantasy sport was merely a probe of the possible. And that's all it was. This is characteristic of many Culturematics. They don't begin as great, honking ideas. They don't fill the room with light and sound. No one shouts "Eureka!" They merely come tumbling in over the transom. Winkenbach, or someone like him, says, "You know, I've been thinking. This is going to sound weird, so bear with me. But what if . . . "

At this point, it's just a wild idea. I don't mean *wild* as in "wild and crazy." I mean *wild* as in "untested and unthought." At that moment, fantasy football was a will-o'-the-wisp, one of the millions of stray fancies that flow through American heads on any given day. Most of these ideas keep moving, passing back out to the sea marked as "Here Lie Wild Beasts" and, in some circles, "Don't even think about it."

A few of these ideas survive long enough to get a hearing. But not much of a hearing. Friends can be relied upon to offer discouragement, as in "Winkenbach, you are such a loser. You can't win betting on real football, so you make up *fantasy* sports. In your dreams!" But some ideas survive the first cut. If they resonate with culture, they can hope for wider adoption, and if they really speak to something in our culture, they scale up until they attract one in twelve Americans. That's how many play fantasy football. Culturematics are not expected to take the world by storm. But sometimes they do.

Web 2.0

Web 2.0 is a concept created by Tim O'Reilly and Dale Dougherty.[18] It was designed to change the way an industry thought about itself. The aftermath of the dot-com collapse was all doom and gloom, pain and skepticism. Companies had disappeared, share value had imploded, personal wealth had taken a header, venture capital was in retreat, and Silicon Valley was in withdrawal. An entire industry was wondering what the future held.

O'Reilly and Dougherty shared the pessimism. But they could also hear something stirring. Surely, it hadn't all been a dream. Surely, this industry had bones, structural properties that would endure. Surely, this world would right itself. O'Reilly and Dougherty believed the crash might be a sorting out, a chance for the wheat of real enterprise to separate from the chaff of dubious start-ups.

The first question was, Was there something out there, or not? And if it was something, was it a coherent something or a dispersed something? If it was a coherent something, O'Reilly and Dougherty were going to have to give it more shape and form. First, they would have to find a name. "Web 2.0" felt right, a term robust enough to start and sustain discussion. Next, they would have to develop the concept, finding something that would make some part of the world make more sense. Their next step was a conference where they could solicit comment, provoke debate, build a consensus, and publicly launch Web 2.0, now without its training wheels. O'Reilly and Dougherty had a

Culturematic mission: fire their little idea into the world, and see what happened.

Of course, O'Reilly and Dougherty could have simply announced Web 2.0 from their publishing house. The trouble is, many things get launched this way, and most of them fail. (We only see the successes, so it's easy to suppose that new ideas take root easily. In fact, the world is ruled by a dandelion ratio: thousands of parachutes are necessary for one to take.) Wishing will not make it so. Pronouncements usually fail.

"Web 2.0" was a strategic term. It said, "Listen. Calm yourselves. Here's the future. It's what you know . . . in a new iteration." This same-but-different technique is reassuring in times of crisis. Here, it comforted people about the dot-com crash. "That? Oh, that was just Silicon Valley 1.0. Bound to happen." People were accustomed to things being rocky in beta. Web 2.0 obeyed the convention that gave us Windows 5, Netscape 6, Word 7, and OS X. Naming by numbering is the way this industry works . . . and reassures.[19]

Web 2.0 worked. It won a toehold in the world. People started rallying around. It might be the triumph of concept over reality, but it created value immediately. The concept said, "Our industry is not a hopeless heterogeneity of practices and approaches. It is some *thing*. Google AdSense, Flickr, BitTorrent, Napster, Wikipedia, blogging, search engine optimization, Web services, wikis, tagging, and syndication—all of this is not an experiment in free fall, but an industry charging forward." Web 2.0 bundled nicely, and as it bundled, it clarified and galvanized.

Talk about putting your reputation on the line. O'Reilly and Dougherty ran a flourishing publishing house, specializing in software and new media titles. If they were wrong about Web 2.0, well, that could be the end of everything. They could make themselves a laughing stock. Who was going to buy books about the

Internet from a publishing house that had been spectacularly wrong about the Internet?

Web 2.0 took. Within a couple of years, it was coin of the realm, the term you could use in a meeting and count on nodding heads. Eighteen months into its launch, Web 2.0 had 9.5 million citations in Google. The Web 2.0 Conference, first held in 2004 in San Francisco, drew seven hundred people and an array of distinguished speakers. Of course, there were real differences of opinion about what the term meant. But at least people were now conducting the discussion under one umbrella instead of all over the place. In fact, a world of faint signals, tremendous confusion, ceaseless experiments, and a lot of skepticism was beginning to cohere. Now we could be more like hedgehogs (who, as Isaiah Berlin told us, think about a few things) instead of foxes (who are obliged to think about many things). Our culture was a little more organized.[20]

As a Culturematic, Web 2.0 delivered that most extraordinary thing: a category in our heads that would help us see the world. And from this could come a conference, a consensus, and a community. An industry pulled itself back from chaos and began again, now more confident and more purposeful. It helped coax nervous investors back into the market. It helped reignite the entrepreneurial culture of Silicon Valley. Not bad for a word, two numbers, and a dot.[21]

Burning Man

Larry Harvey and Jerry James took an eight-foot wooden man to San Francisco's Baker Beach on June 21, 1986, and set him on fire. People came sprinting up the beach to have a look. As the winds drove the flames to one side, a woman rushed in to hold the Burning Man's hand. A stranger with a guitar improvised a song. Sparks flew into the night air, and the Burning Man burned.

Harvey and James resolved to burn another man the following year. Volunteers assembled to help. Friends brought friends. These friends brought friends. More songs were written. And after a couple of years, Burning Man was an annual fixture of Baker Beach. Eventually, the city said no to a fire on the beach, and Burning Man moved to the desert. This meant creating Black Rock City, an economy and a culture that now exist for a week each year, about ninety miles from Reno. Some forty-eight thousand people come to participate. Burning Man makes the desert bloom and then vanishes without a trace.[22]

Some twenty-five years after it was founded, Burning Man has a credo: "Burning Man is about coming together in a beautiful yet unforgiving environment to celebrate radical self-expression." But at the moment of the first event, he was just a guy on fire. No back story. No story at all. The Burning Man Web site explains: "During the early years of growth on Baker Beach . . . organizers or workers [never] asked what it meant . . . no self-conscious meaning or symbolism seemed necessary."[23]

Harvey and James didn't need meaning or symbolism. They had started with a simple what-if, as in "What if we build a man out of wood, take him down to the beach, and set him on fire?" It was a little Culturematic, an event with a very clear start and no clear outcome. The two men didn't know what the Burning Man was for. They just wanted to see.

Like every Culturematic, Burning Man is both a cause and an effect. It's a cause, because it pushes parts of American culture to new intensity, especially the democratization of art and the notion of "random kindness, senseless beauty."[24] It's an effect, because it is riding what Daniel Bell called America's "expressive individualism," our need to explore our own and the community's creativity.[25]

Culturematics can't flourish unless they catch something in our culture. But when they do, they have an accelerating effect. This makes Burning Man a little like Chez Panisse, the restaurant that Alice Waters created in 1971 and that helped express and intensify the local-food movement. Culturematics begin as innovations tiny and obscure. But when they speak to Americans, they end up speaking for Americans.

Some Culturematics make it. But all of them begin as a shot in the dark, a tiny what-if. They cost so little, we can afford to be wrong. We can use them to probe even remote possibilities and unlikely scenarios. These days, this is sometimes the best place to look for the future.

Culturematics and the World of Innovation

British researcher John Kearon recently looked at the innovation record of Unilever, a Dutch-British corporation. The results were surprising. Unilever has a great track record, creating not just new brands and products but entire categories in the U.K. consumer market: laundry powder, fabric softener, margarine, and moisturizing soap. Kearon noticed that none of these discoveries came from the innovation centers Unilever set up in the 1990s.

Everything about the innovation centers looked right. They hired the best people. They spent real money. They centralized Unilever's creative efforts. And as Kearon explains, by and large they failed:

> The innovation center model is good at creatively farming existing brands and has added significant value to the likes of Dove, Lynx and Flora. However, as a model of innovation it is too centralized, too evidence-based, too

marketing-science orientated to have the freedom and contrariness to originate new categories that can create even greater value.[26]

Kearon recommends another approach. If you want to innovate as Google, Apple, and Red Bull have, he says, you should follow a couple of rules:

1. Don't look for big ideas. Seek small ideas that can grow.

2. Fail fast. Fail often. Keep learning and never give up.

Excellent, very Culturematic advice.

2 Why Culturematics Matter

Strictly speaking, the Culturematic doesn't look like a promising way to discover the next new thing. How can innovation come from something so clumsy, so random, so risky?

Culturematics matter because the world is becoming more and more inscrutable. As business management expert Michael Raynor says, "The future is deeply unpredictable."[1] We know change is coming, but for Intel's Andy Grove, this change is something "no amount of formal planning can anticipate."[2] Normally, in situations like this, we would turn to the experts and gurus. But they give us book titles that fan our anxiety instead of calm it: *Faster, Blur, Out of Control, Blown to Bits, Fast Forward, Creative Destruction*.[3]

Lucky us! We have to steer our personal lives through a world that churns with constant change.[4] And if we work for an organization, this problem is compounded. In their study of IBM, Richard Foster and Sarah Kaplan conclude:

> Discontinuities challenge the most basic assumptions of
> continuity that companies create for themselves . . .
> Discontinuities of [the sort facing IBM] present manage-
> ment with an almost unending stream of enigmas,

dilemmas, paradoxes, puzzles, riddles and mysteries, which remain unsolved until the mental context of the viewer changes. They present management with a maelstrom of disorder.[5]

The growing inscrutability of the world haunts all the traditional producers of culture: movie studios, design houses, advertising agencies, publishing houses, magazines, corporate R&D labs, and newspapers. Bret Easton Ellis recently observed that no writer will ever shape our culture as Steinbeck and Hemingway did.[6] The failure rate for TV shows is 95 percent, and at this writing, NBC cannot pull out of its downward spiral.[7] Outside of the blockbuster, Hollywood is no longer sure it can predict what will work at the box office. Even blockbusters, with their giant marketing campaigns, sometimes fail. When asked to predict whether *Charlie Wilson's War* was going to be a success, actor Tom Hanks replied that not even his stardom could promise results:

> I am no guarantee that a movie is going to be a success . . . The audience has become smart about stars. So it's chaos out there now. Nobody has any idea why people are going to see a movie. Nobody knows what's going to be a hit or what's going to be irrelevant. There are no new models. The new paradigm in Hollywood is that there is no new paradigm.[8]

And as if to make this point, Colin Hanks, Tom's son, signed up for a TV show called *The Good Guys*, which did not survive its first season.[9]

Tina Brown asked Leslie Moonves, chair of CBS Television, what he thought the next wave in television would be. He replied, "It's impossible to say. If five years ago, you had said to me, Leslie, the show that's going to help CBS emerge to number one is going to be about sixteen people on a desert island, I would have said, 'Tina, you're crazy.'"[10]

Yikes! Hollywood used to shape our culture almost at will. What would Adolph Zukor have made of Tom Hanks's conclusion? I think the head of 1930s Paramount studio would have replied, "No one knows how to make a hit? Just watch me." An inscrutable future is new for us.

Marketing has fallen in love with the idea of tipping points, media viruses, and runaway memes. But it is almost impossible to manufacture these media cascades. We don't know what's going to take off. Tim Harford reports on the work of Duncan Watts, who looked at popularity and fads developed online:

> The typical Twitter cascade is both rare and tiny. Ninety per cent of tweets are never retweeted, and most of the remainder are retweeted only by a person's immediate followers, not by those at two or three removes. The second surprise is that beyond the mind-numbingly obvious, it's impossible to predict which tweets will start cascades.[11]

An inscrutable future is antithetical to the corporation. After all, the corporation is designed to be a problem-solving machine. And in the twentieth century, the corporation could deal with just about anything. It had a system. It had managers. Material shortfall? We know what to do. Miscommunication with the consumer? We can fix that. This is the world at A in figure 2-1.

The world got a little more difficult when there arose clear problems (B in figure 2-1) that the system didn't anticipate. Never mind. The corporation was good at healing itself. Given a brief period of thinking and reform, the system would be improved and we could go back to A.

FIGURE 2-1

Varieties of dynamism for the corporation

No problem (A)	Clear problem (B)	Unclear problem (C)	??? (D)
We have a system, the system works; worst case: the occasional "hiccup"	System falters but we see what's wrong and put things right	We can't tell what's wrong; our system and assumptions are getting in the way; we need to change the systems; time to reread Roger Martin	The world "grays" out; we don't know what to think and we don't know where to start. We are stuck: we might brainstorm our way out of this, but . . .

Source: Grant McCracken, "A 'Special Teams' Unit for the Corporation," CultureBy: This Blog Sits at the Intersection of Anthropology and Economics, October 25, 2010, http://cultureby.com/2010/10/a-special-teams-unit-for-the-corporation.html.

Then we entered a period in which problems were harder to reckon with. It wasn't clear what we needed to do to fix the system. And that's because it wasn't clear what the problem was. Now we were at C. Living at C is no fun at all. We contort the corporation to fix one problem, only to discover or create another. These problems are not just difficult; they are sometimes intractable. Usually, we fight our way through to a solution. But even our best efforts don't seem to get us out of C. All solutions feel temporary.

And now we're learning how to live at D, in a world that is, as Raynor says, deeply unpredictable. This world churns with mysterious forces. This is the world of the blind-side hit. What systems apply here? We're honestly not sure. How do we find our way back to stability and calm? Well, perhaps those days are gone.

To make matters worse, the corporation is now a cause of the problem. At the urging of the likes of A. G. Lafley and *Business Week*, the corporation engages in constant innovation. This creates fresh chaos, black swans, and blind-side hits for every other corporation. Corporations now take turns producing commotion for one another.[12]

Which of these innovations will take? We don't know. The ones that do work frequently seem to be sleepers, hits that come out of nowhere, unanticipated and bewildering. Their success leaves us none the wiser. We continue to live in an inscrutable world, where value creation and management are vexing. Even the great student of "creative destruction," the economist Joseph Schumpeter, probably could not foresee a world in which great corporations routinely fall from grace. Jim Collins tells us, "Of the 500 companies that appeared on the first [*Fortune* 500] list in 1955, only 71 have a place on the list today." Harris Collingwood puts it less qualitatively but just as clearly: "Idiosyncratic volatility is the signature of our economic age."[13]

In this world, reading the consumer is increasingly difficult. The head of design at Coca-Cola, David Butler, points out, "Nobody, not one single organization predicted that texting would work. Not one." The designer Wally Olins echoes this observation: "I think that finding out how consumers act and react, and what they do and feel when they see things is useful. I think that trying to predict proves valueless—again and again and again." Enterprise struggles to anticipate what the consumer wants. Fully 95 percent of new products fail; that's 28,500 unsuccessful launches a year.[14]

To make matters worse, the corporation is called upon to act with new vigor in the creation of new worlds. Not so long ago, the name of the game was steady growth, interspersed with moments of technological advantage, market penetration, or marketing genius. Growth would spike until, eventually, we would return to "slow and steady wins the race." But we are beginning to see that real competitive advantage belongs to corporations that can create new worlds. I refer, of course, to the likes of Apple, Nike, Cirque du Soleil, Four Seasons, and Starbucks, each of which managed to create not just a competitive brand, but a new market.

W. Chan Kim and Renée Mauborgne call these "blue oceans," great expanses where value is rich because competition is scarce. Cirque du Soleil might have entered the market as it had been defined by Ringling Brothers. Instead, the Canadian company invented a new kind of circus that spoke to a new clientele at new price points in new venues, in the process colonizing a creative territory that was as dynamic as the Ringling Brothers was traditional. In sum, Cirque du Soleil created a market where none had existed before. Mark Johnson calls these new worlds "white spaces." Southwest Airlines created a new territory in the airline industry by acting like a bus company. Finding new territory takes heroic acts of imagination, initiative, and strategy. The corporation must effectively leave the rules and processes it knows, and cultivate ones it does not. But the outcomes can be spectacular for the winner and violently disruptive, to use Christensen's term, for all the rest.[15]

Pity the corporation. There is trouble on the one side. The future is going dark. Strategy and planning are losing their powers of illumination. And trouble on the other. In this murky, muddled world, the corporation is being asked to solve a new and daunting problem, aggressive innovations that sometimes give us entirely new worlds. Argh! That's the standard anthropological term for problems of this order: argh.

Launch a Thousand Ships

Everyone's first reaction is to become more responsive. This was what Tim Brown did when he redesigned IDEO. He wanted an organization that was "flexible, nimble, relevant and responsive."

Almost all organizations have made themselves flatter and more egalitarian. We have ripped out office walls to give everyone faster access to one another. Social media give managers instant access to one another. We have consulted new and sometimes exotic management models. The idea, according to Andy Grove, is simple: become a fire department. We can't predict where the fires are going to break out. We can only get faster at fighting them.[16]

Well, maybe. Culturematics say otherwise. They say the corporation can be batlike. It can see while flying blind. It can send little pings into the world to read what's there and to find a path through. More responsiveness is always a great idea. But it's a passive response. It waits for the world to act, and only then does it react, trapping the corporation in a feverish game of catch up. The Culturematic is more aggressive and proactive. It engages the world. Enough Culturematics, and we begin to see the shape and substance of what's out there. This isn't a perfect substitute for planning and strategy. But it's better than building a nimbler fire department. It's better than catch-up.

When John McArthur was transforming the Harvard Business School as its dean, he couldn't be certain which strategies would work. His response was to experiment:

> "I adopted a kind of Elizabethan strategy—Elizabeth the First, that is. She sent thousands of little ships down the Thames, and those sailors went all around the world. Some got boiled and eaten in the South Pacific. Others ran onto the rocks in New England. And in some cases, Elizabeth had to send the navy out to bring them back in chains. But somehow or other, they eventually got back home to the Thames—after three years, or thirteen years, or whatever. And that was my belief about this place. I thought we should try to encourage as many as

possible who had an idea to head down the Thames, and see what they would do with it."[17]

This idea is also cultivated by David Gray of the Boston Consulting Group:

> "[T]he only way to get a good idea is to get lots of them, even to let them proliferate independently and compete for primacy. Such redundancy is expensive but can be crucial to innovation. Credit card issuer Capital One conducts thousands of structured experiments each year to identify profitable new products and segments, knowing that most will turn out to be duds. A few hits, however, can quickly become vast new opportunities . . . managers are prepared to accept false starts and dead ends."[18]

Randomness is sometimes the path to riches, even for organizations that pride themselves on being ferociously capable and deliberate. Jim Collins and Jerry Porras say that history sometimes bears this out: "In examining the history of the visionary companies, we were struck by how often they made some of their best moves not by detailed strategic planning, but rather by experimentation, trial and error, opportunism, and 'purposeful accidents.'"[19]

Robert Austin takes on the issue directly: "Working without a clear definition of your objective is considered wasteful, inefficient. But if you are trying to get outside what you can anticipate, if you are going after the truly new and valuable, this way of thinking can be a problem."[20]

When conducting research for *Little Bets*, Peter Sims found a corporation obsessed with scale. For instance, Hewlett Packard was reluctant to pursue any idea that didn't promise to become a billion-dollar business.[21] Sims argues for spreading the risk, a strategy he sees in the comedy career of Chris Rock, in the management style of Amazon.com's Jeff Bezos, and in the counterinsurgency strategies of Col. Casey Haskins. And he sees it in the approach taken by Pixar's Andrew Stanton, the man who directed *Finding Nemo* and *WALL-E*:

> My strategy has always been: be wrong as fast as we can. Which basically means, we're gonna screw up, let's just admit that. Let's not be afraid of that. But let's do it as fast as we can so we can get to the answer. You can't get to adulthood before you go through puberty. I won't get it right the first time, but I will get it wrong really soon, really quickly.[22]

Innovation is a messy, multiple business. There is no single method. The sensible approach is to keep trying stuff—to provoke the world and let it start talking to you. As Sims puts it, invention and discovery emanate from the ability to try seemingly wild possibilities; to feel comfortable being wrong before being right; to live in the world as a careful observer, open to different experiences; to play with ideas without prematurely judging oneself or others; to persist through difficulties; and to have a willingness to be misunderstood, sometimes for long periods, despite the conventional wisdom.[23]

In his TED talk, Tim Hartford argued that the secret truth of organizations is that they succeed through trial and error. Corporations like to think that success comes from deep thought and grand ideas, that it springs perfectly formed from strategy. These days, it makes more sense to "try stuff," see how the world responds, and go again. In her TED talk, Kathryn Schulz says that this trial-and-error approach will take a new frame of mind, a comfort with error, and an understanding that truth begins in failure.[24]

This Culturematic impulse is proliferating. It's been evident in one version or another in the corporate world for twenty years.

Take, for instance, the "skunk works," which Tom Peters describes as "bands of eight or ten zealots off in the corner, often out producing product development groups that numbered in the hundreds."[25] These little operations signify an organization prepared to protect innovation from bureaucratic meddling and nay-saying committees. Skunk works anticipate the Culturematic. They move experiment out of the corporation and point it toward the real world (figure 2-2). But they are mere anticipations, because there is usually just *one* skunk work and it tends to be expensive and committed to a single evolutionary strategy.

Corporations have unconsciously struggled to be more Culturematic in other ways. When John Mackey founded Whole Foods in 1980, he wasn't sure how to go from being a tiny company to a large one. He decided to organize the employees of each store into small teams and to encourage them to experiment.

FIGURE 2-2

The corporation learns to escape its own gravitational field

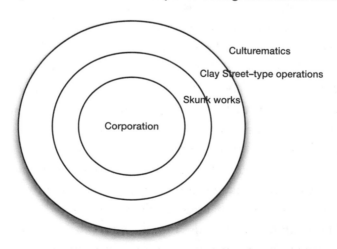

Whole Foods is now the world's largest retailer of natural and organic foods. Google has engaged in Culturematic experimentalism as well. Some of its best ideas, including Gmail and Google Earth, came from engineers set free to spend a day each week working on whatever caught their fancy. 3M pioneered this approach with a "15 percent program" that allows employees to devote time to their own projects. This is how Art Fry invented the Post-it. Procter & Gamble created a place called Clay Street, a converted building at the corner of 14th Street and Clay Street in Cincinnati, chosen deliberately for its distance from P&G headquarters. Culturematics seek to move things out of the gravitational field of the corporation. As Clay Street manager Brice Westring says, "If you ideate in the same space as you work in, you are going to come up with the same solutions."[26]

The Culturematic spirit manifests itself when corporations struggle to make themselves more porous, embracing open-source innovation and the wisdom of crowds. As P&G discovered, the corporation can't think of everything. Under the influence of A. G. Lafley, it began to let things in. The Culturematic impulse can also be seen in our new feeling for iterative innovation and rapid prototyping. Thus does the corporation improve its ability to let things out.[27]

In a sense, this is merely the corporation taking advantage of its good fortune. It is filled with people who have richer, deeper creative gifts. As Henry Jenkins, Eric von Hippel and Clay Shirky have demonstrated, we now have an abundance of inventive capacity.[28] Every individual is more likely to be active when it comes to the creation of culture. And this means every corporation is, in a sense, sitting on a great oil reserve. In the olden days, the corporation didn't care that an employee might be an expert in anime or social networking. His or her skill was, in a sense, considered the employee's "problem." It is time to see the problem as a gift.

A Culturematic impulse is becoming more evident in the very structure of capitalism. In his novel *Makers*, Cory Doctorow paints a world that is McArthurian and Culturematic: "The days of companies with names like General Electric and General Mills and General Motors are over. The money on the table is like krill: a billion little entrepreneurial opportunities that can be discovered and exploited by smart, creative people."[29]

The start-up world is the way we do a lot of business now. Giant corporations can be slow and clumsy. The start-up world takes big business and breaks it into smaller parts, each of them a Culturematic testing the world with its own what-if. And it turns out that entrepreneurs proceed as "brilliant improvisers" developing their "goals on the fly . . . creatively reacting to contingencies."[30] It's as if capitalism is shifting its center of gravity from large and stationary to small, mobile, and experimental. We embrace the famous mantra of IDEO's founder and chairman David Kelley: "Fail early and fail often." At the extreme, we are drawn to things that are in Errol Morris's famous phrase, "fast, cheap, and out of control."[31]

Here's the weird thing. Our best ideas are not always the best idea. Using our own strategic vision will not always get us where we want to go. Indeed, in a turbulent world, conscious planning and invention will sometimes take us in precisely the wrong direction. It's not our fault. We are simply the product of the corporation's present mind-set and trajectory. Furthermore, we are the product of a culture that has long insisted that the individual is the "locus of production." Both managers and creatives believe themselves sufficient to the problem-solving task. As the world moves on, this is only sometimes right.[32]

We know two things. First, we are obliged to innovate. This is the only way to survive the killing fields of the contemporary marketplace (where only 14 percent of the *Fortune* 500 survive for more than fifty years). Second, we're hard-pressed to tell which innovations will flourish and which will die. Sometimes, we are not even sure where to start. In a world like this, we want lots of little experiments. So says the IPO prospectus for Google in an almost perfect expression of the Culturematic logic:

> We will not shy away from high-risk, high-reward projects because of short-term earnings pressure. For example, we would fund projects that have a 10 percent chance, [placing] smaller bets in areas that seem very speculative or even strange. As the ratio of reward to risk increases, we will accept projects further outside our normal areas, especially when the initial investment is small . . . Most risky projects fizzle, often teaching us something. Others succeed and become attractive businesses.[33]

Gareth Kay sums it up nicely:

> Of course we want big business results and brands and communication that feel big, pervasive and central to culture. But, perhaps counter-intuitively, to achieve this we need to think and act small, not big . . . Build a culture of experimentation in which we do stuff and learn from it rather than learning from research. It's about bootstrapping ideas, placing lots of bets and . . . making communication products, not PowerPoint presentations.[34]

We Will Know It When We See It

Our strategic intelligence has not abandoned us. We can still spot good ideas. We can still innovate. But our best efforts are sometimes no longer good enough. What's left is a process called "we'll know it when we see it." When the problem at hand is too complex, too uncertain, or just too difficult for us, we wait for the world to make a suggestion. "Yes," we say, "that could work." And if the world isn't offering suggestions? That's where Culturematics come in.

The good news is that our pattern recognition is very strong. We need only to see something for an instant to see that it will work for us. I had a chance to see how fast this process can be when I visited the offices of *Allure* magazine.[35] I was introduced to a woman in a small room. She was standing on a platform watching images pass below her in a kind of photo pour. What surprised me was how fast the photos moved. This didn't matter. The woman needed only a fraction of a second to spot the photo she wanted for the pages of *Allure*.

It's odd, isn't it, that we can *see* when we can't *say*.[36] As Malcolm Gladwell has noted, we harbor a deep, cognitive talent that makes this not just possible, but effortless.[37] This is also sometimes called the serendipity effect.[38] The history of science is filled with stories of investigators who were engaged in one inquiry when some accident in the lab gave them a very different way to solve the problem. (Well, accident and years of training. As Louis Pasteur said, "Chance only favors the well-prepared mind.")

Lucky us. We may not be able to find the innovation by dint of our own efforts, but we do know it when we see it. The trick, then, is to give the world a chance to surprise us. We need a photo pour, a stream of possibilities neither too formed by our expectations nor completely random. We need a series of experiments. Mary-Ellis Bunim and Jonathan Murray had several experiments going in the early 1990s as they searched for the future of TV. The reality TV experiment was a shot in the dark, but when the results came in, they knew they had something. Ah, they said, this could work.

It is a sociological verity. People who escape familiar groups and make contact with unfamiliar ones become smarter and more creative.[39] They have what Ronald Burt calls a "vision advantage." They are no longer captives of their cultures. They no longer have to think what they have always thought. Burt's subjects leap "structural holes" to discover things "they didn't know they didn't know." With Culturematics, we leap conceptual holes to discover things we didn't know we couldn't think.

In a world like this, advantage goes to those who can launch a hundred ships. For, as Steven Johnson says, "Good ideas . . . want to connect, fuse, recombine. They want to reinvent themselves by crossing conceptual borders. They want to complete each other."[40] Insisting that we can plot a course to get to the future is ill advised. No doubt, we can spend a lot of money and make a little progress, but in an inscrutable world, there's no guarantee that our future will correspond with anyone else's. The trick is to invent our own serendipity, to establish a cloud of possibilities in which we can spot the telling pattern. We may not be able to read the future, but happily, we can say with some confidence that we will know it when we see it.

So That's Why There Are So Many Laboratories?

It's the weirdest thing. All of a sudden, laboratories are springing up everywhere. We see them in subcultures like Steampunk, TV shows like *Fringe* and *Warehouse 13*, institutions inside the university like David Edwards's Artscience Lab at Harvard, commercial enterprises like IDEO, the Syyn Labs in Los Angeles, the Culture Lab in Mumbai, Le Laboratoire in Paris, the FreedomLab in Amsterdam, the Ars Electronica Futurelab in Austria, the management laboratory being created by Gary

Hamel, and, yes, the Pie Lab of Project M.[41] Still weirder. As I pointed out in the introduction, most of them are not real laboratories at all. No beakers, test tubes, lab coats, nor indeed, in most cases, any scientists! These laboratories are more about culture than science.

Even ad agencies have labs. Bartle Bogle Hegarty (BBH) has one. So does Ogilvy. Ed Cotton notes how strange this is. It is, he says, impossible to imagine a lab at Sterling-Cooper, the agency in the TV show *Mad Men*.[42] On balance, Cotton likes the lab idea. He thinks it's a good way for the ad industry "to keep up with technological and consumer change."

BBH Labs was founded by Ben Malbon and Mel Exon in 2008. Here's the mission statement:

> Labs is BBH's global innovation unit. We're tasked with pioneering new outputs and approaches: exploring emerging platforms and behaviors on behalf of brands, and developing new agency models along the way. Our overall ambition is to ~~save the world~~ find ways in which marketing innovation can be a powerful force for good (more effective, more engaging, more sustainable, more exciting). We're particularly interested in:
>
> - Innovative new forms of creativity
> - Novel approaches that are rapid, iterative & curatorial
> - The mashup of thinking from radically different sources & industries
> - Sustainable marketing at scale
> - Co-creation and mass collaboration

- Social ideas and how they propagate

- Marketing as product or service

- AI[43]

I am an unabashed admirer of Ben Malbon. (His study of the London club scene is a thing of glory.[44]) But this mission statement feels shapeless and abstract. "New," "original," "innovation" "creativity," "exploring," "engaging," "pioneering"—it's like something out of Baudrillard, empty signifiers chasing one another without the production of meaning. Of course, all mission statements have an abstract quality. But I can't help wondering whether this sort of thing ever touches down.

This is the advantage of the Culturematic. It's not stuck in a lab. It's out there in the world. And it's not a grand idea. It's a hunch and a gamble. It has no sense of entitlement. It doesn't insist on its glamor or its usefulness. It's prepared to sink or swim. It's unassuming and hardworking. When an ad agency or a corporation creates a laboratory, I think it is responding to the Culturematic impulse. But when it makes innovation a captive of this laboratory, it misses the point of the exercise entirely. Laboratories matter. But experiments, with or without laboratories, matter more.

I prefer the approach suggested by David Edwards in his recent book *The Lab: Creativity and Culture*. Edwards thinks of his laboratories—the ones at Harvard, where he teaches, and in Paris, where he consults—as part of an "idea funnel." As I understand it, the point of the funnel is to move ideas briskly, from the point of origin out into the world, where they may be exposed to and oxygenated by ever-broader audiences. Edwards's labs expose new ideas to more ideas. Labs do not take ideas captive.

Indeed, Edwards's lab funnel begins by wrestling ideas away from the university, those reluctant headwaters of what should be a Mississippi of invention. Edwards's "artscience" liberates innovation:

> In an age when society and culture are rapidly
> evolving, large institutions need to adapt if they are
> to respond positively to the needs and opportunities
> of a changing world. Innovation is paramount. But
> institutions where specialization of information
> and function discourage innovators and dampen
> dreams . . . are not well suited to innovative practice.
> They innovate best through association with innovation
> catalysts. And that is what artscience labs can be.
> Artscience labs provide interdisciplinary conditions
> and expressive environments.[45]

Edwards's model makes public exhibition the equivalent of academic publication, and this means the new idea gets the benefit of scrutiny of a querulous press and inquisitive crowd, not the much smaller community of people and opinion in the academic world. He oxygenates ideas with controversy, instead of inoculating them against it.

Still, Edwards's model is too managed for my taste, too hands-on, too institution heavy. All those labs! Not just one, but a network of them. All those grants! Edwards has found commercial applications, but finally, his model is, for all its dislike of the university bureaucracy, a place that will take bureaucrats to staff it. This is the virtue of the Culturematic. What it fires into the world is removed from academic interference. The Culturematic doesn't require a lot of aid or supervision. Mostly what it needs is an idea and a dare.

And there is, in Edwards's vision, too much of the romantic concept of creativity. He asserts that the "passion" of an idea's creators acts "like a gravitational force that propels [them] through the various stages of maturation."[46] There are overwrought statements of the power, drama, and, oh, I don't know, the sheer intellectual grandeur of the innovator. Perhaps it's the dour Protestant Scottish Canadian in me speaking, but I find this all a little too self-dramatizing. "Do you have an idea?" I want to ask. "You do? Very good. Let's get on with it."

Edwards makes Paris and Le Laboratoire the epicenter of his world, and this strikes me as a bad idea. The French, to the extent that one can generalize (and as an anthropologist, that's my job), have lost some of their feeling for cultural invention. This is because popular culture remains a smelly, bastard child who is just wrong for the garden party of public life. (The French can't quite forgive pop culture its commercial origins.) And at the high end, the intellectuals, as postmodernists, sold for scrap (and their own celebrity) the ideas we need to make sense of culture now. Paris, with its centrist tendency, state sponsorship, and patrician intellectuals, is a dangerous place for ideas.

Edwards's model for innovation is the sort of thing only an academic could love, clinging as it does to the notion that ideas come into the world most surely in the convivial circumstances of a common room. But more likely, invention comes from the pinball machine of contemporary culture and markets.[47] Edwards's model holds us too much in the gravitational field we noted in figure 2-2. There is no willingness here to blow it out the air lock and see if it survives.

The idea is to escape the lab, the university, Paris, and the expert and to explore serendipity. I learned something about serendipity on a recent train trip to Rochester. (And normally the only thing one learns on the train to Rochester is, given the state of Amtrak, not to take the train to Rochester.) My traveling companion was Steve Crandall, a physicist.[48] Crandall was telling me about Bell Labs, a place where he had worked for some twenty years.[49] People applied themselves to lab problems around the clock, but sometimes, he said, it was when they went to lunch that the best progress was made. And this is serendipity in action. When we stop thinking about the problem, we see the idea we need to solve the problem.

What does lunch do? It gives the world a chance to supply its metaphoric materials. We are working on a problem about, say, system logics, and someone starts talking about the organization of ganglia in the brain, and we say, "But of course. That's the pattern I was looking for. Thank you." Left to our own devices, we never would have thought to look at ganglia research. But when someone else tosses it into the conversation, we can see at once that it is an excellent solution. We know it when we see it.

Blame the Dewey decimal system! It clusters like things together. And that's what we do when we try to solve a problem. We gather the data, theories, methods, and colleagues we think we'll need. But now we know it is sometimes better to open ourselves to serendipity and the world's metaphoric materials. The innovation paradox is this: we need ideas we can't possibly guess we need. We must canvass concepts that are entirely unrelated to our present problem set. Only thus do we give our deeper powers of pattern recognition a chance to work.

Every lunch table, especially when staffed with smart, interesting people, can serve to help us harness the innovation paradox. But we can do better than this. There is a way to narrow the range of our stimuli and increase the chances of "contact." The problem is to punch our way out of what we know and the communities in which we know it, and open the idea to other things. That's what the Culturematic is for.

What Culturematic Is and Isn't

Is Bethenny Frankel a Culturematic? (See chapter 7 for a discussion of how a person can be a Culturematic.) According to the *Wall Street Journal* , she is one hell of an experiment.

> Currently filming two shows, preparing to publish her
> third book and putting the finishing touches on her
> lines of mixed drinks, skin-care products and shapewear,
> Ms. Frankel offers a glimpse of what it's like when no
> corner of your world is private and everything belongs
> to the brand.[50]

Frankel is relentless. She left college for an acting career in Hollywood. When this didn't work out, she returned to New York City to go to culinary school and start Bethenny Bakes. When this failed, she took a part on *The Apprentice: Martha Stewart* and eventually joined the *Real Housewives* cast. Success! As a reward, she was given her own reality show, *Bethenny Getting Married,* in which the camera is present for engagement, marriage, pregnancy, and even childbirth. Her new show is called *Bethenny Ever After.*

Outwardly, Frankel looks like a Culturematic. She is relentlessly searching for her place in the world. And she tries a range of things. But what's missing is anything that looks genuinely experimental. Frankel is not testing out possibilities, waiting for the world to surrender its secrets. No, she is trying only the things likely to bring her celebrity. To be sure, some of these vehicles have an experimental air. But there is nothing questing about Frankel's motives, nothing intrinsic about her interests. Hers is a simple opportunism, driven apparently by desperation and, perhaps, the fear of obscurity.

I do not mean to be judgmental. Opportunism drives us all. Obscurity frightens us all. Desperation haunts us all. But Frankel shows no sign of curiosity, play, or what-if abandon. Not to be unkind, but Frankel's climb to celebrity appears to be idea-free. I don't mean to sneer. I like *Bethenny Ever After*. There just isn't anything Culturematic about this life. Strictly speaking, the spirit of the Culturematic sends us not in the narrow pursuit of opportunity but in a broader search for meaning.

James Franco is another story. Yes, *that* James Franco, the stoner from *Pineapple Express*, the arch-enemy from *Spider-Man*, and the host of the 2011 Oscars. Sam Anderson examines the diversity of Franco's career and asks, "Movie star, conceptual artist, fiction writer, grad student, cipher—he's turned a Hollywood career into an elaborate piece of performance art. But does it mean anything?"[51]

Franco acted a little in high school and dropped out of University of California–Los Angeles to do some TV. With *Spider-Man*, he ascended to stardom. This might have been the moment when he started to manage and augment his celebrity in conventional ways. After all, he was now a bona fide star with lots of options and a string of new roles: *Eat Pray Love, Howl, 127 Hours, Your Highness, William Vincent, Maladies*, and *Rise of the Apes*. But Franco decided to augment his movie work with distinctly non-Hollywood engagements. He has gone back to college and then to graduate school, in not one but four institutions (New York University, Columbia University, Brooklyn College, Warren Wilson College). He has appeared in the soap opera *General Hospital*, a solo art show, and the pages of several literary magazines. As Anderson puts it, "Plenty of actors dabble in side projects—rock bands, horse racing, college, veganism—but none of them, and maybe no one else in the history of anything, anywhere, seems to approach extracurricular activities with the ferocity of Franco."

We can eliminate one possibility. Franco is not a virtuoso showing off as Orson Welles did when the latter took on new projects to show how easily he could dispatch them. Franco struggles, says Anderson: "He's not a savant or an obvious genius—he's someone of mortal abilities who seems to be working immortally hard."

Franco is the opposite of Frankel. The point of his explorations is not celebrity. Indeed, he appears almost in flight from celebrity. More likely, his motive is curiosity. In the old Hollywood, stardom brought the actor a kind of completion. Nowadays, for some actors, it is seen to close off options and experiences the actor cares about. Franco doesn't know what he needs to be an actor or a person. And he doesn't know what he needs to know to stop being an actor. So he needs to find what's out there.

Franco is an open-ended experiment. And this is how Culturematics work. They can't say where they're headed till they get there. And they can't get there till they strike off in several directions, at least one or two of them unexpected. And they can't even be certain they have arrived when they get there.

What is and what isn't a Culturematic? Franco is. Frankel isn't. Does that help? Is the idea of Culturematic coming into focus? The danger is that I will act like that proverbial man with a hammer and treat everything as a Culturematic. Let me reassure you. I don't want Culturematic to apply to everything. Then it wouldn't mean anything.[52] Here are a couple more examples.

A *seed bomb* is a little packet made out of a seed and some clay.[53] It is carried by guerrilla gardeners into the industrial parts of a city and hurled into empty lots that have been shut off by chain-link fences and No Trespassing notices. The bomb is designed to carry the seed into the lot and then supply the soil that helps it germinate and grow.

There is something a little Culturematic about a seed bomb. It's interesting and odd. We don't expect to see *seed* and *bomb* in the same sentence, let alone the same package. And there is something

Culturematic about people gliding around the inner city under the cover of darkness, committing tiny crimes in the name of public good. There is something Culturematic about finding a way to penetrate security with so little risk. There is something Culturematic about making desperate places bloom with plant life. Many good things happen: a no-man's-land is reclaimed for the senses, the city is made more humane, and for all we know, the lot that is bombed and now flowering may have the "no broken windows" effect that helped transform American cities.[54]

But a seed bomb is not a Culturematic, because it knows (or, better, we know) exactly what it's for and almost exactly what its outcome will be. Seed bombs are not experimental. They are not shots in the dark, even when thrown in the dark. They may have longer-term consequences we cannot anticipate, such as a role in the transformation and "florification" of the urban neighborhood, but unless they are created for this reason and thrown for this purpose, they are not Culturematics.

Culturematics *can* be a little stuntlike. They are attention seeking, so counterexpectational that it's hard to turn away from them. But this does not mean Culturematics refuse serious thinking. They merely prefer to begin as something that is playful and unpretentious. They take on big questions, but they like to sneak up on these questions. We can't search out all the people with our name in our state without giving a thought or two to the question of identity. Morgan Spurlock's McDonald's stunt naturally gives rise to thoughts of diet, obesity, and wellness in America, as he knew it would. Culturematics smuggle in their profundity.

The Ritz-Carlton decided to ask every employee in the hotel to greet hotel guests. This marked a big change in the culture of the hotel world. Traditionally, housekeeping staff, servers, gardeners, and maintenance people had been previously classified as "noncombatants," to be seen but not heard, present but not part of the hotel's public face. Now they were called upon to produce what Tom Peters calls "The Ritz Pause." When he passed them in the hall, "they took a couple of seconds, stopped, looked me in the eye, and asked 'How is everything going? Is there anything I can do for you?'"[55]

This looks like a Culturematic. It sees an opportunity that's been there since the invention of the hotel but was ignored by virtually all big chains. It reaches in and changes some part of life in the corporation. It moves the goalposts. But it's not a Culturematic, because it has a clear and simple objective: to make the Ritz-Carlton friendlier. Culturematics typically aren't exactly sure where they're going.

Starbucks embarked on the creation of what it calls a "third space," a place between home and work.[56] In effect, it was opening up the possibility that people might entertain private behaviors in public spaces, that they might relax and work at a café without being self-conscious. Previously, people who were sitting around in public were seen to be loitering. Starbucks was trying to refashion the rules of public life.

This *is* a Culturematic. In the early days, no one could be sure what was going to happen. What if "undesirables" moved in and took over? What if paying customers were driven out? What if Starbucks damaged its brand? The third-space notion was a risky proposition. Starbucks knew it wanted a third space, but not whether this idea would work, how it would work, or what it would look like. The company would know it only when it got there.

Many are called to the status of a Culturematic, but few are chosen. The world is filled with things that look Culturematic-ish. As the book proceeds, I will distinguish between half-matics, full-matics, and no-matics at all.

Are Culturematics Stunts?

Putting people in a house and turning on the cameras, how odd! Giving away pie on the street, how droll! Taking a wooden man down to the beach and setting him on fire, how strange! Many Culturematics look like stunts, pranks, or hacks. But they are not merely attention-seeking. They do not engage in mischief just for the sake of mischief. They are not the brainchild of the puerile or the juvenile.

Stunts are easy to spot. Consider the one played by Dick Tuck on Richard Nixon. Tuck filled a political rally with very pregnant African Americans wearing Nixon's official campaign button: "Nixon's the one." This isn't a Culturematic, because it isn't exploratory. It had a simple objective: embarrassment. When Tuck donned a trainman's outfit and waved a train out of the station while Nixon was still talking from it, this wasn't a Culturematic, either. The objective was to make Nixon look ridiculous. It wasn't to discover some aspect of the man or the world we didn't know before.[57]

College pranks don't qualify, either. When fraternity brothers clothe statues of university founders in bras and panties, no Culturematic is accomplished. The motive is mischief and the objective is the diminishment of the dignity of the institution. When cows are tipped, no one is any the wiser. Nothing larger or more imaginative is sought for. MIT has a long tradition of hacks that display a certain wit and a technical virtuosity—placing an MIT Fire Dept. truck on the great dome of the campus, for instance. But this isn't a Culturematic, either, because the actors know exactly what the outcome will be. Pranks can't be Culturematics, unless they mean to explore or discover.[58]

The trouble is that pranks are self-conscious, sometimes even coy. They know they are breaking the rules, and they hope for a reaction.

Culturematic-makers tend to be a little more literal. When they engage in exploration, they really want to know. When they query the world, even with play, they expect an answer. They leave the box of ordinary thinking not because it is mischievous to do so, but because there might be a world out there and it might be interesting to find out what this world is.[59]

The answer, then, is no, Culturematics are not stunts.

Hackers, Hipsters, and Harem Pants

If not a prankster, then what? What is a Culturematic-maker? A hacker? A hipster? Or just a little odd?

People who make Culturematics are certainly like hackers. Hackers create something interesting, often unprecedented. They do so by breaking into a system of some kind and using it for an unanticipated purpose.[60] They hack computer networks, stock exchanges, iPhones, or Xboxes. They find a way into the lighting system of an apartment building to make a smiley face appear on its exterior. Or figure out how to make a car run on coffee (the famous Carpuccino).[61] This takes technical virtuosity, imagination, cunning, and, often, daring.

But those who make Culturematics are not trying to break into or commandeer anything. They are provoking the world, to see what happens. Hackers have a clear objective. Culturematic-makers are playing a hunch. Hackers are cunning. Culturematic-makers can be a little clueless. Hackers are worldly; Culturematic-makers are wandering.

We *could* say that when John Bielenberg and friends are giving away pie in Greensboro, Alabama, they are trying to hack the community there. But it doesn't really work. It's more plausible to say that Wilfred Winkenbach and friends were hacking the NFL when they created fantasy football, but even here it feels a little forced. After all, Winkenbach wasn't trying to take over any part of the NFL, merely to repurpose something that NFL was throwing off. At least in the early days, the NFL never felt a thing. We could say that a grave-marker project described in chapter 3 was hacking the history of the Negro Leagues (more on this in the next chapter). And here the phrase feels a little more apt. But again, this doesn't resemble breaking into the database of a bank or a government institution. Culturematics are a kind of hack, but they are usually the gentlest of interventions.

What about hipsters? Hipsters are experimental. They are searching the world for new messages. Still and all, they belong to a community, and this community supplies some of the things that define them: art, music, politics, styles of clothing, patterns of language. We may call these styles alternative, but they all tend to be alternative in the same way. For instance, hipsters will refuse clothing found in the mainstream, but their clothing preferences tend to fall into a narrow range. There is something conventional about their unconventionality.

Culturematic-makers are not necessarily like this. They are, for instance, prepared to wear harem pants. I am thinking of an MIT student who does wear harem pants. It is not a fashion statement. It is not a gender statement. He is not being ironic. As far as I know, he is not a fan of MC Hammer. I believe that he doesn't fully appreciate how unfashionable these pants are. If asked, he would likely say he likes these pants because they are colorful and comfortable. My guess is he has *no* idea these pants are Jupiterian in their oddity. Hipsters, on the other hand, would *never* wear these pants. *Ever.*

Hipsters are aware of what's going on. We say of them, and they say of one another, that they get it. Culturematic-makers don't always get it. And if they do, they don't always care about "it." They are immune to what Mark Earls calls the "herd effect."[62] Hipsters are, well, hip. They are hip to the con, hip to the game, hip to the joke. Culturematic-makers, on the other hand, can be a little clueless, a little literal. Not only are they not in on the joke, but they are surprised to hear that a joke was on offer.

In effect, Culturematic-makers are a little blind to cool. Take this book, for instance. I dare praise reality TV, a form of television that everyone knows is bad, stupid, and wrong. I praise fantasy football, which everyone knows is just about sports. I praise Chuck Lorre, the maker of *Two and a Half Men*, a show everyone knows is the product (and producer) of dumb-and-dumber culture. I even praise Steve-O and other knuckleheads, known by everyone to be philistines of the first order. Everyone, that is, except me and other Culturematic-makers. We are not going along with what everybody supposedly knows. Because going along with what everyone knows makes you the captive of convention.

Culturematic-makers can look like people with autism, like people who are somehow oblivious to social rules and cultural understandings.[63] But this is wrong. They are not oblivious. They are trying to see *through* these rules and understandings. They mean to escape the dead hand of cool. Culturematic-makers want to see with their own eyes, work with their own judgment.

If this gives them a slightly Martian quality, well, too bad. We can try to jolly Culturematic-makers along, with that "Oh, come on, everybody knows this, right?" But we can expect them to reply with a look that says, "Not really." Most of culture is an arbitrary arrangement that presents itself as natural and inevitable. But for Culturematic-makers, this is the point of the exercise: to see the artifice in the inevitable. This is the path to cultural innovation.

Being Creative *and* Useful

Culturematics are nothing if not versatile. They create innovation in the worlds of TV, sports, social media, the Internet, festivals, advertising, marketing, and public life. When Culturematics ping the universe, many things return.

In all of this, Culturematics are interdenominational. They serve the teenager working in a basement laboratory just as well as the GE employee looking for the next new thing. For Culturematics, there is no important difference between the personal projects and corporate ones, no difference between things that are useful and things that are artistic. Both begin as an inkling, a stirring suspicion that the present order of things is not the inevitable order of things, that there is something else out there. This is what the Culturematic is for, exploring a suspicion. What if . . .

A Culturematic resists the usual categories. It is not merely creative or useful, but usually both. At the moment of invention, there isn't much difference between imagination and pragmatism. The great American sociologist Daniel Bell divided the world into the expressive and the instrumental.[64] Culturematics are inclined to refuse the distinction and put this Humpty Dumpty back together again.

The next chapter will look at twenty Culturematics. We will see this dual character everywhere. When Chuck Lorre seizes the opportunity created by the vanity card and begins to beam his messages to the TV viewing public, we can't actually say whether he is being expressive or instrumental. When people create or participate in Ford's Fiesta Movement, again we can't tell whether they are driven by curiosity or the pragmatic. In point of fact, these boundaries are breaking down. Thanks to influential business writers Tom Peters, Seth Godin, Bill Taylor, and Polly Labarre, we expect to play at work and to work at play. In Mihaly Csikszentmihalyi's famous term, what interests us is "flow."[65]

Culturematics are ecumenical. They should aid the corporation, encouraging it to play, embracing even projects that are quirky and inconsiderable. And they should inspire the girl running a lab in her parents' basement to keep an eye out for commercial application. Somewhere in her many projects may be the beginning of a career as a medical researcher or an entrepreneur. Many Culturematics will start just for the fun of it and become a going concern, perhaps even a lifelong enterprise.

Since the seventeenth century, the American economy has run through a succession of forms: agricultural, industrial, service, knowledge, information, digital, and creative.[66] With each new economy, the world became less tangible and less literal. It becomes less about utility and more about value, broadly defined. It becomes less about objects and more about ideas, less about present realities and more about possible outcomes. And as this new world has unfolded, two things became obvious. First, we live in a world of constant change. And second, we must adapt to this constant change with an experimental stream of new ideas. This is why Culturematics matter.

3 Twenty Culturematics

Culturematics come in all shapes and sizes. They have popped up online, on TV, and in the real world. They have changed the way we think about marketing, sports, advertising, and food. We might think of the Culturematic as an all-purpose innovation engine.

Viva Rube Goldberg

Seen a Rube Goldberg contraption lately? Rube Goldberg was an engineer, an inventor, and a prolific cartoonist active in the 1920s, 1930s, and 1940s.[1] He created wonderful devices in which household objects took turns being cause and effect: a mallet hits a ball, which rolls down a plank, which tips a can of paint, which drips into a pan, which . . . In most cases, a mouse ends up getting a bit of cheese. These intricate cartoons made Rube a minor celebrity. Then he hit a dry spell. For many years, no one cared about Rube Goldberg or his nutty contraptions.

How things change! Rube is now *the man*. Dorm rooms are routinely taken over by his fiendishly complicated devices. (Plug Rube's name into YouTube if you want to see some examples.) Tom Baynham and Ben Tyers were engineering students at Cambridge

University when they made their Goldberg machine. It took them weeks and weeks to complete, and by the time they were done, the contraption took up the whole of their apartment. It's an exercise in absolute ingenuity, bringing together pool cues, golf balls, polo mallets, paper towels, forks, cell phones, wine bottles, a chess board, an arrow, a boot, a burning candle, and several Slinky toys, in a chain reaction that runs for three minutes and eighteen seconds.[2]

Recently, the band OK Go treated us to a Rube Goldberg contraption that ends with the band's getting blasted by primary colors. *MythBusters* did one to celebrate the holidays. (And yes, Mentos and cola were involved.) The marketing world has embraced Rube. Planning mastermind Russell Davies turned the components of a Honda Accord into a Goldberg machine. Guinness staged a Goldberg that took up the whole of a small town in Argentina. A Sprint ad uses a Rube Goldberg device to show the history of technology. That's to name a few. Rube Goldberg's devices are happening everywhere.[3]

After World War II, when America was conducting a love affair with technology and science, Rube's contraptions looked silly, old-fashioned, and frivolous. America was a world of push-button efficacy and wonderful new gadgets that actually helped get real things done: blenders, toasters, lawn mowers, mechanized washing machines. This technology was formidably capable. Who cared about Rube's completely contrived contrivances? Rube's creations look like whimsy of the most pointless kind, and Rube looked like, well, a rube who didn't know any better.

What made Rube so irritating after World War II endears him to us now. We love the idea that the disparate pieces of our world might be made to cooperate after all. What a lovely surprise. But there is something irreducibly, inexplicably charming about ordinary objects that take on a magical synchronicity. Order out of accident. Magic out of banality. We love Rube now.

Ford's Fiesta Movement

For a marketing campaign in 2010, Ford gave one hundred Fiestas to one hundred drivers. The drivers were free to keep the car for six months. All Ford asked was that they complete a different mission each month. And away the drivers went. They delivered Meals On Wheels. They took treats from Harry and David to the national guard. They went looking for adventure, some to wrestle alligators, others to elope. Oh, and the other condition of having a Fiesta: drivers were to document their stories on YouTube, Flickr, Facebook, and Twitter.

Mystery Guitar Man (MGM) was asked to drive his Fiesta until it ran out of gas. This makes for a charming video. We see MGM driving around burning gas, waiting for the inevitable. There's a fuel gauge in the upper right-hand corner of the screen. MGM doesn't know when the gas will run out, so he just keeps driving. In the meantime, he flirts with girls in the drive-thru lane at McDonald's. He stands around in parking lots and answers the kinds of questions men ask about cars. People give him unsolicited advice (specifically, that if he's thinking of running away from home, he shouldn't). And he keeps driving into upstate New York, where, eventually, some 432 miles from home, he coasts to a stop. It's kind of a letdown, but then it's a mystery that any of this held our attention. After all, this is a weird enterprise, isn't it? Well, yes, and really pretty interesting.[4]

In another mission, we are introduced to Bridget O, a beautiful chatterbox. The Fiesta camera finds Bridget wandering the streets of Seattle in search of her car keys. Yes, charged with a Fiesta mission, Bridget actually managed to lose her keys. Go, Bridget! Bridget has roped a boy into a search for the keys, when, wait, what is this vision they see before them? It is a woman doing some sort of interpretive dance in the middle of the street. Bridget and the boy watch, transfixed. The dancer engages Bridget in the dance, and then, hey presto, returns her keys! Bridget and the boy are flabbergasted! Was this a setup? Well, probably. Bridget plays it out as if it were the real deal, and she does this with just enough dramatic conviction that we are prepared to give her the benefit of the doubt. Maybe. OK, we're not sure. (And that, our uncertainty, is the point.)[5]

These missions don't actually amount to much. but they are interesting in their way. They represent a departure for the world of marketing, which used to prefer the thirty-second TV spot or the four-color print ad. Invented by Bud Caddell, Jim Farly, and Connie Fontaine, the Fiesta Movement was the most visible and interesting social media experiment the automotive world had tried to date.[6]

Dan Harmon's Channel 101

Dan Harmon makes television. He created *Community* for NBC and *The Sarah Silverman Program* for Comedy Central. Harmon could have made TV the old-fashioned way, coming up with ideas, pitching them to network and cable executives, rolling out pilots, going on air, and, with luck, running the table of contemporary culture, creating a hit series that brought him fame and fortune.

But that's the risky proposition. All the world is trying to make hit television. So many are called, so few are chosen.

Harmon settled on another, Culturematic approach. With his friend Rob Schrab, he created a forum called Channel 101.

> Since 2001, every month in a small bar-turned-screening-room in Hollywood, audiences of a hundred or so people—often in, or aspiring to be in, the entertainment

industry—gather to watch mini-pilots, each up to five minutes long, of varying DIY types of production, submitted by whoever has enough spare time and interest to make them. The audience watches ten of these super-condensed shows: a CSI spoof, a surreal animation about a horde of murderous, Gremlins-esque Bill Cosby clones. At the end of the screening, the audience votes for five of these pilots to be "picked up," or given the green light to make a new episode for the next month's screening. Each series continues its run for as long as the show remains popular in this underground television network. Over the last decade, Channel 101 has helped launch the careers of many comedians—from Andy Samberg and the SNL digital shorts creators to Jack Black, Sarah Silverman, and Adult Swim's Tim and Eric.[7]

With Channel 101, Harmon made a laboratory, a place where new ideas could be tested without the whopping, great investments normally required. If some pilots cost, as we have noted, $2 million, a Channel 101 experimental minipilot could be funded with comparatively tiny investments of time and money. If it doesn't work, well, it doesn't work. The sky doesn't fall. Careers don't end.

Channel 101 has all the earmarks of a Culturematic. It keeps innovation cheap. It lets people experiment fast. They can fail early and often. They can see what strikes a chord, treating their competitors as collaborators. They are now viewing a stream of new ideas giving themselves a chance to "know it when we see it." If this were 1950s television, Channel 101 would make much less sense. But Harmon knows he lives in a world in which he can't see more than one hundred feet ahead of himself. In this case, Channel 101 makes all the sense in the world.

SETI (Search for Extraterrestrial Intelligence)

Working late at the Harvard Business School, I would button up my office and start my walk home. This would take me past the windows of colleagues, and I would notice with pleasure and interest that sitting on several desks were computer screens glowing with a search for life in the universe. The year was 1990, and the Search for Extraterrestrial Intelligence (SETI) had come to Morgan Hall.[8]

SETI was founded on the idea that someone out there in the universe might have started beaming us messages and that we really should start listening more carefully. Actually, the SETI idea was that we should be listening more broadly. We needed to scrutinize every piece of the night sky in all directions, listening for something, anything that wasn't noise. This is a vast computational undertaking, and someone had the bright idea of enlisting ordinary desktop computers that sit idle every night. These computers were ordinary HPs and Macs, not very powerful, but together they could crunch a lot of data. Hence those glowing screens in Morgan Hall.[9]

Now, the SETI could have said, "Listen: frankly, this is way too complicated for you to understand, so just give us access to your computer, all right?" (We are the Borg. Resistance is futile.) Instead, someone decided to create a little Culturematic. Now the pitch was more like, "We need to canvass the entire night sky. We are going to give you a tiny piece of it. Your own little patch. And if we find what we're looking for there, you get the credit. Hey, it could be you who discovers intelligent life in the universe. This will look good on your résumé and make a great story to tell over dinner."

It was like getting a ticket in the world's greatest lottery. What if our computer was the one that discovered life on Planet x54192?! The press was not going to want to talk to geeky scientists. It was going to want to talk to Jim Urbina, owner of the Dell desktop that took the call from deep space. The family phone would never ever stop ringing. "Where was Urbina at the time of the discovery?" "Did he have any inkling of what was happening in his study?" "What does he think of the universe now?" There's a good chance that Urbina and his wife were watching *CSI: Miami* and debating why David Caruso is always putzing around with his sunglasses, but the press knows that Jim will rise to the occasion and solemnly report that at 10:17 on the night in question he was standing in his backyard staring up into the great, celestial theater that vaults Metuchen, New Jersey. What a coincidence!

Gatorade's Replay

On November 25, 1993, two high school football teams played to a tie.[10]

Not the worst thing in the world, perhaps. But it happened in small-town America, where football can matter extraordinarily. And it happened to two teams that have a hundred-year rivalry that *Sports Illustrated* describes as one of the most intense in the country.

And a tie, as they say in American sports, is like kissing your sister. The world is made symmetrical, when the point of sports (and Western cultures) is to produce events, outcomes, and asymmetries. Ties erase the event. It's like nothing ever happened.

Someone at Gatorade had a great idea. What if fifteen years later, the teams of Easton and Phillipsburg were reassembled and the game replayed? Athletes now in their thirties got a second chance. So did the fans. Ten thousand tickets sold out in ninety minutes. And the rest of us went, "How completely interesting."[11]

It's an irresistible story line, isn't it? But it's not clear why, especially if we don't particularly care about football, small towns, or the ignominy of a tie. It's not because football greats, the Manning brothers, were brought in to help with the coaching. It just happens to be flat-out, eye-poppingly interesting.

Gatorade's *Replay* reactivates men who are no longer in their physical prime, now playing more for honor than heroism. We glimpse immediately that these men will have to be retrieved from wherever the biographic tide has taken them. The solidarity of the old days will have to be reasserted over all the differences that have sprung up in fifteen years. We don't have to be a culture creative to think, "Hmm, this is going to be dramatically juicy." We have all seen conventional football heroics. There are only so many things that can happen. *Replay* gives us something more authentic, where life and sport will share the field.

And what makes this a Culturematic is that all this grist and gusto comes from an entirely simple, mechanical premise: what if we brought these teams back together again? So much drama from so little pretext!

Gatorade is well compensated for its use of a Culturematic. The Gatorade message is "It doesn't matter how old you are. Eight to eighty, you are always an athlete." *Replay* talks to all of us, and the brand gets to escape the gilded palace of professional sports and enter a domain that looks a lot more like life.[12]

SNL Digital Shorts

When Andy Samberg joined the cast of *Saturday Night Live*, he found his own way to make a contribution.

> If you don't ask your boss, he can't say "no." And when you're new and young and your ideas are kind of weird, "yes" is a hard answer to get. So Andy Samberg, the new guy at the highly competitive *Saturday Night Live* ideas

meetings, borrowed a friend's wife's camera, made a short film and never told producer Lorne Michaels what he was doing until he handed him the tape.[13]

Andy Samberg has since made lots of digital shorts for NBC's *Saturday Night Live*. With the help of two friends from high school, Jorma Taccone and Akiva Schaffer, and their production company called The Lonely Island, Samberg is one of the new producing wells in popular culture.

Samberg, Taccone, and Schaffer found their way to *SNL* thanks to the intercession of Jimmy Fallon. What passed between *SNL*'s show runner Lorne Michaels and Samberg in their first conversation, we can only guess. Michaels has had this conversation hundreds of times, with the likes of Bill Murray, Eddie Murphy, Amy Poehler, Mike Myers, Adam Sandler, and Tina Fey. In many cases, Michaels was dealing with a brash talent who needed to learn the rules of the game. In Samberg's case, the traditional approach from Michaels would have been something like, "This is the big time, kid. I know you love your high school friends, but it's time to say good-bye. You can't take them with you."

But this time, Michaels took a new approach. Instead of making Samberg a fully integrated, fully socialized, member of the *SNL* culture, Michaels allowed him to remain in loose orbit. Samberg could keep working with Taccone and Shaffer, and the three of them could punt their work into *SNL* as digital shorts. Thus did Michaels enable *SNL*'s first Culturematic.

Michaels's motives were entirely Culturematic. Digital shorts could go places and do things that were out of the range of *SNL*. Typically, the cast has one week to get from inspiration to air-ready work. Ideas have to produce quickly, and there's no room for dithering. Digital shorts gave Michaels an experimental zone. The Lonely Island guys could try things. If something didn't work, it didn't work. Failure was acceptable, because as Michaels put it, it's the guys who "take the risk."[14]

With risk managed in the Culturematic way, *SNL* could break out of what Ethan Thompson calls "the residual boomer sensibility that still permeates the show." *SNL* was famous for creating characters and catchphrases (e.g., Mike Myers as host Linda Richman: "I'm all verklempt"). Samberg and his pals were mocking pop culture in the *SNL* tradition, but this work was more carefully observed, more finely executed than sketch comedy would allow. *SNL* has ridiculed youthful pretension before, but only SNL Digital Shorts could have done this as well, as fully, as "Ras Trent." Digital shorts could also take on topics outside standard *SNL* daring. "Dick in a Box" and "Jizz in My Pants" were extremely daring. Most of all, digital shorts could leverage celebrity firepower in new ways. In the old model, *SNL* would bring in a star and hope that he or she wouldn't make a hash of things. (Good performances from the guest host usually win *grateful* laughter, as if everyone is thinking, "Whew, that wasn't so bad.") The digital shorts model leveraged celebrity firepower in new ways. "Shy Ronny" could never have happened in studio. Finally, digital shorts gave *SNL* a digital presence it needed badly. The YouTube views generated by SNL Digital Shorts run into the hundreds of millions. ("Jizz in My Pants" has been viewed more than 100 million times.) Digital shorts created a robust old-media, new-media collaboration.[15]

The Japanese Torch Run

In 1998, something odd happened during the torch run in Nagano, Japan. Traditionally, this has been a sedate affair. The Olympic flame is flown to the new host country from Greece. Runners deliver it by stages to the Olympic stadium. People show up to salute the runners as they pass in the street. Polite applause is the order of the day. Not in Nagano. Not this Olympics. People turned out by the thousands, and they were demonstrative. They wept. They shouted. They exulted.[16]

The torch run is by definition a Culturematic. It creates a little, bounded, mechanical event. And, blammo, it got a huge response.

The Olympic torch run transmits the torch from runner to runner in the manner of a relay. Getting three torches from far-flung places by one-kilometer intervals through thousands of hands for simultaneous arrival at the stadium requires a small miracle of logistics and execution.

But this is always true. Every Olympics has a torch run. And in every case, people come out to show their appreciation. They applaud. They wave. And they go home. Not in Nagano. Here in Japan, people wept.

It's still not clear why the torch run had extra oomph in Nagano. It might have been that the flame passed through almost every prefecture in Japan, touching many little towns normally left to slumber in obscurity. Observers liked the fact that the far margin was being articulated with a national center at the very moment that this was being articulated with the world community. This run had the magical ability to express differences *and* commonality. To borrow technologist David Weinberger's wonderful book title, it made Japan "small pieces loosely joined."[17]

The torchbearers were wonderfully diverse, including local schoolchildren, public officials, and homemakers. Perhaps that also helped. Perhaps it was that some torchbearers were participating out of deeply personal motives. A Taiwan TV celebrity, Pai Ping-ping, was running, she said, to demonstrate to her daughter, murdered a year before, that "Mum is back on her feet again." Chris Moon, a British activist who had lost an arm and a leg to a mine in Mozambique, was running to help end the use of land mines. The flames told extraordinary stories everywhere they went.

There were other reasons to love the run. This Olympics came at a time when some people were feeling that scandals, banking difficulties, and other frustrations were diminishing Japan's standing as the "best in show" of the capitalist economies. The Olympics would not restore this vaunted position, but it might help augment Japan's international profile.

The Olympic ideal is a very large—one might say, billowing—idea. The torch run helped make it local, little, and literal, something like clockwork, kinda Rube Goldberg, and very Culturematic.

Negro Leagues Grave Marker Project

Recently, three men assembled in Columbia, Missouri, at the unmarked grave of William M. Gatewood, a star pitcher in the early Negro Leagues, who died in Columbia in 1962. They had come to put a new headstone on Gatewood's grave. As an anesthesiologist, an historian, and an insurance agent, the men didn't have much in common, but they did share the conviction that Negro Leagues baseball was very good baseball and that it deserved to be rescued from the obscurity into which the game and its heroes had fallen.[18]

They could have taken a more conventional approach. They could have done their research, created a book or a documentary, issued a press release, and done the talk shows. Instead, they decided to hit the road, in personal journeys to very particular places, to find and honor players they had never seen play. They stood there on bleak, fall days, in largely forgotten graveyards, and paid their respects. They created a mission; they created a Culturematic.

Why not a book or a documentary? Well, yawn, that's why. Certainly, they would have gotten reviews. The documentary would have done the circuit. The project would have won an award from national organizations dedicated to baseball or black history. And the whole thing would have disappeared. "Interesting," we would have said. "Important. Got it. Next!"

But the Negro Leagues Grave Marker Project, as it was officially known, did much better than create a small stir. It got coverage on the front page of the *New York Times*, leaping over the most expensive PR that money can buy. Everyone wants to get into the *Times*. And front-page coverage? Forget about it. This is the holy grail of the media world. Corporations and countries spend millions trying to get there. This Culturematic got it for free.

Why? Because this is a story we want to hear. This is something that comes up off the page and goes straight into the imagination. We can picture it: three perfect strangers standing in a graveyard in the wind, the rain, and the middle of nowhere, honoring men they have never met. Irresistible. This leaps to the front page because it has the qualities of the Culturematic: little, manageable, vivid, thought-provoking, and oh-so-very actual. We are there, standing in the middle of a graveyard. Documentary, schockumentary. This Culturematic captures us.

Twitter as a Culturematic

Twitter is now five years old. It has around 200 million users, who, between them, send around a billion tweets a month. That's about 140 million tweets a day and around 4,000 tweets in the time it will take you to read this paragraph. To be sure, some of this is noise, bursts of data that don't matter very much. (We don't *really* need to know someone just fed the cat.) But for many people, Twitter is also a raw feed of new intelligence, one of the organs of democracy, and a great enabler of the Arab revolt that began in the spring of 2011.[19]

It was not always thus. In the early days, the founders of Twitter, Biz Stone, Jack Dorsey, and Evan Williams, thought Twitter might appeal to "technical geeks" in San Francisco, who would use it "to fool around with and to find out what each other's up to." Like the founders of fantasy football, they had no idea what they were about to release into the world.

And frankly, they didn't care. Williams happened to have a fascination with dispatch software, the kind of thing that could be used for taxicabs, emergency vehicles, and couriers. Mobile phones had made short message service (SMS) communication ubiquitous, and the guys thought, "Well, we could build on top of that." At this early stage, they were driven by personal passion. So it didn't especially bother them that, as Stone recalls, "for the first nine months or so everyone just thought we were fools [and that Twitter] was the most ridiculous thing they'd ever heard of." For Stone and company, Twitter was a "very simple side project [we did] almost to scratch an itch."

Culture was on their side. More people were using new media to create more messages. The world was filling up with communication. One way to manage the chaos was to establish a new "maximum headroom." The intellectual forum called TED was giving the stage to smart, talented people, but then it said, "Oh, and by the way, keep it under eighteen minutes." And to everyone's surprise, what would once have taken a full forty-five minutes could be captured in one-third the time. A new parsimony was in effect.

Lo and behold, 140 characters were enough. Enough to alert other people about your existence, share an article, track a changing world, and occasionally stage a revolution. And it was created as an experiment on the side. Williams said, "Why don't some of us just take two weeks and build something that really . . . inspires us." Twitter was a simple what-if. What if we all had access to dispatch software? What if we could speak in bursts of 140 characters? What started as a what-if for Stone and company became a what-if for the rest of us.

You may remember those early days. We didn't really know how to use the technology. What if I said this? What if I said that? And eventually, we began to find our way. We tinkered our way into the future. But if someone had said, you can only have the technology if you are prepared to tell us how you will use it, well, Twitter would never have found a place in the world. We didn't know. We couldn't tell. How was anyone going to use 140 characters to good effect? We had to use it to see. We had to "what if" it. First, we make the tech, then the tech makes us. A certain blind experimentalism is the order of the day.

NFL Films

Ed Sabol was selected for the U.S. Olympic team going to Berlin in 1936. He chose not to go because of Hitler's influence on the games. He went instead to war, serving as a rifleman in the Fourth Infantry. When he returned from Europe, he became an early owner of a 16 mm camera. He used it to film "my wife getting into and out of the car" and football games played by his ten-year-old.[20]

In the early 1960s, professional football had no real presence on the screen, as Greg Eno explains:

> Pro football was archived as newsreel footage, shown in two-minute increments in the movie houses across America.
>
> It was filmed in black and white, always from the same high angle with the camera perched at the 50-yard line.
>
> The images were sterile, the music usually a cheesy version of some college fight song.

> During the 1940s and 50s, nothing was compelling
> about pro football on film. [It was like watching] a
> fish tank.[21]

Sabol asked the National Football League if he could film the 1962 championship game between the Packers and the Giants. In those days, the NFL didn't have the scale or grandeur it does now. Many players had second jobs, and not just in the off-season. Stadiums were little and exposed to the elements. Audiences were small. Baseball was still America's game. After it had got over its surprise, the NFL said that Sabol could film the game and they sold him the rights for $3,000.

Film was expensive. To make matters worse, Sabol used several cameras. Worse still, he used a slow-motion camera that burned film like crazy. Every minute of football cost Sabol a small fortune. This approach struck some people (and certainly the NFL) as entirely excess to requirement. The newsreel-footage approach was fine. No one could quite believe the game deserved better.

But Sabol had a strategy. "We're storytellers," he said. "We're romanticists. If 'Lord of the Rings' had been shot on videotape, it wouldn't have the same sense of wonder, of majesty, of magic about it. We're historians, we're storytellers, we're mythmakers. We'll always stay on film."[22]

What the NFL was selling was a game, working-class heroes laboring on the frozen tundra. What Sabol was buying was a platform for telling stories. And to tell stories, Sabol was going to have to capture the game in new ways. He shot players close up. He miked huddles, coaches, and collisions. He shot exertion and emotion invisible on newsreel. Using slow-motion camera, powerful music, and voice-over, Sabol made journeymen players stand for something larger than themselves. The voice-over came from a newscaster called John Facenda, a guy Sabol had discovered when Facenda was doing impromptu voice-over at a bar. As Sabol later joked, Facenda couldn't tell the difference between a "trap block and a Greek salad," but the voice! "If the Last Supper ever had an after-dinner speaker, it would be John Facenda." Sabol has managed to make football feel somehow mythical and the men who bagged groceries in the off-season somehow heroic.

NFL Films is a Culturematic. It posted a powerful what-if: "What if we treat football not as a sport but as a story? What if we treat tough guys as mythic heroes?" It took a flyer on an emerging sport and an emerging medium. It transformed an athletic undertaking into something larger than itself. It discovered value where no one suspected value existed. In this process, it did great things for professional football. If football has supplanted baseball as America's game, it is largely due to Ed Sabol. Or put another way, if Sabol had gone to work for professional baseball, it might still be America's game. (Yes, Sabol could have made myth even out of guys standing around scratching themselves.)

WhySoSerious.com

WhySoSerious.com was a promotion for the 2008 film *The Dark Knight*. It proved an effective marketing device, running for fourteen months up to the launch of the movie and drawing an astounding ten million visitors. WhySoSerious.com helped give new life to the sixty-nine-year-old Batman franchise and helped propel *The Dark Knight* to sales of $1 billion worldwide.

Happily, the site is still up. (Have a look.) We begin with a screen filled with fragments, a page torn from the phone book, playing cards, a defaced one-dollar bill. It turns out that the phone numbers are "live." So I called the *Gotham Times* at 866-237-6480. (Try it!) A recorded message told me new subscriptions were suspended due to production difficulties. Trouble at the *Gotham Times*? Clicking on the bits and pieces on screen gave me Gotham Police Department circulars and newspaper articles, both of which document the chaos caused by Batman's nemesis, the Joker. There are also ferry schedules, ads, and restaurant menus, all of them defaced by the Joker. I was beginning to see a pattern.

Somewhere in this blizzard of information and artifact, there's a trailer for the movie. But it's easy to miss. Apparently, for these movie makers, a trailer is old media designed according to the old logic of Hollywood, the one that says, "Sit there and listen while we tell you all about this movie." The point of WhySoSerious.com is to engage the moviegoer in new ways.

In his excellent book *The Art of Immersion*, Frank Rose explains how this promotional Web site works:

> [WhySoSerious.com is] a new kind of interactive fiction, one that blurred the line between entertainment and advertising, as well as between fiction and reality . . . The story is told in fragments; the game comes in piecing the fragments together. The task is too complicated for any one person. But through the connective power of the Web, a group intelligence emerges to assemble the pieces, solve the mysteries, and, in the process, tell and retell the story online. Ultimately, the audience comes to own the story, in ways that movies themselves can't match.[23]

Thus does the ad for the film become a part of the film. Indeed, the ad allows the story to live outside the film. Broken into all these pieces and now accessible to millions of people, the Batman story is turned loose in the world. What happens to it here is, well, hard to say. In this transmedia approach to filmmaking, the creatives give up some control.[24] But they take on new opportunities. Now the story is messy, multiple, indeterminate, and, for a certain generation of filmgoers, more engaging than anything they could hope to see at their local cinema. Thus did these filmmakers turn *The Dark Knight* into a Culturematic. Thus did the Dark Knight escape.

Old Spice: "The Man Your Man Could Smell Like"

The first salvo in the Old Spice "The Man Your Man Could Smell Like" campaign was very "old media" and not at all Culturematic. It consisted of a spot during the Super Bowl and was big-message advertising addressed to a mass (the massest) audience. As the work of Wieden + Kennedy, it was not an average ad. It was shot through with the sly, self-mocking intelligence that had characterized their work for Old Spice from its Bruce Campbell beginnings.[25]

It was what happened next that was Culturematic. The world so liked the Super Bowl ad that it began to comment on blog posts and Twitter. And then there was a great flood of YouTube videos that celebrated, satirized, and copied it. Wieden + Kennedy is not a shop famous for its new-media enthusiasm, but Dan Wieden had recently announced his interest in taking up the digital opportunity.[26] With this and client encouragement, Wieden + Kennedy created the Response campaign.

> A team of creatives, tech geeks, marketers and writers gathered in an undisclosed location in Portland, Oregon yesterday and produced 87 short comedic YouTube videos about Old Spice. In real time. They leveraged Twitter, Facebook, Reddit and blogs.[27]

And this is very Culturematic. The Wieden + Kennedy team worked for three days in a fury of creative activity, trying just about anything people thought was funny, firing the result into the world to see what worked and what did not. The campaign was entirely experimental.

> Nothing was pre-written. Nothing was promoted in advance. The [creative team's] prop table included money, a fake monocle, fake fish and other artifacts that they suspected would come in handy. Their process was completely collaborative. One writer would write jokes, the others would review, delete some, build on others. This advertising effort was more similar to a stage performance than advertising. As the responses came in it was completely exhilarating.[28]

Fake fish! Improv meets vaudeville. And no one has any idea what's coming.

The world replied in a flood. Nearly forty thousand comments on YouTube. Responses came in from (and went out to) Biz Stone, Ryan Seacrest, Kevin Rose (founder of Digg), Guy Kawasaki, and Perez Hilton.

The Response campaign proved one of the great success stories in the world of marketing, winning a Grand Prix at Cannes in the Cyber category. Between February and July 2010, there were roughly 34 million views on YouTube.[29]

Two-Dollar Holler

I recently came across a two-dollar bill. This was remarkable all by itself; fewer than 1 percent of the bills in circulation in the United States are two-dollar bills. But this bill also had a sticker on it that read "Life, Liberty and the Pursuit of Happiness." On the sticker, there is a large arrow pointing to the part of the bill that reproduces John Trumbull's famous nineteenth-century painting that shows the founding fathers signing the Declaration of Independence. The point? The Seattle Art Museum had commandeered these bills to promote its exhibit of American art.[30]

It looks like a stunt. And a daring one, at that. Since when did an art museum deface federal currency? On closer examination, something more is going on. "Life, Liberty and the Pursuit of Happiness" is the great phrase that leaps from the Declaration into American life. (We may think of it as the starter's gun of American life.) It is the name of Trumbull's painting that captures the Declaration's signing. And it happens to be the name of the exhibit in question, at the center of which stands Trumbull's painting. What a bit of good luck. The two-dollar bill created a message with which to circulate news of the exhibit. And the message, as a measure of currency, is a part of the economic experiment that makes up so much of the American experiment. It was very like a gift from the gods of communication. No mere stunt, this Culturematic, but something intricately, wickedly clever.

Reckless and strange for an art museum, to be sure, but entirely in character for a Culturematic. Culturematics are inclined to interfere with convention and the rules of the game, and this one is prepared to bewilder and offend people in the process. It digs deep into culture, finds the meanings and rules that define culture, and deliberately violates them. It makes meaning by making mischief.

Chez Panisse

Chez Panisse is a restaurant that opened in Berkeley in 1971. In the early days, it was a "slapdash, make-it-up-as-we-go-along little hangout."[31] No one, not the founders, Alice Waters and Paul Aratow, and not the chef, Victoria Kroyer, had ever cooked in a restaurant before. Things were chaotic from the beginning, and the place was an exercise in the principle that what can go wrong will go wrong. But within a few years, it was clear that something remarkable was being accomplished.

The first big review of Chez Panisse hinted at good things to come:

> Right now in an unassuming, circa 1900 wood-frame house on Berkeley's Shattuck Avenue, an exciting experiment in restaurant dining is being carried out. That is how I view Chez Panisse—as a vibrantly alive, ongoing experiment, not always meeting with unqualified success, but never anything less than stimulating and often positively.[32]

What drove this restaurant was not experience or system, but the conviction that American food should change. In 1971, a postwar food regime was still in effect. Factory farming, industrial processing, and fast-food distribution were in the ascendancy. The most organic substance in the world was subject to interventions and adulterations of every kind. The 1950s was a Cambrian era for processed food. (Sugar Pops were created in 1950. Cheez Whiz in 1953. Tang in 1958.) Most of our fast-food chains were created in the period. (Dunkin' Donuts was created in 1950. Denny's in 1953. Pizza Hut in 1958.) People were taking resort vacations where they exposed themselves to heroic quantities of sugar, fat, sun, salt, monosodium glutamate (MSG), alcohol, caffeine, nicotine, and chlorine. Every glorious day ended with a floor show, florid, insincere, and loaded with aesthetic toxins of its own. Something had to give.

The creative genius and indomitable spirit at the center of the Chez Panisse was Alice Waters. She did not have imperial pretensions. She didn't like what America was doing to food, but she saw no hope of changing it: "All I knew was that Chez Panisse could be better than it was."[33] So many of the ideas on politics, gender, class, and technology that come out of North California are self-consciously revolutionary; they mean to change every-thing. Waters just wanted to improve Chez Panisse.

But Waters had greatness thrust upon her. When Michelle Obama put a vegetable garden on the lawn of the White House, one of the lines of influence went straight back to the little restau-rant on Shattuck Avenue. Chez Panisse is now a shrine for the restaurant world. It has transformed the eating habits and food expectations of most Americans. California cuisine and the arti-sanal trend are largely its creation.

But again, in the beginning, there was no big idea. No strategic plan. The success of Chez Panisse came from many things.[34] Waters's perfect palate, her education in France, a succession of lovers from each of whom she appears to have learned something essential, even her training as a Montessori teacher played a role. The restaurant proved equally syncretic. It drew a succession of bril-liant chefs, making it seem as if the very point of Berkley's diversity was the promotion of Chez Panisse. Academics, gardeners, hippies, filmmakers, farmers, even drug dealers were called upon to serve.

Chez Panisse is an odd Culturematic in some ways. There is nothing little or inexpensive about a restaurant. Even when cre-ated in a dilapidated building in a college town, it requires a large investment of time and capital. The risks are enormous. But it is a classic Culturematic in other ways. It breaks with conviction. It's as if this Culturematic can hear a navigational signal that is inaudible to everyone else. And it follows this signal, even though no one can tell where it's coming from or where it must lead. It provokes the world, it discovers value, it unleashes meaning.

Restaurants are the outcome of thousands of decisions, large and small. Should the light in the restaurant be white or yellow? Crème in this dish or yogurt? Shallots, not garlic? Waters and company made these choices with conviction, and with each choice, Chez Panisse moved farther and farther out of the mainstream of

American cuisine and culture. None of the Chez Panisse people quite knew where they were headed. No doubt they had the explorer's classic anxiety that they were too long out of sight of land and must eventually fall off the edge of the world. At some level, everyone knew that if Chez Panisse failed, there would be misery all round. Staff and even customers were ruined for any other restaurant. They could not go home again. But they carried on, making choices that no one had quite made before, in conformity to a grammar no one could quite make out. It looks as if for all her modesty and diffidence, Waters never met a risk she didn't take.

Culturematic-makers carry on. Chez Panisse worked. It was so in touch with the larger forces of American culture and so formative of the popular will that it fashioned our future. Many of us watched Chez Panisse pull away from American culture and make its way onto uncharted waters. And then we followed in its wake.

The Unconference by Evelyn Rodriguez

I saw this float past in my Google+ stream. When I read the following blog by Evelyn Rodriguez, I thought, "Wow, this is a Culturematic in the meeting world":

> I'm in the early stage of percolating ideas around some kind of gathering that's a mix between an unconference and an urban game. First up is Las Vegas; but don't see why not other places as well.
>
> The purpose is barn-raising—by cross-fertilizing and sharing our individual objectives, dreams, desires[,] we'll find partners, new ideas, and who can predict what else to move forward. We can take individual dreams also into the collective realm as well when we come together. I cannot do sit-down board meetings or lecture-type

conferences. This has got to be fun, useful, [and] participatory for me to even bother to engage any of my own energy into it, much less ask anyone else to pitch in. The spirit would be vision-oriented rather than problem-focused, like this article outlines:

"We understand that for every high-spirited 'Why not?' there is a swift and cruel answer these days: 'Because we don't have the money, that's why not.' But that's a conversation killer. And we're not going to get much of anywhere by killing the conversation. How can we ever talk about plausible dreams for our city when it turns out that all dreams are implausible? Isn't it worth it, just for a moment, to clear the cluttered actuarial tables and make room for a few wildly diverse proposals, ideas that at first glance seem far-fetched, but at second thought leave you wondering, 'Why not?' Let's set some thoughts loose to contend with one another, to compete and collide and start productive, creative arguments." —["Why Not? 21 arguably plausible, definitely outrageous ideas for our city, from downtown to the mountains," *Seven*, December 2, 2010, http://weeklyseven.com/news/2010/december/ 02/why-not]

p.s. Mind you, this story comes from the city that has the most foreclosures and the highest unemployment rate in the USA—at least, that's what they keep harping [on] in the papers and saying in the news. Las Vegas also closed [its] only art museum[,] due to funding.

If you have suggestions, examples, etc. of things that might help with inspiration, please let me know.[35]

Rodriguez is a leading light in the blogging world. She blogged so prolifically and so well in the early days that some bloggers, including me, began to wonder whether we had fully grasped the blogging proposition. This call for an unconference fulfills most of the conditions of the Culturematic. It is broadly focused, highly experimental, and a real shot in the dark. It is ill defined and is proposed with a view to identifying and capturing ideas that are themselves ill defined. And this indeterminacy is not only OK, but also the very point of the undertaking.[36]

Apple Genius Bar

When something goes wrong with an Apple product, the consumer is invited to take the ailing object to a Genius Bar in an Apple store.[37] So when something went wrong with my iPhone, I took it in. Bracing myself. Because you know how this usually goes. The seller doesn't really want to see the buyer. Except when it comes time to buy a new product. Warrantees and return policies are honored under protest and with reluctance. And then, of course, they are not honored at all.

This is the standing bargain in capitalism. Caveat emptor. It's up to the buyer to do his or her due diligence and buy things only when persuaded of their quality. If something goes wrong, well, tough luck. The relationship ends with the purchase. Indeed, this is the genius of Adam Smith's vision of capitalism. The exchange was something that could pass between perfect strangers. No relationship need exist before or after the exchange. This is the *transactional* view.

So I approached with trepidation. I knew what I was in for. I would ask for a repair, replacement, or refund. They would push back with some excuse. The warranty was up. Or the problem was off warranty. Or I had damaged my phone and all warranties were null and void, in any case. The seller would find a way to slither out of every obligation.

The Genius Bar experience was completely opposite. The staff person was actually sorry that something was wrong with my iPhone.

I can remember thinking to myself, "Boy, are you in the wrong line of work." Not only was he sorry, but he was also solicitous. And then the stunner. He asked what he could do to help me. Replace the phone? Fix the phone? Apparently, he wanted me to have a working phone as soon as possible. I know, I didn't believe it, either. Clearly, this guy had not read the capitalism handbook.

I left the store feeling better about Apple than when I had gone in. Somehow, Apple had found a way to reverse the polarity of this event. The company had found a way to build the relationship rather than abuse it. And this was a brilliant what-if. As in, "What if we treated an unhappy customer as if we were glad to see him or her and eager to help?"

The question is, why Apple? Why did Apple rewrite the rules of retail? Why did it change that fundamental terms of the transaction? It could have been caprice. But nothing, and I mean nothing, about Apple suggests the capricious. It could have been a burst of sheer, good-humored sunniness. Um, no. There were many terms that described the late Steve Jobs, the Apple godhead, but sunniness was not one of them. So why do it? Apple has such customer loyalty, it really didn't need to create any more. It didn't just own the category. Apple was the category.

The answer here has to be that Apple did its anthropology and performed a Culturematic analysis. The company looked at the underlying assumptions of the marketplace and saw an opportunity. And what an opportunity it was. This was a chance to delight the customer with service in the very way that Apple products were meant to delight the customer with performance. Except here the opportunity was richer. In the world of badly behaved corporations, this was going to have a big effect. Apple was going to look like a genius, bar none. And all it had to do was to spot existing practice and fix it. Hey, presto, *terra nova* that belonged entirely to the brand.

This Culturematic is a little different from the run-of-the-mill Culturematic, and we will come back to it in chapter 8. It's not experimental. But it is designed to dig down into the cultural assumptions that organize our world, and then rework these assumptions to create new value.

Wordle

Wordle is a little program Jonathan Feinberg created while he was working at IBM. It takes words and turns them into images. If we enter the words of this paragraph, the one you're reading now, into Wordle, it gives us back an image that supersizes some words (*Wordle, program, one, back, image,* and *words*); eliminates the work-a-day language (*a, of, and, then*); and then jumbles, stacks, and colors the rest (figure 3-1). We can submit text to Wordle over and over; the images (aka *clouds*) come back, each more beautiful than the last. No one has ever accused the tech world of being obsessed with aesthetics, but Wordle seems always to return a thing of beauty.

FIGURE 3-1

Wordle at work

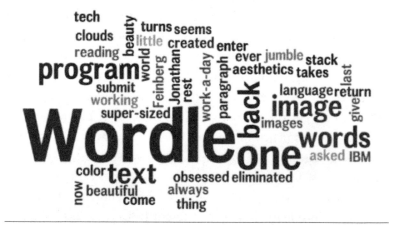

Wordle comes from a tradition called *visualization*. Many gifted programmers have thought about turning text (or other data) into something visual, interesting, and useful. IBM has been one of the centers for this work, and the Many Eyes Web site will give you an idea of how various this work can be.[38] At present, there are around eighty-five thousand visualizations on the Many Eyes site. This site and others like it are driven by the notion that as we enter an increasingly turbulent world, we would be well served by visualizations that can make complexity less complicated and give us new powers of pattern recognition.

IBM wasn't entirely sure what it had in Wordle. As a visualization engine, the program was a little odd and unorthodox. It gave Feinberg leave to create his own Web site and the rest of us the right to use it without charge. And use it we did. There are some 1.4 million clouds on the Wordle Web site. The total number of Wordles is much higher. (I haven't saved any of my Wordles to the Web site. How about you?) Wordles are now a standard way of dramatizing a PowerPoint deck or a blog post. Quietly and without fanfare, Wordle made itself indispensable. When future archaeologists and historians gather to give accounts of the present day, they will treat Twitter as a sign of the time and Wordle as a signature.

Feinberg himself was a little ambivalent about his experiment. It violated several of the rules of information visualization. Feinberg says the word size in his program is "naïve," the color "meaningless," and the fonts "fanciful."[39] If it appeals to us, it is not for its technical excellence. What it gives us, he says, is "delight, surprise, and perhaps some of the same sense of recognition and insight that poetry evokes."

Wordle is one of the delights of the digital world. We bought all that software and hardware on the grounds that it would make us creative. And while it's been terrific to create text and images in new ways, some of us are still waiting for our digital apotheosis. Making anything with the new technology has not been easy, and making beautiful things has been especially hard. Wordle delivers both.

I like that Wordle is a little mysterious. We put words in. We get clouds back. How does this happen? Well, not by the rules of visualization. Wordle is a bit of a black box. Feinberg stuffed his image engine with beautiful colors and typefaces and turned it loose. He created a device that could be relied on to deliver images with a certain something. We're not sure what. In spite of this uncertainty, we have used Wordle over a million times. Let's restate that. *Because* of this uncertainly, we have used Wordle over a million times.

It reminds me of a jewelry store I used to pass in Chicago late at night. There was a small light left burning far, far in the back of the shop. It illuminated a workbench covered in tools, wires, and projects. As you were staring in, you'd notice a small note in the window that read: "All my work made by elves while I sleep." And of course, you would look again, and sure enough, as your eyes obligingly played tricks on you, you *could* see elves hammering away. (If you really listened, you could hear them whistling while they worked.) Max Weber helped us understand that our world has been disenchanted by rationality and routinization.[40] Feinberg created a means of reenchantment, a way to turn the rational, the effable, the text, into something mysterious and engaging.

Smart Mobs

With his book *Smart Mobs*, Howard Rheingold encouraged people to assemble in public on scant notice for just-in-time purposes. And assemble they did, to freeze for a moment in Grand

Central Station, to shop in slow motion at Wal-Mart, or to act out letters in a department store window. Actually, smart mobs were more smart than mob. They represented beautiful moments of orchestrated order. No mob these.[41]

T-Mobile staged a spectacular smart mob in the Liverpool Street Station in London. Music rings out, and a handful of people begin to dance. People nearby recoil in astonishment . . . until they too begin to dance. The dance ripples through the crowd until everyone has been transformed from an alarmed bystander into a Dionysian celebrant. Suddenly, the music ceases and the dancers melt back into the crowd. The virus spreads through the crowd and then dies.[42]

In each of these cases, Culturematics make something happen in the world. And we're not sure what or why. From a rational or an economics point of view, they are futile gestures. No tangible good will return from this investment of time and effort. Odder still, no tangible record will remain, except, of course, for the inevitable YouTube video. But participants believe their time was well spent. When the smart mobs demob, they leave well satisfied. Observers are thrilled. "What was that?" they ask, grinning sometimes wildly. It feels as if something magical just happened. Order that emerges and then disappears. It's as though someone has been practicing senseless acts of beauty.

Reworking Wagner's Parsifal

Rodney Graham is a contemporary artist with pieces in all the great art museums. His art is remarkable for its range and complexity. In a recent piece, we find him reworking a Wagnerian opera called *Parsifal*, which was first performed in 1882. Graham noticed that

Wagner's assistant had added a small passage, and Graham seizes on this addition to stage a musical intervention of his own.

> [My] work supplements Humperdinck's supplement by introducing a system of epicycles within his loop. My method was to create a number of musical loops of incommensurable lengths using the fourteen prime numbers between 3 and 47. I began by adding to the 7 bars commencing at Wagner section no. 89 a total of 40 bars of rests to produce a "new" expanded 47 bar passage. Then working down from the top score at No. 89, I assigned prime number values in ascending order from 3 to 47 bars to each of the 14 instrumental voices of the orchestra. Thus I had the flutes repeat the first 3 bars of the 47-bar passage, while I assigned to the second oboe a repetition of 5 bars, and to the first oboe a repetition of 7 bars. The alto oboe repeated the first 11 bars (7 bars plus 4 bars of rests), while the first and second horns repeated the first 13 bars (7 bars plus 6 bars of rests) and so on.[43]

With this supplement, Wagner's work is changed. Graham introduces asynchronous loops that will play out over many bars, indeed many years. Graham believes that the opera that started in 1882 will not return to sync until 307,444,891,294,246,706 bars have elapsed. By his estimate, this will take 39 billion years to happen. Graham estimates that his version of *Parsifal* would finish on June 18 in the year 38,969,364,735. That's a Monday. For practical purposes, Graham's version of Wagner's opera will play forever.

Graham's *Parsifal* is crafty, measured, mechanical, and experimental. Of course, it is also sublime, mysterious, and more or less insane. And this is because it comes to us from the most difficult laboratory in the Culturematic universe. We don't expect things to make perfect sense here. We're not surprised when a Culture-matic generates disorder of a kind.

The Two and a Half Men Man

Chuck Lorre is perhaps the most inventive man in television. He is certainly the most durable.[44] In a world where making one TV show breaks some people, Lorre is making three: *Two and a Half Men*, *The Big Bang Theory*, and *Mike and Molly*. And it's not as if Lorre is playing out variations on a theme, as Dick Wolf has done with *Law and Order*.[45] *Two and a Half Men*, *The Big Bang Theory*, and *Mike and Molly* are very different shows. Apparently, Lorre doesn't need a formula.

Early in his career, Lorre spotted an opportunity. To my knowl-edge, he is the first person to see this opportunity and the only one to take advantage of it in the intervening fourteen years.

Every producer is entitled to a production logo (or *closing logo*) as a way of announcing their production company and briefly blowing their own horn. You've seen them, I'm sure. Bryan Singer ends *House* with the logo for Bad Hat Harry Productions. It's an amateurish cartoon of two men sitting on the beach. One says to the other, "That's some bad hat, Harry." Terrible stuff, really, but that may be the point. Here the producer can do anything he or she wants.[46]

And then along came the videotape machine. Now people could record a show and, if they wanted to, watch it frame by frame. And Chuck Lorre thought, "Hmm." He turned his closing logo into a vanity card. Here's what the first one said:

> Thank you for videotaping "Dharma and Greg," and
> freeze-framing on my vanity card. I'd like to take this
> opportunity to share with you some of my personal

beliefs. I believe everyone thinks they can write. This is not true. It is true, however, that everyone can direct. I believe that the laws of Karma do not apply to show business, where good things happen to bad people on a fairly regular basis. I believe that what doesn't kill us makes us bitter. I believe that the obsessive worship of movie, TV and sports figures is less likely to produce spiritual gain than praying to Thor. I believe that Larry was an underrated Stooge without whom Moe and Curly could not conform to the comedy law of three (thanks, Lee). I believe my kids are secretly proud of me. I believe that if you can't find anything nice to say about people whom you've helped to make widely successful and then they stabbed you in the back, then don't say anything at all. I believe I have a great dog, maybe the greatest dog in the whole wide world, yes, he is! I believe that beer is a gateway drug that leads, inevitably, to vodka and somebody oughta do something about it. I believe that when ABC reads this, I'm gonna be in biiig trouble. I believe that Tina Turner's "River Deep, Mountain High", is the greatest rock song ever recorded. Once again, thanks for watching "Dharma & Greg". Please be sure to tune in again to this vanity card for more of my personal beliefs.[47]

Lorre found a way to turn the freeze-frame into a personal message. He now owned his own split second, which he managed to turn into a window on his soul.[48]

So what's this Culturematic for? The jury is still out. Lorre gets stuff off his chest. And in a town like Hollywood, where injustice is a way of life, that's important. He gets to report his life in a feverish, slightly alarming, *Postcards from the Edge* kind of way.[49] How does someone work this hard, this well? Now we know. Lorre also gets to build a bond with his audience in a way he could never do otherwise. Every other producer in Hollywood, with the exception of Ron Howard or Jerry Bruckheimer, is the captive of a certain anonymity. (We may see a producer's picture in the *Hollywood Reporter* or *Entertainment Weekly*. But it's not good for much more than, "Look, he's standing beside Julia Roberts!") And Lorre gets to speak to us in a voice that is not just personal, but also candid, scathing, witty, and revelatory. (And this counted for something when he was crossing swords with Charlie Sheen.) By this standard, every other producer is a talking head. What does this Culturematic accomplish? Well, we're still waiting to see, because, you see, it's an *experiment*.

4 Culturematic Clockworks

Here are nine properties that define something as a Culturematic. Not every Culturematic has all these properties, but most Culturematics have most of them.

Culturematics Start Playing in Our Heads Immediately

Culturematics capture our attention. They leap to the mind's eye. Most of all, they engage us with a problem we begin to solve the moment we hear of it. This means, among other things, that they make good titles for books. *The 100-Mile Diet: A Year of Local Eating.* "Hmm," we say, "how would that work?" Alisa Smith, the author, could have called her book *Eat Where You Live*, as Lou Bendrick did. Or *Animal, Vegetable, Miracle: A Year of Food Life*, as Barbara Kingsolver did. But neither of these titles works quite as well as *The 100-Mile Diet*. It's catchy, and we're caught. The title inducts us into a problem.

Culturematics can also prove catchy because they have an inherent drama. This is what makes the Gatorade *Replay* event so compelling. Replaying a game that ended in a tie? Fifteen years later? In a community obsessed with football? With athletes beyond their prime? This is instantly interesting. In the SETI case: A message from outer space? On my computer? Irresistible.

Culturematics can also be catchy because they have a certain strangeness. The Negro Leagues Grave Marker Project works because it brings together an anesthesiologist, an historian, and an insurance agent in places they wouldn't otherwise go for reasons that wouldn't normally move them. We can picture them enduring a succession of too-small rental cars and crummy motel suites to honor men they never saw play. There's something touching, poignant, unexpected. Images start in our heads immediately. Narratives take hold. "Wow," we say, "I wonder what that's like."

Catchiness is in the eye of the beholder. The torch run proved compelling in Japan during the Winter Olympics of 1998, but generally, it gets polite applause elsewhere. Indeed, this may be the only time it will capture the attention in Japan. Both the place and the time made it matter. Good Culturematics have a way of speaking to the underlying preoccupations of a particular culture at a particular moment.

These days, we are treated to books about word of mouth, as if this were the true secret to how news of an innovation spreads through a social world. But surely what matters more (and first) is that the innovation appeals to us, that it catches our attention. And this is the great advantage of the Culturematic: that it appeals to us so intensely that it begins to play itself out in us. It is fashionable to treat innovations as memes or viruses, but as USC's Annenberg School Provost Professor Henry Jenkins and I have pointed out, this metaphor is ill advised.[1] There is no natural propagation of the kind that distributes genes and no natural contagion of the kind with which viruses infect the world. Ideas, artifacts, and media creations don't move from one person to another of their own accord. They move only if and when a human *chooses* to embrace and communicate them. There must be something there that makes us go, "Hmm."

This is another way of saying that Culturematics are good at the holy grail of social media marketing: they spread quickly and well. People like to tell other people about them, extracting a little cultural capital for their trouble.

Culturematics Make the World Manageable

Is there anything vaster than the vastness of the heavens? Probably not. So when it came time to ask people to help search those heavens, the Search for Extraterrestrial Intelligence (SETI) community had its work cut out for it. The "baby step" principle tells us that humans are sensitive to moments when the scale of a problem threatens to render their action insignificant. In fact, even trace elements of futility will cause most humans to give up and go home. Searching the vastness of space? Oh, please.

Someone on the SETI team (and I wish I knew who) had the good idea of making the world's biggest problem tidy and bite-size. As if to say, "We don't want you to search all the world. We just want you to search this tiny part of it." To which we reply, "Ah, that we can do."

When Julie Powell tired of life in Queens, she resolved to prepare the recipes of Julia Child. This is a gigantic undertaking, to do and to read about. Julie decided to do one recipe a day for a year. Not so gigantic.

When Morgan Spurlock resolved to test the nutritional powers of a McDonald's diet, he could have eaten there for an indefinite period. He could have eaten there for a year. He chose instead to eat at McDonald's for a month. There is something about this duration that makes the thing plausible, somehow more thinkable.

United Way takes our philanthropic dollar and spends it on something for someone. We have no way of telling who the recipient is and what good our dollar creates for someone. DonorsChoose.org invites us to help buy a projector for the Ms. Miller's third-grade classroom in P.S. 293 in Rochester, New York. One act of philanthropy is abstract. The other is about as particular as, well, the kids in Ms. Miller's third-grade class in P.S. 293. And that's very particular, not to mention noisy and rambunctious.

In 2005, Kyle MacDonald was twenty-eight and living in Montreal, where he worked as a fridge deliveryman.[2] For reasons of his own, he placed a notice on Craigslist saying that he wished to trade a single red paper clip for a house. And then he started to barter. The clip became a pen, which MacDonald traded for a doorknob, which eventually became a stove. By 2006, MacDonald had traded all the way up to a role alongside movie actor Corbin Bernsen. And that's what he traded for a house in Saskatchewan. It's a little like a serial Rube Goldberg, isn't it? A child's vision of the economy, with the abstractions called *work* and *value* made literal and visual.

The poet Frank O'Hara wrote a series called *Lunch Poems*. Each day, he walked out of his Midtown Manhattan office to the Olivetti showroom, and composed a poem.

This inspired the photographer Gus Powell:

> For the past few years I have worked behind a desk not far from where O'Hara once sat. After I was given O'Hara's book, my lunch breaks started to get longer. Sliding out of the revolving door I found myself transformed into a hungry sailor with one hour of liberty from his ship. Some days the sidewalk offered a dramatic or romantic one-act play; a pedestrian might fall, a couple might kiss . . . but most of the time

I was looking at people who walked towards and away from me. The quiet gestures of strangers in daylight became significant, and these photographs became my lunch pictures.[3]

Making these poems and photographs hour-bound performs two simplifications. It says to the artist, "Here, you don't have to address everything. Just do what you can in a lunch hour." And it says to us, "Look, this is not art about everything. It's about a lunch hour in New York City." And the writer and the artist gave themselves over to a certain Culturematic openness. They turned New York City into an editing machine.[4]

Culturematics Are Something We Want to Try

Poetry and photography are difficult for most of us. But putting them in a lunch hour makes them manageable and something we can imagine doing. Culturematics have a you-could-do-this-too quality. They make us wonder, almost involuntarily, "What would that be like?"

But of course, we still follow the exploits of our heroes, astronauts, quarterbacks, and winners of the Tour de France. We admire these people, precisely because they do what we cannot. But increasingly, we are interested in expanding the things we can do. Call it our vanity.[5] In a postmodern world, the measure is "me." Could I do this? What would it be like if I did this?

Often, this ends up as a kind of surrogate experience-seeking, to be sure. We are not really going to eat all our meals for a month at McDonald's. We are not going to drive our cars until they run out of gas. But we are pleased to imagine doing this, if only for a moment. And even more pleased to have someone do it for us. So we don't have to. We get the pleasure of seeing what it would be like, without having to eat all those fries.

This is one of the reasons reality TV has done so well. We are now in a position to see what it would be like to be (a) an ice road trucker, (b) a young designer, (c) a crazy kid on the Jersey Shore, (d) a sous chef in a high-powered restaurant, and (e) an explorer lost in the wilderness—sometimes all on the same evening. Culturematics honor this new condition of our culture: that no one is excluded and anyone can participate at least by an act of the imagination.

Culturematics are riding a clear cultural trend. We have a new appetite for experience. We are no longer a culture that prizes conformity. We cultivate a multitude of selves. We take this as our due.

Culturematics Like Order Out of Accident

One of the things about Culturematics is their affection for a disorderly order. The Rube Goldberg contraptions, for instance, are wonky. There's no rhyme or reason to what goes into them. It can be a cue ball, bowling ball, or hatbox. As long as it rolls, it doesn't matter. Heterogeneity is the order of the day.

Reality TV is quite deliberately about emergent order. We don't know the outcome of seven kids in a household, who is going to win the *Amazing Race*, or who the next winner of *American Idol* will be. That's the advantage of reality TV over scripted TV. The outcome is not predestined. Burning Man is about setting a start point and then seeing what happens, and the diversity of what happens is breathtaking.

Culturematics like order that trembles on the edge of chaos. In the Russell Davies version of a Goldberg contraption, near-disorder is everywhere. The whatsit only *just* makes contact with the thingamajig. This is order that threatens to stop being orderly. This makes the Culturematic the opposite of the classical French garden, the one so rigidly structured it looks almost exactly like the diagram from which it sprang. The Culturematic is the opposite of a well-edited magazine, one dominated by a single editorial voice. We prefer things that pile up in a great, glorious mess. More Boing Boing, perhaps, than *Daily Beast*.

Culturematics don't file a flight plan, so we can't tell where they will end up. A literal example: the Ford Fiesta mission in which Mystery Guitar Man drives his car until it runs out of gas. Culturematics revel in indeterminacy. We don't mind waiting to see where things end up. In fact, we like randomness. It feels fresh.

Culturematics sometimes look like the "emergent order" contemplated by the physicists at the Santa Fe Institute.[6] Emergent order is messy, multiple, noisy, and complex. Culturematics are, too. They are generative grammars that create lots of surface speech. They are designed to be prolific, to take up as much of the world as possible, and, sometimes, to take over as much of the world as possible.

Why? Surely, it's because Culturematics are exploratory. They go looking for something, anything, in our noisy future.

Culturematics Find Value Invisible to Others

Culturematics glory in discovery. They find neglected value in the world and mine it. Fantasy football is one example. Winkenbach and friends found a way to create an entire new professional universe by borrowing the numbers thrown off by the NFL. These numbers, once ignored, now generated an industry worth nearly a billion dollars.

Chuck Lorre made a discovery of his own. He captured the value of a single frame of video. For others this is merely a fraction of a second. For Lorre it was an opportunity to communicate with his viewers. We wouldn't be pushing it altogether to say Lorre found a way to create his own channel within a channel. At this writing, he has used his channel to publish some four hundred personal communications to the American viewing public. Talk about a brand builder. When the Charlie Sheen story broke and Sheen began making accusations, Lorre might have been defenseless. Thanks to his vanity cards, we felt we knew him. We had endured his battles, experienced his frustrations. And in this context, we felt for him. Sheen looked very much like another frustration.

Eugene Pack and Dayle Reyfel found a fortune on the remaindered pile at the bookstore. They found autobiographies written by celebrities. Their big idea: merely to read these books aloud.

"My gift is simply this: to be here with you as fully as the gods will allow, and just let you love me."[7] So speaks Kenny Loggins in his autobiography. Suzanne Somers reads her poetry. Loni Anderson and Burt Reynolds declare their love for one another. (Hey, it *was* undying . . . for a while.) Celebrities wearing their hearts on their sleeves—it is so childlike and trusting, so spectacularly vain. And available to Pack and Reyfel for about a buck a book.

Pack and Reyfel turned this free material into a show called *Celebrity Autobiography*. They staged it in New York City. Audiences loved it. Coverage and awards poured in. *Sunday Morning* wanted an interview. Pack and Reyfel did not add or subtract a word to the material. They merely had the wit to see that in a new context, these passages would be hilarious. They found a way to invent culture out of culture, to extract new value from old value. With no investment beyond their own ingenuity, they augmented their place in the world.

The clever thing about *Celebrity Autobiography* is that it didn't depend on stealing anyone's intellectual property. The play consists of having people reading what is there for anyone to read. It takes only a change of emphasis and a knowing look to invite the audience to think about the text in new ways. Pack and Reyfel had a second good idea, and that was to have other celebrities do the reading. Florence Henderson read Pamela Anderson. Brooke Shields read Elizabeth Taylor. Ryan Reynolds read Burt Reynolds. Delicious. Having celebrities help scorn celebrities, it was a nice job of having your cake and eating it, too.

Does this make the Culturematic a little leechlike? Was fantasy sports exploiting professional sports? Was Rodney Graham exploiting Wagner with his remix of *Parsifal*? Was Gatorade exploiting small-town athletes? Was the Seattle Art Museum exploiting the U.S. Treasury? I don't think so. Property rights are respected even as value is extracted. A Culturematic isn't about stealing value. It's merely repurposing value. It discovers value in the artifact the maker does not know is there. Who owns this value? Surely, this is a case of finders, keepers.

Culturematics Are Both Playful and Deadly Serious

Culturematics are two-faced. Just when they seem most arcane and irrelevant, they end up getting things done. Just when they are producing results, they seem most whimsical. This distinguishes Culturematics from some of the culture created in the 1990s, when everyone was inclined to be ironic and not of this world. Culturematics can "do" irony, but they are earnest in a very twenty-first-century way.

Rodney Graham's *Parsifal* has this quality. It is not of this world. Graham's *Parsifal* can't be played to completion. This is nothing if not playful. But Graham never talks about his creation except in a tone of high seriousness.

Art critic Jerry Saltz sees this playing out in the art world today:

> I'm noticing a new approach to artmaking in recent
> museum and gallery shows. It flickered into focus at the
> New Museum's "Younger Than Jesus" last year and ran
> through the Whitney Biennial, and I'm seeing it blossom
> and bear fruit at "Greater New York," MoMA P.S. 1's
> twice-a-decade extravaganza of emerging local talent. It's
> an attitude that says, I know that the art I'm creating
> may seem silly, even stupid, or that it might have been
> done before, but that doesn't mean this isn't serious. At
> once knowingly self-conscious about art, unafraid, and
> unashamed, these young artists not only see the
> distinction between earnestness and detachment as
> artificial; they grasp that they can be ironic and sincere
> at the same time, and they are making art from this
> compound-complex state of mind—what Emerson
> called "alienated majesty."[8]

The Culturematic says, "Take me seriously, but don't take me seriously." It loves to keep us guessing. It delights in playing both sides of the street. And this gives it versatility. Ultimately, Culturematics err on the side of the earnest. They can do irony, but when they explore the world, they mean it.

Culturematics Aim to Change the Contents of Our Heads

Consider Margaret and Christine Wertheim, identical twins who were born in Australia in the late 1950s. Margaret became a physicist. Christine became a painter. They moved to Los Angeles, where, in 2003, they founded the Institute for Figuring. The point of the institute is to show the intersection of art and science. The Wertheim sisters believe that both math and art are "figuring." This isn't word play. Margaret and Christine see them as the same.[9]

Culturematics have the power to reconfigure the culture in our heads. After we see or participate in the Culturematic, the hope is that we are changed. We see the world differently because the lens through which we see the world has been tampered with. That puts the Culturematic on a par with good data visualization. John Tukey, the renowned Princeton statistician, said that visualizations "force us to notice what we never expected to see."[10] We might say Culturematics force us to reckon with things we never expected to think.

As described earlier, Web 2.0 is a good case in point. It sought to persuade us that disparate things—blogging, Google, wikis, tagging, syndication, and Flickr—were really one thing. We were now mobilized for thought and action. With this term in place, we can think and act differently. I think the books that prove to be formative in our culture can be seen in this light. *The Whole Earth Catalog* cast a single net over many bits and pieces, and in the process, it helped people see the world in new ways. So says Steve Jobs.[11]

Gaea, or Gaia, the mother earth of Greek mythology, was adapted by British biochemist James Lovelock, who invited us to think of the planet as a living, breathing creature. It is not an idea to be taken entirely seriously. The earth is *not* a sentient creature. But this Culturematic invites us to think again. If the earth is vast, limitless, unthinkably large, there is plenty of room for expansion and waste. But if the earth is a living, breathing creature, we can't throw things away. There is no "away." Everything done on earth is done to earth.[12]

Culturematics have the ability to reshape the categories in our head. Indeed, this little book is a Culturematic. It says, "All these various things, Web 2.0, fantasy football, and Burning Man, look diverse. Actually, they're one thing."

Some Culturematics are explicitly about changing the way we think. The Negro Leagues Grave Marker Project asks us to see that these neglected ball players deserve our esteem. Other Culturematics are sneakier about it. The Pie Lab wants us to rethink how we think about community, but officially, it's just about pie. The torch run changed the way the Japanese thought about Japan, but it never claimed to be more than an Olympic ritual. The Ford Fiesta Movement hoped to engage the creative efforts of the Mystery Guitar Man and bring credit to the brand. But the secret mission was to change the character of social media in America. We use Culturematics to find the future, but some of these probes actually invent it.

Culturematics Work from Native Curiosity

We live in an era of great change and some mystery. When strategy and planning fail us, we plunge ahead anyhow, now working without navigational equipment or even clear objectives. What directs us? In many cases, all we have left is our native curiosity. We begin by looking for the things that interest us, not as employees or problem solvers, but as people.

Culturematics spring from our own enthusiasm. Wilfred Winkenbach, Bill Tunnel, and Scotty Starling didn't invent fantasy football because they thought it would revolutionize professional sports in America. They did it because it looked fun and possible. Could they do this? How would they do this? Not an idle curiosity, exactly. But an open curiosity.

Only if we are intrinsically interested in something are we likely to follow it into the unknown. Intrinsic interest matters here because it means we're "getting paid" even if the Culturematic fails. Native curiosity is its own reward.

Intrinsic interest makes us persevere in the face of difficulty and skepticism. When we produce a new what-if, a skeptical soul in the room can be relied upon to say, "Oh, please. That's a stupid idea!" But by that time, it's too late. By that time, our curiosity has been activated. We're hooked. And of course, things will go badly before they go well, and the skeptics will take courage from this. But because there's just something we love about this idea, we keep at it. In some circumstances, especially corporate situations, native curiosity looks like the worst motive to help us identify the innovations that matter. But in fact, it's a pretty good indicator that there's something out there, even when we cannot say exactly what it is. And it remains an excellent source of motivation even when the sledding gets hard.

Culturematics Make Scientists, Social Chemists, and Adventurers of Us All

Miguel Nelson and Sherry Walsh decided to create a secret restaurant. They installed it in their home, a converted car showroom on the edge of LA's Chinatown. The idea was to mix music and talk and food in new ways. On balance, Nelson says, the thing failed spectacularly:

> It was supposed to be this [synesthesia] experience that happened between the ears and the mouth, and even the eyes. At the end of the day it turned into this cacophonous mess. Some people were shushing other people who were talking. The people who were talking were angry that they couldn't talk during the dinner. A fight

broke out afterward. I felt like Robert De Niro at the end of *Raging Bull* standing up there, holding the microphone. I just wanted to have a fun, alternative type of dinner party. It wasn't for profit. It wasn't a business model . . . Really, it was a social experiment.[13]

LA Weekly writer Linda Immediato calls Nelson and Walsh social chemists, and this is apt. They are combining things that normally do not go together. They were treating the world as a laboratory, a place to try new things. And the laboratory can be an LA laboratory or the *World of Warcraft*. We can stage our Culturematics just about anywhere.

When we create reality TV, search for community in the deep South, reinvent professional sports, revivify Silicon Valley, or burn a wooden man on a city beach, we are acting in a deeply experimental mode. We are trying stuff, even when this means trying things that, on their face, are implausible and in fact unprecedented. Giving away pie? Insisting on a new term? Burning something wooden on a beach? At their moment of conception, these are just plain odd. And at the moment of their enactment, they are not much better. They have leaped out of our heads into the world, but they are not very much more plausible for all that. They still exist as frail hopes the world might just as easily scorn as embrace. And in this event, we will just have to take it on the chin. We are called upon to act in the manner of scientists, chemists, and adventurers. The thing is to try. Failure is inevitable.

Summing Up

Culturematics start small. *The Blair Witch Project* cost $20,000 to shoot and around $500,000 to complete.[14] In a Hollywood where the average blockbuster is now $100 million, these are ludicrous numbers. Culturematics are often puny, typically funded out of someone's spare time and modest resources. Happily, at this stage, Culturematics often take only tiny investments to initiate and sustain.

Culturematics can be counterintuitive and even downright puzzling. Burning a wooden man on a beach—it looks very like a mere literary device (or stunt). But the oddity of the Culturematic is deliberate. It's this oddity that makes it a useful test for atmosphere, to see what the world will sustain. Culturematics are odd to a purpose.

Culturematics are charming, even when they don't make a fortune. We love them, even when they are just plain strange. They have made the world little and manageable. That what-if statement sets a condition to which the world must conform. (Which recipes? Julia Child's recipes. How many recipes? A year's worth.) The Culturematic sets a focus and a boundary. Suddenly, we are working in a world constructed according to human scale. In a world of commotion, there is something pleasing about this.

The Culturematic is let loose . . . and stuff happens. We can't be sure, in the event of the Ford Fiesta Culturematic, when Mystery Guitar Man is going to run out of gas. Or what will happen when that happens. We have exposed ourselves to randomness. Someday, this is going to make a great story; in the meantime, for Mystery Guitar Man, it's a little nerve-wracking. The Culturematic puts the world in uncontrolled motion. It "disintermediates" the traditional producers of culture—the directors, producers, writers, and stars—and it lets in spontaneity. What will happen on the reality TV island? Until the Culturematic runs for a while, we don't know. Culturematics manage a tension between the order of the starting point and the unpredictability and disorder of the ending point. Some of these experiments scale up ferociously, bootstrapping as they go. Not bad for the tiniest and cheapest of creative appliances.

In economics, disintermediation is the removal of intermediaries from the supply chain. The manufacturer dispenses with middle men: the distributor, wholesaler, and retailer. The point of the exercise is efficiency and profit. The manufacturer keeps the value that otherwise would have been shared. In some ways, a Culturematic's disintermediation resembles its economic counterpart. We have removed or demoted players who were once essential to the cultural production process. Reality TV still has producers, directors, and writers, but they matter much less. Their job is to manage the start conditions, to crank up the Culturematic . . . and then live with what happens.

But there is a deeper disintermediation at work here. Popular culture was once thoroughly formed by the genre and the producers at hand. The soap opera, for instance, was created according to a strict set of rules. It was the job of the creative and executive team to see that these rules were honored. The audience demanded it. The surest way to lose an audience was to confuse it by straying off genre. Reality TV is *designed* to go off genre. No one really knows what the kids in *Jersey Shore* are going to do when turned lose in a Miami Beach club. The Culturematic is less mediated. It's less genre, more warts and all.

Culturematics are an excellent way to respond to an inscrutable world. They allow us to produce small and inexpensive outcomes. We may not know exactly what we want, but with Culturematics, we don't have to. Culturematics will generate a range of options, and we can choose. We will know it when we see it. And if we can't see it, never mind. Culturematics put a range of outcomes before the consumer, user, reader, or fan, and *they* will know it when they see it.

But we don't love Culturematics merely because they are adaptive. We love them because they are charming. They engage us. At a time when so many things look predictable and even jejune,

Culturematics are interesting and fun. When someone announces that he intends to eat all his meals at McDonald's, we say, "Really?" and rock forward. We want to hear what happens next. Spurlock could have given us a laborious treatment of the fast-food industry and the American diet. Instead, he created a Culturematic.

Culturematics may look like stunts, but this accusation will appeal only to those wedded to old models of creativity. Culture may once have come from tortured artists living in unheated garrets, from the deep well, that is to say, of individual inspiration. And by this convention, anything that is *not* from the artist's well is inauthentic, a cheat, perhaps even a con. But the Culturematic is stuntlike to a purpose. It allows us to turn an idea loose in the world and to see where it takes us.

5 Finding Your Vector

Culturematics are shots in the dark, but we would be wrong to point the cannon in just any old direction. After all, the possibilities are endless. In a truly random exercise, it would take thousands of years to work out the possibilities. And that exceeds my attention span. (Most of us have until the end of the month.) It makes sense to look in places we think are promising with the instruments and strategies we think are apt. Here, then, are the "vectors" that we might consider working on.

Every Culturematic is working with the culture in place. Reality TV spoke to our new feeling for improv and authenticity, Pie Lab to our growing confidence in the power of the gift, fantasy football to the shift from the passive to the active, Web 2.0 to the new fluidity of consensus, Burning Man to our belief in the artistic powers of every individual, Rube Goldberg to our new fondness for accidental order, the Ford Fiesta Movement to our enthusiasm for the new content providers, SETI to our inclination to give the world artisanal proportions, NFL Films for our new conviction for storytelling. And so on.

Here are a couple of culture developments to keep in mind.

No Boots in the Shower: Mine the Particular

Sitting on an airplane not so long ago, I fell into conversation with a guy from Nike. He told me about a campaign Nike was creating for its soccer brand. To do its research, Nike people went to England to visit a famous soccer pitch. They found a sign in the clubhouse that read something like No Boots in the Shower. "Perfect," someone said. "This is exactly what we need for Nike packaging and advertising."

No Boots in the Shower captures the ambience of men's sports: the hectoring tone of the clubhouse, the sheer density of the male athlete, the inextinguishable need to spell out the obvious. You could put ten creatives in a room for a week and not get something half as good, funny, or authentic.

Traditional brands have taken a different road. If they needed to capture the game of soccer, they would summon a creative team to work with image and sound. And we would be given soccer with a capital *S*, soccer as everyone understands it.[1] To be fair, this was our preference. But now—perhaps it's a matter of overexposure, or perhaps it's just ingratitude—we find this kind of thing a little predictable, pallid, jejune. "Fine, another ad." "Great, soccer, whatever."

There is something about No Boots in the Shower that demands our attention. Suddenly, we are right there. This must be the real thing. No roomful of creatives could make this up. It rings with authenticity. It is too actual not to have come from life. This is the Culturematic breaking the rules of cultural production to make newly vivid cultural materials . . . and to change the rules of cultural production.

Disney hired Johnny Depp for *Pirates of the Caribbean* because he was the "sexiest man in the world." But when Depp appeared on set, he didn't seem very much like a matinee idol. His Captain

Sparrow had matted hair, a mincing gate, bad teeth, a braided goatee, eyeliner, weird headgear, a cartoon run, and a visible disregard for personal hygiene.

Disney executives were horrified. They peppered filmmakers Gore Verbinski and Jerry Bruckheimer with questions. Why was Depp walking funny? Why was he lisping? Was he drunk? Was he gay? There were shouting matches. With $150 million at stake, this Captain Jack Sparrow looked like a risk Disney couldn't afford.

As it turned out, *Pirates* made $46 million in the opening weekend and a final profit of $655 million. The *Pirates* trilogy went on to make Disney more than $2 billion. Now, of course, Depp looks like a hero. Hollywood generally agrees that without Captain Sparrow, *Pirates* would have been a dreary exercise in genre filmmaking.

Depp remembers:

> There was one executive in particular who really went out of their way to investigate what the fuck I was up to, and after the release of Pirates, I got a letter from that executive saying, "Look, I apologize. I was wrong. You were right. Thank you for sticking to your guns. I appreciate the fact that you didn't listen to me."[2]

The public didn't want another swashbuckling hero, an Errol Flynn. Been there, done that. It wanted a guy in eyeliner who ran funny. Much more interesting. So much more particular, actual, and authentic.

Before it was a prime-time entertainment on NBC, *Ugly Betty* was a staple of television in Latin America. Producers Ben Silverman and Salma Hayek figured that it would also be a hit in the American market. Naturally, a little bit of adaptation would be called for. Silverman and Hayek decided to make the show a little more glittering and upscale. And then came the hard part. How ugly to make Ugly Betty?

Finally, they decided to make America Ferrera, the star of *Ugly Betty*, quite unappealing. Her eyebrows were, well, actually, one eyebrow. Her teeth sported braces. And Betty went to work in a terrifying poncho that read "Guadalajara!" Maureen Ryan of the *Chicago Tribune* describes the show's rule-breaking approach:

> It's a good thing Betty Suarez's poncho is roomy. Under that billowing bright-red garment, which Suarez famously wore in the first episode of ABC's "Ugly Betty," Suarez sneaked in the tools of a television revolution. The success of the Thursday night show, one of the few real hits of the new season, has upended as many rules of television as you care to count.[3]

No Boots in the Shower, Captain Jack Sparrow, and *Ugly Betty* have something in common. They are particular where before they would have been general. In another time, Nike might have *started* with No Boots in the Shower, but someone would have said, "Well, that's just going to confuse people. How about we helicopter over a stadium and get the big shot?" Depp's Sparrow would have had cartoon imperfections. His hair and teeth would have been comically wrong; his affectations goofy, not gay. And Ugly Betty would have been cosmetically imperfect, not unattractive. Her Guadalajara poncho would have been a little more pastel, a little less terrifying.

Culturematics excavate the particular. They break out of the genre, out of the blandification with which culture is sometimes served up, and give us something closer to the here and now, the real, the robust, the actual and the authentic. Where once we were storytellers addicted to big themes and the situating helicopter shot, now we are archaeologists. We drill down into the topic, looking for the telling detail. It's as if popular culture is learning what artistic culture has always known, that the particular has a certain power, that the particular is the gateway to the general, William Blake's "world in a grain of sand."[4]

THE CULTUREMATIC TAKEAWAY: Point your Culturematic not at the general but at the particular. Not at soccer, but at boots in the shower. Not at a pirate, but at a braided beard. Work with particular materials.

Playing with Meaning

Some years ago, *The Onion* pictured Alan Greenspan and his Federal Reserve Board team destroying the penthouse of the Beverly Hills Hotel. In its "coverage," *The Onion* gives us a dispassionate treatment of televisions being kicked in and mattresses hurled from the balcony:

> Monday's arrest is only the latest in a long string of legal troubles for the controversial Greenspan, who has had 22 court dates since becoming Fed chief in 1987. Economists recall his drunken 1994 appearance on CNN's *Moneyline*, during which he unleashed a profanity-laden tirade against Bureau of Engraving & Printing director Larry Rolufs and punched host Lou Dobbs when he challenged Greenspan's reluctance to lower interest rates. In November 1993, he was arrested after running shirtless through D.C. traffic while waving a gun. And some world-market watchers believe the international gold standard has still not recovered from a May 1998 incident in which he allegedly exposed his genitals on the floor of the Tokyo Stock Exchange. The Tokyo case is still pending.[5]

Thus did *The Onion* bring together two things: the dour keeper of the economy and the self-indulgent chaos of the rock star. It performed a careful act of transposition. Every line of *The Onion* "story" is lifted from a typical newspaper report. Journalistic details are lovingly preserved. ("The Tokyo case is still pending.") Only the names and occupations are changed.

Culturematics often bring together what our culture has put asunder. And this is sometimes the source of their power. We don't expect two worlds to cross. Indeed, we rarely think of them at the same time. On the one hand, there's Alan Greenspan, Washington, the Federal Reserve, men and women in suits, capital markets, economics, statistics, business, the *Wall Street Journal*—matters solemn and grave. On the other, there's tour buses, hairspray, drugs, mayhem, screaming fans, electrifying performances, packed stadiums, matching M&M's, and self-indulgent tantrums. These are separate worlds, sitting in distant corners of our culture. We can think about one or the other. But as the French theoretician Michel Foucault might have pointed out, it's hard to think about them at the same time.[6] Crossing these wires releases something in us, a giddy laughter, a vertiginous feeling.

Culture distributes meaning. It's one of the ways it makes a world make sense. The meanings assigned to the head of the Federal Reserve must be different from the ones we assign to a rock star. Our world must be stretched to be etched. Otherwise, distinctions are insufficiently vivid, differences are insufficiently different. The world is pallid, ill organized, and hard to read. We distribute meanings to make them more meaningful.

As a result, we contain multitudes. Alan Greenspan and Axl Rose. Dale Earnhardt Jr. and Phil Mickelson. Alice Waters and Lou Pearlman. Tom Waits and Donny Osmond. Jim Jarmusch and Rosie O'Donnell. Bill Gates and Ron Popeil.[7] Michael Bloomberg and Ed Koch. These are the latitudes and longitudes of our cultural world, and they describe a vastness. Indeed, the very statement of these pairs tests the idea of a shared culture. Could Bill Gates and Ron Popeil have managed lunch together? Or would the occasion be overwhelmed by awkward silences and great dollops of incomprehension?

Some Culturematics are designed to collapse the space between these distributed meanings. It is not quite as bad as the natural disaster, the cataclysmic event that leaves people unhinged. The effect we are looking for is delight, amusement, happy amazement. A little bit of disorder is a powerful aid to the imagination. It refreshes our sense of understanding by briefly and carefully violating that sense. It allows us to create culture by moving away from culture.

In the early days of popular culture, we were given gentle "buddy movies." Now the Culturematic formula is something like this: take two actors of different races, ages, and outlooks, shake well, confine to a squad car. This was the mechanism of *48 Hours*, which succeeded in colliding Eddie Murphy and Nick Nolte. Bruce Willis and Samuel Jackson were brought together this way in *Die Hard with a Vengeance*. Mel Gibson and Danny Glover were so combined in *Lethal Weapon*. (Joel Silver produced all three of these projects.) Most interestingly, Mos Def and Bruce Willis were combined in *16 Blocks*. And it was precisely the absence of collision that caused one buddy picture, *Miami Vice*, to fail to flourish. Colin Farrell and Jamie Foxx were both so totally cool, there was almost no difference between them. We stayed away in droves.[8]

We can address this problem with a Culturematic machine that creates new combinations for us. In figure 5-1, we are giving a way of randomizing our choices. I have entered the names of existing buddy combos. And if the Java programming were in place, we could simple "pull the lever" and get a new buddy picture combo. (Go to Culturematic.com to see this Culturematic live.) Some of the combos are merely strange: Jackie Chan and

FIGURE 5-1

Culturematic machine for the buddy movie

Mel Gibson	Danny Glover
Jackie Chan	Chris Tucker
Nick Nolte	Eddie Murphy
Thelma	Louise
Bruce Willis	Tracy Morgan
Steve Buscemi	Gary Busey
Bruce Willis	Mos Def
Denzel Washington	Chris Pine

Louise (of *Thelma and Louise*). But others are kind of interesting: Denzel Washington and Gary Busey? Wow. Now that could be fascinating.

A more sinister version of this combinatorial logic took Hollywood by storm in the 1990s, when the movies of Quentin Tarantino appeared. In *Pulp Fiction*, thugs have a conversation about Big Macs in France before breaking into someone's apartment. Samuel Jackson recites biblical passages before shooting someone in cold blood. Banality and terror are combined in the first case, high moral discourse and murder in the second. Hollywood was impressed with this new way of bringing tension to the screen and promptly began turning out quite a lot of Tarantino-lite cinema (e.g., *Excess Baggage*) until this practice became formula and it was time to move on.

This Culturematic principle appears in the restaurant world. Ma Maison and Spago dared to mix high- and low-design signatures in the same restaurant. Founded in the early 1970s, Ma Maison installed AstroTurf, cheap flatware, and plastic chairs without offending Hollywood's rich and famous. Spago was founded in the early 1980s because Wolfgang Puck believed that New York was "completely boxed into French or Italian" and that in California, new risks and combinations were possible. He introduced pizza as high cuisine, daring to serve Italian convenience food on Villeroy & Boch plates with Christofle silverware.

The strategy also appears in the world of fashion:

> Designers found magic in the drama of what happens when they put together different textures. [Calvin] Klein recalls, "To me the contrast between rough fabrics and satin fabrics against a woman's body was really sexy . . . It's the combination that has always intrigued me. The contrast between soft and hard."[9]

And in popular music:

> Ms. [Erykah] Badu's Vortex Tour was a visit to her eccentric pop cosmos, which encompasses silliness and hard-nosed realism, idealism and bawdiness, choreography and whim, R&B and hip-hop, funk and jazz. Ms. Badu listed some of her aliases soon after she arrived onstage— Medulla Oblongata, Sarah Bellum, Analog Girl in a Digital World, Lowdown Loretta Brown—and those weren't nearly enough to sum her up.[10]

The potential in cultural mashups has always been with us. Until quite recently, it was seen as error. The unexpected combination of things indicated that the cultural creator had made a mistake. Combining different cuisines, combining different styles of interior design, combining articles of clothing high and low— all of these were code violations. The punishment was critical disdain, audience confusion, and social exclusion. Now it is precisely these code violations that make our culture live.

CULTUREMATIC TAKEAWAY: Find things that do not go together, and put them together. Collect what spills out of the collision, and publish it.

Bad Is Often Better Than Bland

Paul Fussell, then professor of English at the University of Pennsylvania, wrote a book in the early 1980s called *Class*. In the book, he managed both to ridicule the middle class for caring about status and to scold them for getting it wrong. Apparently, he was following the example of Peter York, who, a year before, had published a book in England called *Style Wars*, which scorned the idea of class *and* those to whom it was a mystery. Fussell and York were apparently writing for readers so desperate for the secrets of class they would submit to mockery as the cost of entry.

About a decade later, Fussell published *Bad*, his study of excrescences, lapses, and accidents of taste in America. In his now familiar lordly, smirking tone, Fussell implied that bad taste was usually a problem of class. Good taste came from high standing, bad taste from low. (It was a ramshackle argument, but it found support in the work of the eminent French sociologist Pierre Bourdieu.) We may think of Fussell as the grand inquisitor. The point of his book was trial and punishment. Those responsible for bad taste would pay for their sins with swift demotion in the status world. In a selfless act of public service, Fussell had decided to protect Americans from themselves.[11]

Taste had many friends in American culture, especially in the chattering classes. Writers all, Russell Lynes scorned "low brow"; Dwight Macdonald, "masscult"; George W. S. Trow, "no context"; and Northrop Frye, "uniformity."[12] As a result, bad was thoroughly cowed after World War II, confined to B movies, Las Vegas, trailer parks, pulp fiction, muscle cars, and mah-jongg parlors. People might engage in bad art, bad design, bad media, bad products, bad taste, but in some way, at some level, they knew they were shameful and, er, bad. Anyone who dared to offend good taste was subject to big fines and strict punishment. America's intellectual elite stood on guard.

Then bad broke out. It became a kind of a cultural producer, instead of a cultural mistake. Sometime since the early 1990s, bad began to animate popular, mainstream culture. Things once banned were now visible even to the middle class: wrestling, pulp fiction, tattooing, comic books, tractor pulls, blue-collar comedy, Steve-O, and *Jackass* were no longer shameful secrets. They were no longer "infra dig" (i.e., beneath one's dignity). They were now visible in mainstream society. They were now *reshaping* mainstream society.

As much as anything, it is the eruption of bad that persuades some people that our culture is going to hell in a handbasket. I was giving a talk about contemporary culture for an electronics company, and someone asked, a little sternly, whether we should be alarmed at how uncontrolled culture is now. The picture I had painted was not the one supplied by the Victorian writer Matthew Arnold, who encouraged readers to think of culture as something that moved ever upward from the crude to the refined and that policed crude people, bad manners, reckless behavior, and otherwise kept "a lid on things." I have real sympathy for this argument, but as an anthropologist, I am persuaded that bad is pretty harmless. It is not the beginning of the end of standards and decency. It is just another way to arrange things. The existing system was pretty arbitrary. This new one is the same.

Bad broke out for a number of reasons. But the greatest of these might be that it looked like a new, unexploited source of cultural energy. Bad was like wind or solar power. It had been there all along, but now it was getting new attention. People saw that when the rules of middle-class society were broken, something powerful was released. This is, in fact, the secret of bad's vitality. Refusing the possibility of shame or embarrassment, it lets rip where others demur. This principle enjoys rude health. (But it is not, for all that, so very dangerous.)

We used to think of Las Vegas as a place of extravagant, garish kitsch. When Wayne Newton took up residence there, this seemed right. After all, this is where kitsch belonged. Las Vegas was something like an atomic experiment, removed to the desert to protect the rest of the country from harm.

But Las Vegas is now mainstream. It trades shamelessly in spectacle. Cirque du Soleil is, among other things, a deliberate investigation of scale and an unabashed return to the sublime. Liberace, were he to return from the grave, would no longer be so patently ludicrous.

Tattoos fired a shot across the bow of middle-class taste. Academics and the rest of the middle class thought of tattoos as self-stigmatization, a way for kids without hope of advancement to declare that they were kids without hope of advancement. Tattoos were a way of saying, "I'm a loser," when the phrase still meant something. (Like tattoos, "loser" was to be rehabilitated and redefined.) Then came the great rehabilitation, and now tattoos are increasingly common. (Forty percent of Generation X has a tattoo; 36 percent of Generation Y does.[13]) Tattoos still have a certain air of daring and menace, useful if you live in a middle-class world, where menace is usually hard to come by, and daring rarely called for.

Jeff Foxworthy released an album called *You Might Be a Redneck* in 1993 and an autobiography titled *No Shirt, No Shoes, No Problem!* in 1996. In the early 2000s, he launched the Blue Collar Comedy Tour. His comedy is designed to defy the redneck stereotype even as he wore it as a badge of honor. Bad humor was conducting its tests above ground. And we take Foxworthy as precursor of the TV show *My Name Is Earl*. By this time, redneck humor was upscale enough to get Jason Lee as its male lead and NBC as its network.

Steve-O is famous for a stunt called "The Butterfly," in which he staples his scrotum to his leg. He has also been arrested for urinating in public, a stunt recently appropriated by a French film star. His TV show *Jackass* featured stunts of stunning recklessness. A series of movies followed, with Steve-O and Johnny Knoxville pulling stunts that went past college status into an astounding disregard for personal safety. Normally, elite taste would have ignored these shenanigans and the new "Jackass players" theater.

Instead, it excoriated them. It was as if Steve-O and his crew were an American answer to English punk. And they had struck a nerve. They had violated the value a bourgeois culture puts on the sanctity and safety of the physical self. (Where Johnny Rotten used safety pins, Steve-O used staples.) *Jackass* took aim at what the political philosopher Crawford Macpherson calls our "possessive individualism," and the world declared a direct hit by announcing its outrage.[14] Puerile, yes. Dangerous, no.

Bad springs also from what we might call sociological stunts. TV and Hollywood had typically depended upon gentle violations of the social code. On *The Mary Tyler Moore Show*, Mary would sometimes worry that Mr. Grant was mad at her. This small contretemps would lead to further misunderstanding and still more laughs. Ben Stiller's *There's Something About Mary* represents a new order of difficulty. He catches his penis in a zipper and must leave the house in this humiliating condition. For her part, Mary wanders around unaware that she has semen in her hair. Bad has created something *Wikipedia* calls "humiliation comedy."

Bad also features in what is called *cringe comedy*. According to the master, anthropologist Erving Goffman, social situations are designed and negotiated to protect social actors from the risk of embarrassment. That's what social rules are for. This is why, normally, we take care not to ignore, insult, ridicule, or otherwise diminish the people with whom we interact. It's a hidden contract of social life. But bad comedy breaks this contract. It opens up the social actor to the loss of social protection, to the sting of social diminishment, to our unabashed ridicule.

In every episode of *Curb Your Enthusiasm*, Larry David goes looking for an excruciatingly embarrassing situation. Our hero is a heat-seeking missile, searching out yet another of Goffman's rules to violate. Ricky Gervais's series *The Office* is still more cringe-worthy. His own character, David Brent, is self-centered, pompous, and vain. He uses his power to behave in ways maximally insensitive and obnoxious. He is, of course, appalling. Cringing was not a usual reaction to *The Mary Tyler Moore Show*. With Larry David and Ricky Gervais, cringing is the objective. (The American version of *The Office*, staring Steve Carrell, is a little less cringe-worthy. His violations of the social code are more like infringements than felonies; his self-destruction is, as a result, less self-destructive. We identify more and cringe less.)

In each of these cases, bad escapes its excluded status. In the comedy of Jeff Foxworthy, it rushes up from blue-collar circumstances. In the comedy of Steve-O, it shows itself as the damage that can be inflicted upon that most precious value of bourgeois society, the value of the physical body. In the comedy of Ben Stiller and Larry David, it comes from the humiliation that can be inflicted on the social self. In the comedy of Ricky Gervais, it comes from the ridicule little men bring upon themselves through their pomposity and self-regard. All of these are social misbehaviors that a middle-class culture had banished from the charmed circle of polite company. Bad was corralled. Then it broke free.

Bad has been a gold mine for cultural producers. HBO could not have flourished without the ascendancy of the marginal. The cable channel appears to have explored every margin in our culture, including the prison (*Oz*), organized crime (*The Sopranos*), the ghetto (*The Wire*), the circus (*Carnivale*), the frontier town (*Deadwood*), polygamy (*Big Love*), and that ultimate margin, death (*Six Feet Under*). (Maybe the problem with *Rome* was that it was just not marginal enough.) Other cable channels have been alert to the programming possibilities and graced us with shows on tattoos (*Ink* on TLC), gypsies (*The Riches* on FX), families swimming in bling (*Growing Up Gotti* on A&E), and bad manners (*Jersey Shore* on MTV). Surely, it can't be long before strip clubs, massage parlors, and porn theaters get their own programs.

Why should bad flourish as a culture producer in our time? Well, it had its own hydraulic pressure. Were it not for the tut-tutting of middle-class taste, bad would have taken over years ago. So of course, it was going to flourish when those middle-class tastemakers lost their powers of influence. As old elites began to fall silent, popular culture became decentralized, more inventive, and more difficult to police. The ability to control popular taste was now almost impossible. High and low are now unreliable compass points in the world we were becoming.

Furthermore, bad had many powerful friends. Almost every generation after World War II embraced bad as a corrective against its own middle-class origins, parents, and other influences. The Beats took to the company of unsavory neighborhoods and rough customers. William Burroughs left his upper-class home in St. Louis for the north side of Chicago, where this Harvard grad took a job as bug exterminator. Of *Naked Lunch*, he said, "I am shitting out my educated Middlewest background once and for all. By the time I finish this book I'll be pure as an angel, my dear."[15]

Each in their turn, hippies, punks, hipsters, scorned middle-class neighborhoods for places their parents lived in the suburbs to avoid, places that mothers felt obliged to declare NOCD (not our class, dear). The middle class was aspirational. It wanted to climb. Its kids were often headed in the opposite direction. To them, the status anxieties of their parents seemed false and inauthentic. They chose to live in the very neighborhoods their parents had moved to the suburbs to avoid. As the Gordon family documented by Donald Katz's brilliant book shows, children who wanted to escape "suburban falsehood" were keen to burrow into bad.[16] If the suburb seemed like a cliché, there was nothing like the gritty authenticities of the wrong side of town. There was nothing like the press of poverty and the tang of danger to save people from the hypocrisy of good manners.

But there is also a creative advantage here. The world of bad is a little bit unbound. It has escaped the rules and assumptions of the mainstream society. This is a world that wobbles, and this, for some, makes creativity easier. This may have been why Aaron Sorkin, creator of *The West Wing*, would periodically check into a bad motel and stay there till the project was done. Well, one reason, anyhow. Bad neighborhoods have their own disorder, and disorder is, for some, the condition of creativity.

But this principle also has an epistemological advantage. Bad is a kind of dime store version of the sublime. It resists our notion of scale. Edmund Burke, an eighteenth-century philosopher, said of the sublime that it produced "astonishment . . . and astonishment is that state of the soul, in which all its motions are suspended, with some degree of horror. In this case the mind is so entirely filled with its object, that it cannot entertain any other."[17] Burke and his fellow philosophers of the eighteenth century were thinking about the glories of nature, mountain ranges, and waterfalls. But astonishment can also be occasioned by Cirque du Soleil and an arpeggio by Celine Dion. We can look at all of Las Vegas, with its extravagant acts of architecture, as exercises in the sublime. And what should we make of the observation that these cultural artifacts are also corny? Well, that's the magic of Vegas. First, the intimidation of grandeur. Then the apology, "Just kidding."

But bad has fans other than the young. It is also adored by those who like pulp fiction. It is lurid, garish, perhaps a little titillating. It's another world, a netherworld, a place where the physics of ordinary events, action, motive, and emotion take on higher contrast, bigger scale. Melodrama applies here. It is almost as if this world is precultural. And these qualities make it stand opposite not just a standard, middle-class culture, but all culture.

Well across town, there are communities that explore bad for other purposes. Drag queens, diva lip-sync, and revue performances—all of these explore bad by breaking the rules of gender, clothing, emotion. This is bad as camp, an exercise that delights in extravagance. But this is not an escape downward into the demimonde of the wrong part of town, but upward into something more carefully and cleverly aesthetic. Susan Sontag said that one part of the gay community made itself "an improvised self-elected class . . . aristocrats of taste."[18] This bad is designed to trump "the breeders." "Look," it sometimes seems to say, "we control these violations of taste. Here is proof that we are more discerning in all things, and that by comparison, the straight community is aesthetically challenged."

In every case, bad finds another way to burrow out of the received conventions of a middle-class society. And this is a remarkable accomplishment, especially when we consider how many St. Georges nominated themselves to fight this dragon. But Fussell and the others finally lost because the friends of bad proved more powerful. They saw in bad something that was in its way honest and unabashed. For them, bad is not calculated or designed. It is not artifice. It does not spring from a laboratory or a focus group. It is in this respect authentic and possessed of a certain power.

Finally, a middle-class aesthetic seems too bland. A house near mine in Toronto went up for sale. So of course, everyone in the neighborhood posed as a would-be buyer and went in to take a look. Everything inside was a pastel on a pastel. It was the triumph of beige on beige. It was an exercise in matchy-matchy. Someone said it was as if everything had been frosted with modern decorator colors.

Bad may be bad, but it has the advantage of breaking things out of orbit. Gravitational fields be damned. It combines things that are supposed to be held asunder. It mixes things up so that the world becomes a jumble. Less control gives more vibrancy. Things threaten to tumble out of our conceptual grasp. Bad attacks a world that is so controlled and harmonized as to be, finally, insipid and a little dull. Bad says it is better to be in violation of some social or aesthetic code than bland.

THE CULTUREMATIC TAKEAWAY: Find the rules that govern middle-class taste, especially those that govern the presentation of self. Now break these rules. Publish the outcome.

Splicing Culture

Jay-Z was born in Brooklyn in 1969. By the 1990s, he was, by his own account, a Marcy projects hustler hoping for bigger things. Hip-hop looked like bigger things.

He released *Reasonable Doubt* in 1996 and *In My Lifetime, Vol. 1,* in 1997. Both did well, the first reaching twenty-three on the *Billboard* chart, the second climbing to the third spot.

In 1998, Jay-Z released *Vol. 2: Hard Knock Life,* which went to the top of the charts, going platinum in its first week and eventually selling more than eight million copies worldwide. The conventional thing to say about *Vol. 2* is that Jay-Z was playing the opportunist. He shifted from gangsta rap to pop rap in pursuit of a bigger audience and upward mobility. Some were certain that Jay-Z was climbing up by selling out. Many hip-hop artists are unabashedly in it for the money. Some of the point of the exercise is, in the words of 50 Cent, "to get rich or die trying."

Suspicions were especially provoked by one of the songs on *Vol. 2: Hard Knock Life.* The song in question, "Hard Knock Life (Ghetto Anthem)," attracted immediate attention for its use of a refrain from the Broadway musical *Annie*. This looked like a delib-erate effort to make Jay-Z look less threatening and more accessi-ble, less gangsta, more pop. But there were simpler ways for Jay-Z to make his music less threatening. His choice was, in the words of one critic, "completely unexpected," combining as it did "diamet-rically opposed genres." And indeed part of the pleasure of "Hard Knock Life (Ghetto Anthem)" is watching two kinds of music cir-cle one another, coexisting one moment, conflicting the next.

Hip-hop and Broadway are separated by enormous distances on the map of American music. One springs from West Africa, Jamaican toasting, American funk, and soul. The other springs from opera, burlesque, music hall, and vaudeville. They are dif-ferent continents. No, they are mutually exclusive domains. If, in 1997, we were in transit between them and stopped to ask direc-tions from an American musicologist, the answer would likely have been, "Well, no, sorry, you can't get there from here." It was as if Jay-Z had discovered music's Northwest Passage, a conduit all the more remarkable because no one had thought to look for such a thing.

Breaching this distance was controversial. Journalist David Samuels argued that hip-hop was, for all its urban menace, actu-ally something created for white middle-class kids by black middle-class kids.[19] In this view, *more* street credibility was called for, not less. And some American suburbanites were unhappy that the music of Radio Free Brooklyn had found a way over the wall of the gated suburb. Less street credibility could only make this worse, rendering hip-hop more palatable and therefore more present. Most of all, fans who celebrated hip-hop for its gender posturing might be relied upon to take offense. Prepubescent girls singing? Please.

Jay-Z didn't care. He scorned the critics, embracing both the musicologically impossible and sociologically outrageous. In the long term, it's clear he did something good for hip-hop. Under Jay-Z's regime, this musical form has proven immensely adaptive. It survived the alternative challenge of the 1990s, the evolutionary cul-de-sac of gangsta rap, and FUBU (for us, by us) provincialism. It has become ever more catholic and syncretic. (Would Kanye West have dared borrow from Daft Punk without Jay-Z?) Some of the credit for the longevity of hip-hop belongs to the hustler from the Marcy projects. But the anthropological puzzle remains. Why, on the verge of his celebrity, did Jay-Z take a risk of this order?[20]

Jay-Z was engaged in a kind of culture splicing. This is like the cultural mixtures discussed above in "Playing with Meaning," except in this case, we are talking about the combination not of specific cultural artifacts but of entire categories. It's as if we consist of many little cultures, or genres. Each of these is a set of rules for the production of a particular kind of culture. When we talk about TV shows, we treat cop shows, soaps, and talk shows as distinct categories. Literature can be divided into romance, mystery, science fiction, and noir. Music comes not from one set of rules, but from several smaller grammars, or conventions. We have the blues, pop, punk, funk, disco, lounge, and so on. And these rules are exacting. The American band Green Day sings in an English accent because, well, that's what punk called for. Apparently, Green Day didn't care that punk was anarchic. The band was just conforming to genre.

Genres are useful when it comes to the pitch, namely, when the writer and producer make their presentation to the studio executive. The writer will say, "It's sort of romance-meets-action adventure," or "This is basically a crime story, but it's also a psychological thriller . . . with a gothic twist . . . and a noir undertone." Or as Jimmy Kimmel put it when pitching his late-night talk show, "it's going to be a funny version of *The Tonight Show*."

Even in a postmodern period, our culture comes in neat little packages. Genre lets us talk about culture telegraphically, produce it economically, find and consume it efficiently, locate it accurately. Without genre, the Hollywood elevator pitch would be impossible. Airport bookstores would be a mess.

It turns out that Culturematics like to feast on genres, to mix and match and splice them.[21] This is due to many things, chiefly that we have become better at producing and consuming culture, and generic culture holds fewer and fewer surprises for us now. From the opening scene or chord or page, we're able to predict what follows. How dull. So there is now a great passion for splicing culture, for combining what our culture used to keep apart.

The music world shows this Culturematic tendency everywhere. Kanye West has collaborated with Daft Punk, Jamie Foxx, and Maroon 5. Carlos Santana has collaborated with Eric Clapton, Nickelback, Miles Davis, Lauryn Hill, Rob Thomas, and Seal. Rick Rubin brought together Run-DMC and Aerosmith for Island Def Jam. As one critic puts it, "music has come so far, so fast, individual musical genres are practically a thing of the past."[22]

Music from England called grime is described as a "mutt genre" and a "bastard blend" that brings together street English, Jamaican dance hall reggae, drum 'n' bass, and garage. A strange integration is accomplished. Grime is said to be "clean and steely but filthy and ragged, all at once, like battlefield surgery." Lily Allen is said to combine the "mercenary zeal of a ruthless gangsta rapper and the impetuosity of that 'crazy girl' on the junior-high school bus."[23]

We see it also in film. Thus when Charlie Kaufman and Michel Gondry made *Eternal Sunshine of the Spotless Mind*, they brought together a comedy, a love story, mild science fiction, surreal social critique, and art-house appeal. Critic Kevin Flanagan says that this makes the movie impossible to categorize and that we should ask the video store "to fashion a sign with its name and let it sit alone."[24]

Thomas Keller created his restaurant The French Laundry after a straightforward, generic model. He wanted it to be a "three-star Michelin French country restaurant." But as it turned out, he smuggled in a conflicting set of influences. David Kamp describes it in *The United States of Arugula*:

> [Keller] used pop-culture reference points to inspire him, coming up with a "macaroni and cheese" of butter-poached lobster and mascarpone-enriched orzo, a "bacon and eggs" that was really a soft-poached quail egg served on a spoon with crumbles of bacon on top, a "peas and carrots" of lobster pancakes with a pea-shoot salad and a ginger-carrot emulsion, a "surf and turf" that's a cylinder of monkfish medallion on top of braised oxtail, and a "coffee and doughnuts" dessert that's really a cappuccino semifreddo accompanied by little cinnamon-sugar fry cakes.[25]

High cuisine is now largely about splicing. Critic and restaurateur Bryan Miller scorned Escoffier formality for "places that serve lighter, cross-cultural cuisine in a casual, often raucous and visually stimulating setting."[26]

The British actor Daniel Day-Lewis was invited to follow a traditional path as an aspiring actor. He made his own way:

> One of the great privileges of having grown up in a middle-class literary English household, but having gone to school in the front lines in Southeast London, was that I became half-street-urchin and half-good-boy at home. I knew that dichotomy was possible. England is obsessed with where you came from, and they are determined to

keep you in that place, be it in a drawing room or in the gutter . . . I'm a little bit perverse, and I just hate doing the thing that's the most obvious.[27]

The newscast has a distinctive signature: a person, usually a man, sitting at a desk, offering the news and, in some cases, pontificating. This is written into our culture. Over the brief history of TV and the last several years, it has become the televisual way we consume news and opinion. For many years, this formula remained unchallenged. *Saturday Night Live* offered Weekend Update as a conduit for funny stories. The English and Canadians offered their own parodic view (e.g., *That Was the Week That Was* and *This Hour Has 22 Minutes*, respectively). It was left to Jon Stewart and Stephen Colbert to marshal a full-on assault.

It's hard to remember this now, but when *The Daily Show* appeared in 1999, it was regarded as perhaps the last gasp of a struggling comedian. Stewart's previous TV show had suffered dismal ratings, and it was canceled in 1995. He was saved from career limbo only when Comedy Central took him on as an inexpensive risk. But the show worked well. It made glorious fun of cheesy graphics and unashamed hyperbole. Stewart scorned the banalities of the usual talking head. Stephen Colbert, Steve Carrell, and Rob Corddry filed stories as if from the Middle East when actually standing in plain view before the studio audience. Campaign coverage was deliciously bad. The audience cheered the formula's demolishment. Colbert then took aim at Fox Entertainment Group with his magnificently self-congratulatory performance in *The Colbert Report*. It was now difficult to watch conventional news coverage. Every male newscaster seemed to resemble Ron Burgundy. A Culturematic had triumphed.

THE CULTUREMATIC TAKEAWAY: Find genres and other cultural categories. Splice them together.

Kathy Griffin and Other Tricksters in Our Midst

The View was founded by Barbara Walters in 1997. It features lively conversation with diverse cohosts, now consisting of Walters, Joy Behar, Elisabeth Hasselbeck, and Whoopi Goldberg. Rosie O'Donnell had been a cohost, but she proved controversial and left the show in May 2007. While ABC searched for a permanent replacement, the stand-up comedian Kathy Griffin stood in as an occasional cohost.

And so it was that Kathy Griffin came to sit at Barbara Walter's left hand on June 4, 2007.

Walters was talking about the incarceration of Paris Hilton at the Los Angeles County Jail. Griffin was quietly subverting the proceedings. Here is a highly abbreviated account of their conversation. (A clip of the full interaction may be found on YouTube.[28])

Walters's tone is hushed, concerned, solicitous. Clearly, she cares about the Hiltons. She reports that she's spoken to Paris Hilton's mother and to Paris Hilton herself.

> *Kathy Griffin:* Did she actually speak? Did you use flash cards?

Walters says Hilton was moved from the MTV Movie Awards to jail by means of tunnels and press-evading trickery.

> *KG:* What's the point of going to jail unless there's paparazzi?
> *Barbara Walters:* . . . her mother told me, she was very upset . . .

Griffin vamps for the camera in imitation of Paris Hilton's mug shot, with hair swept over one shoulder. She stands up and walks around with her hips slung forward.

BW: This is what Paris said: "My life will change. This is the first time in my life that I will be alone. I think I am supposed to be there. There is a reason and I am ready to face the consequences." She's very frightened. She can only go out one hour a day.

KG: What night club?

BW: People have feelings. In an early conversation, she said I hope my going to jail . . . She refused a lesser jail. She said, "Maybe jail will make people less mean to me." She does have feelings.

KG: It's just publicity spin. The minute she gets out, it's woo! party! dress up!

Joy Behar: Why do people turn on her?

KG: She represents entitlement in America. She's famous for nothing and not doing anything.

Walters is delivering her scoop on one of America's most famous people. Griffin is playing agent of mischief. It's good television.

The collision between Walters and Griffin is being produced for the sake of the show. But there is also a philosophical difference. Walters helped build celebrity culture. Griffin is devoted to tearing it down (or at least sending it up).

Griffin believes that Walters is too close to the celebrity culture. She believes Walters is, as she puts it, "in bed with those famous people":

> [Barbara Walters is] an icon, and I admire her. She's a trail blazer. But what one thing that bothers me . . . She doesn't seem to *ask the question.* She gets the great interviews. And she gets Angelina Jolie, who is super crazy. I have a lot of questions for Angelina Jolie. A lot! That's the only thing about Barbara Walters, she's very soft with the interviews.[29]

Griffin is the enemy of a cozy celebrity world. She pours ridicule on Ozzy Osbourne, Gwyneth Paltrow, the Olsen twins, and Oprah Winfrey. She is "dishing" in the manner of Joan Rivers. She is brawling in the manner of Roseanne Barr. She's the outsider who found a way to sneak into stardom in the manner of Bette Midler. She is the anarchic comedian, a punk, a jester, in the manner of David Cross, Tom Green, and Sacha Baron Cohen. Her job is not to celebrate celebrity. Her job is to puncture it.[30]

Griffin is a comedian in the way Colbert is a journalist. She lives to break into the manufactured appearances and infelicities of a mainstream culture. Some commentators will insist that she is an agent of the new incivility, that we are becoming a merciless culture, indifferent to people's right to privacy, to courtesy, to dignified treatment.

Well, yes. But Griffin is not a barbarian. She is merely the perfect opposite of the traditional PR professional. Our culture now builds itself out of antagonism. We prefer to have many versions of a single reality. Having heard from Walters, we are now too keen to hear from Griffin.

But let us consider what might be the clearest symptom of provocation, the media trickster. This is the media personality who, in the words of Harvard researcher Leora Kornfeld, deemphasizes "control, grace, and refinement," preferring a "childlike spontaneity, a ravenous curiosity, and an uncensored world view."[31] Other tricksters: Larry David, Sarah Silverman, Daniel Tosh of *Tosh.0*, Martin Short as Jiminy Glick, Howard Stern, Steve-O, 4chan, and the Yes Men.

These people are interesting from an anthropological point of view. Our social behavior is bound by two things: hard laws and soft rules. Hard laws apply to acts of aggression against people or property. They are "punishable by law." Soft rules apply to acts of sociality. They are punishable by social criticism or exclusion. If we stand too close to someone while talking to him or her, no law is broken. But we have broken a personal-distance rule. Soft rules govern how we behave while eating, talking, and interacting in public. They determine how we dress, decorate our homes, and otherwise represent ourselves.

Soft rules are generally invisible to us. We obey them without conscious awareness or deliberate compliance. It all comes naturally. Soft rules operate to constrain our behavior, but it's not until a Sarah Silverman says something salacious that we see the rule in question. Silverman likes to break these rules when we least expect it. She presents herself as sweet, corny, and kittenish, and the next thing you know, she is quietly telling us she was just raped by Joe Franklin in the parking lot. She's an ordinary girl who has to tell us about oral sex as practiced by Pamela Anderson . . . in the presence of Pamela Anderson. And she never misses an opportunity to mention that she is the hairiest woman in Hollywood. We are inclined to react with a "I can't believe she just said that!" Silverman scandalizes us by violating the soft rules of social life. (Normally, women do not talk about their body hair.)

Kathy Griffin does something similar. She is talking about Barbara Walters, "dishing," as it were. She is reporting something Walters said to her in the interview, and suddenly, Griffin offers her reaction, something like, "I was, like, bring it, bitch. Let's throw down." The reaction Griffin is looking for, I think, is a horrified "You can't talk about Barbara Walters that way!" We are scandalized because Walters is a senior correspondent and a figure of some reverence in our culture. When Griffin speaks of her as if Walters were a schoolmate in a Brooklyn schoolyard, something goes off in our heads. Griffin has found a soft rule and broken it. She had found a boundary and violated it. (Clearly, white women have been stealing urban language for some time now. Mind you, Griffin may be the only one of them who calls herself a "proud black woman.")

Certainly, this is funny in its way. The fiction that Griffin is confiding in us, and only us, has moved her from the D-list to the A-list. But it is also a humor that fashions an arresting image on the screen. Our reaction is disbelief, perhaps outrage, precisely the reaction Griffin is looking for. And it is the reaction that tells us that Griffin has moved beyond mere jokes to the violation of the soft rules of social life. She is provoking us at a deeper level. This is comedy, but it is something more than comedy.

THE CULTUREMATIC TAKEAWAY: Play the trickster. Find soft rules, and break them.

6 How to Make Culturematics

There are many Culturematics. And each industry has a characteristic approach. Here's a review of precedents and possibilities. It's brief and, I hope, provocative.

For this chapter, I am going to broaden the idea of the Culturematic a little, to let in as much of the world as possible. We will be alert for what-ifs of every kind, even when this is not driven by a pure push for exploration. We will be alert for permutation seeking, even when the Culturematic in question is not in full discovery mode. All of these Culturematics, broadly defined, are acts of innovation designed to punch their way out of conventional wisdom and existing cultural forms. All of them are designed to bring in the new.

TV

Culturematics are everywhere on TV at the moment. In the case of a show called *The Big C*, someone at Showtime said, "What if a woman suddenly contracted cancer? What would happen to her life in the suburbs?" In the case of *Weeds*, someone said, "What if a woman in the suburbs lost her income and took to selling marijuana?" The AMC series *Breaking Bad* says, "What if we took a high school science teacher and turned him into someone who makes illicit drugs?" For the series called *The Riches*, FX asked, "What if gypsies moved into a middle-class home and pretended to be a middle-class family?" Apparently, suburb life is interesting when we stir in commotion in the form of a big what-if like cancer, drugs, or gypsies. But as a Culturematic strategy, this is wise. It takes what many of us know, the suburbs, and mixes in something that destabilizes it. We go, "Oh, that could be interesting," and it often is. A what-if is released into the world.

USA Networks came up with its own Culturematic. Here, the what-if read, "What if we took someone glamorous and powerful and suddenly demoted this person in the world, so he or she had to depend on friends and family and struggle to eke out an existence?" This is the theme of *Burn Notice*, a show about a spy who is thrown out of the profession and must now rely on his mother (among others). It's also the theme of *Royal Pains*, the story of a surgeon who is thrown out of the profession and must now rely on his brother (among others). And it's the theme of *White Collar*, in which a jewel thief who is thrown out of his profession must now rely on his FBI handler (among others). The mastermind of these shows is Bonnie Hammer, the USA Networks executive who came up with the formula. This Culturematic takes what we know about spies, doctors, and jewel thieves and invites us to watch as these people reinvent themselves under duress, with a little help from their friends.[1]

Another approach to a Culturematic is the TV show *Being Human*, which was originally created by the BBC and then recreated by Syfy. The what-if here: what if you took a vampire, a werewolf, and a ghost and put them in a house to live together. (Thus does the *art* of dramatic TV imitate the *life* of reality TV.)

We are now so deep into the vampire trend that most of us have a pretty good idea of what a vampire is. Our knowledge of ghosts is probably less detailed, but not insubstantial. The soft spot is werewolves. Most of us have no clue about them except that they are humans who turn into wolves. This Culturematic says, "Watch as we mix what you know about vampires with what you know about ghosts." We can't really guess how these notions will mix, so we are keen to see what happens. And the Culturematic then throws in a wild card, the werewolf. Hey, presto, the screen comes alive (in a very undead kind of way).

As discussed in chapter 4, when we are making TV, we want to avoid slavish conformity to genres. This was the problem with Fox's recent failure, *The Good Guys*. From the beginning, when promotions for this show were first aired, it was clear that *The Good Guys* would fail. Clearly, it was going to adhere to the buddy-cop picture in a manner that would interest only viewers with limited expectations. The rest of us expect something new. I decided to test my grasp of our culture by predicting the failure of *The Good Guys* well before it went on air.[2] Having put my reputation on the line, I was relieved (but not pleased) when the show was canceled.

Culturematics can help return genres to life. In the case of the Alan Ball novel and the HBO series *True Blood*, someone must have said, "Oh, not another vampire series!" To which someone gave the reply, "Well, what if we make them more human—and a banal part of a human community, at that." Suddenly, all puns intended, the genre came back to life. It is this combination of the thing we know with the thing we don't that is the secret of the Culturematic.

NCIS is one of the success stories of contemporary TV. Audience numbers have risen steadily from a robust 11 million at launch in 2003 to 20 million in the present season. Some of the power of the show came from the way it combined characters with a certain what-if curiosity. The *NCIS* team brought together a formidable boss in Leroy Jethro Gibbs (Mark Harmon) and special agents who were various in standing, gender, ethnicity, and outlook: Anthony "Tony" DiNozzo (Michael Weatherly), Timothy McGee (Sean Murray), Ziva David (Cote de Pablo), and a chief medical examiner, Dr. Donald "Ducky" Mallard (David McCallum). The show even investigated an appealing what-if: "What if we took a Goth and made her a lab tech?" Abigail "Abby" Sciuto (Pauley Perrette) answered this question with some emphasis, inspiring millions of girls to take their science classes more seriously.

But *NCIS* is haunted by a problem. After eight years, familiarity is setting in. The what-ifs are well and truly answered. A Culturematic can help here, giving us a systematic way of canvassing options. Consider figure 6-1, which is designed to force us out of our expectations into possibilities that are illuminating, especially when they are odd. It encourages us to ask what would happen if we teamed Jethro with Tony Shalhoub as the medical examiner, Scott Caan and Ellen Page as special agents, and Snooki as the girl in the lab. Actually, this complicates things too much. Better to start with the simplest what-if possible: what if Jim Parsons (star of *The Big Bang Theory*) replaced Michael Weatherly in the DiNozzo role? What difference would this substitution make? Would it revivify *NCIS* or not?

The spirit of Culturematic is alive in the world of TV. Robert Greenblatt talks about the strategy he intends to use to help bring NBC back:

> I'm a firm believer in moving around until you find
> exactly what the brand is supposed to be. That's part of
> what takes time. You kind of have to muck around in it,
> which doesn't sound very strategic or intelligent but it's

FIGURE 6-1

Recasting *NCIS*: a Culturematic what-if machine

impossible to say, "Here's what our brand is, let's develop to it and let's get these hits on," because that's not going to work. You need a sense of where you're going, cover all your bases and then your brand will help dictate what it should be. Very unscientific but it works.[3]

Hollywood

Hollywood has always used a Culturematic logic on the production side. With each new film, we get a new permutation of director, director of photography, producers, and stars. And this insures a stream of difference within a frame of sameness. And just when even this approach to rejuvenation seems to flag, contemporary culture has a way of throwing up shifts in sensibility and audience expectation (*Easy Rider* in the 1970s, *Reservoir Dogs* in the 1990s). This forces the formation of new genres and the reinvention of old ones.[4]

Another kind of Culturematics for Hollywood has been what might be called "what-if by accident." The old approach was to come to the set with every line scripted, every scene established. (This was the approach of a director like Fritz Lang [active in Hollywood 1936–1957].) Successive generations of Hollywood directors have struggled to break out of the old paradigm and let in randomness and accident. The point of additional takes for Robert Altman was not to get things perfect but to hope that something unanticipated would happen. He loved accident and exploited it to make his movies more interesting.[5]

Mark Wahlberg took this Culturematic a step farther in his recent movie *The Fighter*. Determined to make the picture in record-breaking time, Wahlberg was alarmed by advice he got about the fight scenes.

> Every filmmaker that we talked to [said] "you can't shoot the fights in 20 days, you need 35 days." And I said, "Well, we're going to shoot the whole movie in 33 days and we're going to shoot all the fights in three days" . . . And what I kept telling everybody is that HBO does it in one take and they don't know what's going to happen and they never miss a thing.[6]

Conventional Hollywood wisdom says you are not filming a fight; you are *staging* one. But if the filmmaker is in a what-if frame of mind, it is possible to capture a real fight on film. Getting things off the sound stage and into the world, and then forcing the camera to go to them—this is a Culturematic impulse.[7] The filmmaker surrenders control but is rewarded by discovery.

As we noted in chapter 5, some of the creativity in Hollywood now comes from the juxtaposition of elements that don't normally go together. This play can be left to happen in the mind of the agent, producer, director, or star. Or we can automate the process with a Culturematic. I have chosen a number of dramatic possibilities, and in figure 6-2, I invite you to mix and match them. As you will see, some permutations don't play out in an interesting way. And some permutations are so outlandish as to be hard to imagine

FIGURE 6-2

Culturematic story machine: choose one from each column, then spin again

hero	role	sidekick	victim of	villain	film genre	sound track
Gwyneth Paltrow	U.S. senator	Neil P. Harris	kidnapped by	Snooki	action adventure	Hip-hop
Mark Harmon	talk show host	Jay-Z	supplanted by	Donald Trump	science fiction	Country & Western
Oprah	rock star	Jim Parsons	identity theft	Miley Cyrus	Goth	heavy metal
Robert Pattinson	college prof	Ira Glass	malicious gossip	Lady Gaga	romance	folk
Johnny Depp	entre-prenuer	Donald Trump	managed by	Mel Gibson	scream	world beat

(and are therefore uninteresting in another way). But some play out quite nicely, the combinations being unexpected enough to release some interesting dramatic possibilities without tipping into the preposterous.

Let's say we gave our Culturematic machine a spin and got the following permutation: Robert Pattinson as a U.S. senator with Donald Trump as his sidekick managed by Snooki in a film that has a Gothic mood and a world beat sound track. This is not so bad. Snooki, however, is a problem. Somehow, we doubt that a girl who can't manage "The Situation" is going to work out as a candidate here. But if we spin this class again and get, say, Mel Gibson, well, we might be onto something.

Magazines

Ida Blankenship died at her desk at the advertising agency Sterling Cooper Draper Pryce. She will be remembered as Don Draper's secretary. As one of her colleagues put it, "She died as she lived—surrounded by the people she answered phones for."[8]

The good news is that Ida is a fictional character. Her death was therefore a fictional event. No mourning was called for. But the *Daily Beast* decided to run an obit, anyhow.

Clever. The obit pretends that Ida Blankenship was the real thing. It gives the honor reserved for real humans to a pretend human. This blurs the line between the real world and the fictional world. And this makes us go, "Hmm." A great little cultural artifact has been created. And a series of questions flutters upward. What claim do fictional characters have on us?

Magazines are shaped by cultural conventions. The one that's normally germane for the *Daily Beast* is this: "Everything in these pages is true." But something interesting happens when a magazine runs an obit for someone who never existed. We grin. The world has been let out of its constraints. Our culture has been ever so slightly disobeyed. Real obits take on a new interest. Was this person real? Are these facts true? The magazine, perhaps otherwise a dreary recitation, comes alive.

The spirit of the Culturematic is mischievous. And we like not being able to tell whether something is a real news story or not. This suggests the wisdom of mainstream magazines reaching out to the likes of *The Onion*, that magnificent humor magazine associated with the University of Wisconsin. *The Onion* has made a careful study of the many ways in which it can violate the conventions of the world of journalism, and we are now so comfortable with these violations that we welcome them. This is precisely the tension played upon by Jon Stewart and Stephen Colbert.

I'm not sure when things changed. But at some point, we just gave up that great piety of the intellectual, the one that said there was a magazine (or newspaper) of record, that intelligent people applied themselves to the mastery of the knowledge this record made available, and that they and the body politic were better for it. Indeed, we supposed that only a well-informed citizenry could sustain a democracy, and we visited high condemnation on anyone or anything that risked interference with this sacred mission. And then came Stewart and Colbert. A surprising number of intelligent, well-educated people treat these shows as their exclusive source of news.

As the body politic fragments ever more finely and vigorously, magazines follow these niches down the rabbit hole.[9] And as a result, some become a one-note whistle. We know exactly where they are going. They might as well spring from genre. The possibility of surprise or serendipity has vanished. The spirit of the Culturematic says it is better to mix in messages that are not anticipated by the grammar. This is what gets and holds the reader's attention. I believe that Dave Eggers's magazine *The Believer* is particularly good at this. And I like the *Times Literary Supplement* column that reviews only "a seldom-seen book by an established author, bought from a second-hand bookshop in London or beyond for about a £."[10]

Advertising

An agency called Breakfast is a fountain of Culturematics. These include a bicycle called Precious that reports its experience as it is ridden across the country:

> Precious's brain is an on-board device that captures all of his experiences, combined with a cloud-based system that analyzes those experiences. Put this all together and get a bike that's able to express itself in his own words. He shares his up-to-the-moment thoughts and has a subconscious which allows him to dream about all he's been through.[11]

Breakfast also created a red phone that the agency leaves with prospective clients. (I guess it just sneaks them in.) At some point, the phone begins to ring and a red light begins to flash. Who can resist picking up? Clients love the red phone. Here's one client reaction, transcribed from the Breakfast Web site. It is the senior vice president of entertainment marketing at Turner. "This is the *coolest* thing I have had any agency send! This is *awesome*!!!"

Here's what Breakfast says about what it does:

> Just like the brilliant Edison and Bell discovered, inventing groundbreaking technology doesn't happen first go. Think, draw, prototype, break. Then do it all again. We take pride in the fact that we break a lot of things. With

purpose, and in an effort to invent new and unique ways to help clients reach people. We are BREAKFAST, and we're a crew who've ripped ourselves away from traditional digital to see what happens when we apply our smarts to reality. Let's see if we can make the real world a bit more interesting.[12]

Figure 6-3 is Breakfast's vision of a Culturematic.

Gareth Kay, head planner at Goodby, Silverstein and Partners, was asked to do something for the Dali Museum in St. Petersburg, Florida. There wasn't much money. But Kay and his team went to work, and eventually, they created a brilliant Culturematic. Here's how Kay describes it:

> [We] landed on the idea of helping people release their inner Salvador through a photo App that could create surrealist overlays, a modern day ode to the brilliance that is Dali. We decided to partner with someone to give us critical mass of users and distribution, so we reached

FIGURE 6-3

Culturematic by Breakfast

Source: Breakfast, http://breakfastny.com/2010/03/we-break-stuff-quickly/. Used with permission.

out to Hipstamatic. They liked the idea so much that they have worked with us to create a lens and film pak for the app (the Dali Museum Goodpak), waived their fee and pledged to donate any income from sales of the pak (it costs 99c) to the museum . . . we'll also be projecting images taken with the pak on to the museum's new building on its opening night.[13]

The agency world has long been focused on the thirty-second TV spot. A Culturematic strategy encourages agencies to cast the net wide. On one agency's Web page, Mother New York describes itself with this tumble of nouns: "Advertising, Design, Misc. festivities, Short films, Longer films, Puppetry, Fine spirits, Internet things, Video games, High quality still photography, Business cards, Sausage making, etc."

Sometimes, the Culturematic angle is the creation of radical what-ifs. This appears to be what happens when Fallon London created an ad for Cadbury that combined the Phil Collins song "Something in the Air Tonight" with a man drumming in a gorilla suit. (The man was, in fact, Phil Collins.) The effect was one of those "hmm" sensations. We liked this ad. Somehow it spoke to us. But no, we couldn't quite say why. Half a million people watched the ad on social media in the first week, and over six million did so in the first three months.[14]

Agencies are happiest when coming up with ideas so manifestly good, someone on the client side bursts into applause or tears. Weeping while applauding is, actually, the best reaction. Everyone can see that the new idea is manifestly a good idea. But the gorilla spot was at first merely odd. A lot of Culturematics will have this slightly baffling quality. And this means it will take courage to create and commission. The client, in many cases, will have to be talked into approving the thing. No concrete reassurances can be given. The agency is reduced to saying, "We have a good feeling about this." This was once that kind of thing that made clients deeply and properly suspicious of "what the agency is up to." But now, this "good feeling" talk is almost precisely what the client should want to hear from the agency. Not exactly knowing how and why the thing will work . . . this is evidence that the agency has come up with a Culturematic.

The conventional approach to advertising is to create a single, simple message and to repeat this often and loudly. One Culturematic approach is to run several ads at once. Under the direction of The Martin Agency, GEICO takes this approach with a multiplicity of ads. The GEICO gecko featured a little green creature who speaks with an English accent. The Good News campaign featured a faux news report and the punch line "But the good news is, I just saved a lot of money on my insurance." The campaign called Cavemen featured creatures described by Linda Tischler as "a clutch of metrosexual[s], having somehow eluded extinction while developing a taste for racquet sports, plasma TVs, and 'duck with mango salsa.'"[15] Finally, there have been testimonials from consumers as interpreted by celebrity pitchmen, including Little Richard, Burt Bacharach, and Peter Graves.

This is *noisy* advertising. There is no internal logic, no secret strategy that makes all the campaigns go together. In fact, this strategy forces us to "shift frame" entirely, giving up the meanings cultivated by one campaign to make sense of the next. Complexity of this kind used to be the sign of bad advertising and grounds perhaps for firing the creative director and the agency. Now, it's a competitive opportunity, says Mike Hughes, president and creative director of The Martin Agency: "Once upon a time, an ad was about a company's unique selling position. But people can now accept more complex brands, and I thought we might be able to build a deeper relationship if we built on multiple fronts."

This multiplicity or many-tongued strategy comes from deep within The Martin Agency. The agency decided some years ago to create several creative teams and to "turn them loose to tell multiple, distinct narratives designed to highlight various aspects of the brand." As Tischler puts it, Martin became "a confederation of mini agencies, rather than a single midsize one."

Some advertising can look Culturematic-ish on first glimpse. Take the Alfa Romeo campaign, which claimed to have lowered an ad for the sports car into the Mariana Trench, 36,000 feet below the surface of the ocean. The point of this violation of deep (aquatic) space? "We needed a campaign that really pushed the limits; so if this is the lowest price possible for an Alfa Romeo, [we thought] then maybe we should place the poster at the lowest place possible."[16] So speaks the creative director for Alfa Romeo's ad agency. This campaign is not a Culturematic. It's an old-fashioned stunt. And a moronic one at that.

The Culturematic strategy in advertising is *not* to get flashy and attention seeking. Alex Bogusky created a Burger King monarch dashing onto a football field. It got lots of attention on YouTube, but from a cultural point of view, these are really just empty calories.[17] Once more, stunts are not Culturematics.

Retail and Catalogs

A couple of years ago, while I was visiting Restoration Hardware, I discovered people standing in front of a shelf in a kind of trance. They were holding a "rocket radio," or some other prize from their childhood, an object they believed long gone. And here it was, sitting on the shelf in a store. Very personal memories were now in play.

Before the discovery of experience marketing, artisanal marketing, or a chief culture officer, Restoration Hardware was featuring consumer products that transformed the retail world. When most of capitalism, especially big business retail, was largely tone deaf to culture, Restoration Hardware managed to be interesting and provocative. It did this by putting unlikely little products onto the shelf, tiny Culturematics that got the job done.

There was no precedent for these objects in the retail handbook. They were quirky, retro, odd, hard to find, hard to source—all in all, what the English call a "right bother." I mean, what were these things? Were they toys? Were they decorations? Were they antiques? Come to that, what was Restoration Hardware? Was it a retail or a museum space? These objects blurred boundaries. And vexingly so. After all, people are incredibly vigilant about retail space. Nothing gets on the shelf unless someone is prepared to say it will sell the requisite number of units. There is no room for whimsy, and no room for curios swimming up out of someone's childhood.

Stephen Gordon, the founder of Restoration Hardware, saw these objects very much in the Culturematic spirit. They were cheap, little experiments. They did not all have to make their numbers. Some would move; others would not. But all would give a certain quality to the store, and that quality would be good for the store and the catalog, whatever else happened. Gordon was firing these objects into an inscrutable future. And he was doing so from the inky darkness of our collective past.[18]

There have been a number of experiments in retail. Consider The Liquor Store, which Andy Spade created for J. Crew. Once truly a place for buying liquor, this is now a place that sells a subset of J. Crew products, secondhand and antique goods (e.g., Rolex watches from the 1950s), and a feeling of intimacy that changes the very nature of the retail experience. If The Liquor Store is little and intimate, the sixteen-story building designed by Brian Collins for Hershey's reached for spectacle. The exterior is dressed with props, lights, neon letters, signs, four thousand chasing lights, and not one but four steam machines. Both The Liquor Store and Hershey's challenge the old-fashioned notions that the retail experience is really just a plinth for the product. Following the work of Pine and Gilmore, these places are keen to make the experience of purchase part of the value of the thing being bought.[19]

In the 1990s, people began to warm to the idea of starting a coffeehouse. The earliest adopters of this idea couldn't always say *why* this felt like such a good idea, but as the new coffeehouse took shape, it began to look like an artisanal approach to community. It was if owners were building community one cup of coffee, one conversation, one slam poetry reading, one political meeting, at a time. Most of these coffeehouses were seen as an anti-Starbucks: local, rooted, authentic, and brand-free. It was, in sum, an experiment in community. And an open experiment at that. Of course, some seemed to think coffeehouses existed so that people could have a comfy chair and unlimited Wi-Fi for the price of a decaf latte.[20] Not everyone, that is to say, got it. The rest of us are still working on it.

Food trucks revolutionize retail in another way. They "delink" us from a fixed location. Trucks move constantly, "broadcasting" their location by Twitter, parking wherever they can find enough space, and drawing as many as eight hundred people. There is drama. Finding the truck is fun. There is fusion. Cuisines are combined with daring and imagination. So are people and neighborhoods. Food trucks are designed to bring customers to neighborhoods they don't normally go to and into the company of people they might not otherwise interact with.[21] And the food truck uses a cityscape as its interior design. This is beautiful and it's free. Food trucks are all about the Culturematic economics. Where typical restaurants cost hundreds of thousands and begin to wither the moment they open, food trucks cost tens of thousands, and when they don't like the décor or the clientele, they just move.

The real Culturematic opportunity here is still in its infancy. Eventually, we will treat retail as a full-tilt experiment. The floor will contain many little experiments, in the manner of the objects on the Restoration Hardware shelf. Virtual stores can be created as they were by Tesco Home Plus in Seoul train stations.[22] And retail staff will be deputized as anthropologists, listening and watching as consumers respond.

Storytelling

Jonathan Miller, the English doctor, comedian, and dramatist, made a discovery while preparing a play for the London stage. The harder he worked to define a character, the more inclined he was to fail. Miller was doing the usual thing, draping the character in all the markers that would define him clearly. He had come up with the "correct" clothing, speech, movement, the stuff that defined the character. But the harder Miller worked, the more the character lost clarity and focus on stage. Miller was up against a paradox: what made the character easier to grasp as a character made him harder to see on stage.

Miller discovered a solution. He found that if he added a change to any one dimension, giving the character an unexpectedly youthful voice or counterintuitive manner of dress, he suddenly came alive on stage. Now the audience could *see* him.[23] But doesn't this just put Miller against the grain? Information theory and classical rhetoric insist on redundancy. Good communication is over-determined. Repetition is the road to clarity. Coding the same message in several media is, traditionally, the path to precision. But Culturematic theory says otherwise. Defying expectation is the secret to storytelling.

When the creators of the TV show *Nurse Jackie* began crafting their storyline, they invented a young ER doctor called Dr. Fitch "Coop" Cooper (Peter Fancinelli). They made him an idiot of the first order. Coop is needy and self-satisfied, aggressive *and* passive aggressive, vain and self-aggrandizing. The good thing about Coop for the show was that he made the ER hum with tension and discord. But now the creators had a problem. Coop was a cliché. Once we have watched him inflict his damage on the dynamics of the ER, it felt as if we knew everything about him. This guy was the very picture of an arrogant young doctor. Hmm. Coop was useful, but Coop was obvious. (We had seen plenty of Coops in the world.) How to save him from the young-doctor cliché? Then someone had a good idea: give Coop two mothers, a gay couple played by Judith Light and Swoozie Kurtz. All of a sudden, the stereotype is returned to life. We rethink Coop immediately. Really, what assumptions can we make about this guy? Coop lives.

Transmedia storytelling has taken Hollywood by storm, as we saw in our earlier discussion of WhySoSerious.com. The classic case in point is Batman. This began as a comic book. The story was then taken up by television and Hollywood. Several considerable directors (David Goyer, Joel Schumacher, Tim Burton, Christopher Nolan) offered us their creative visions. It was conventional to think of these properties as distinct stories, so many variations on the theme. And then Henry Jenkins came along and said, "Let's think of variations as the one story, leaping from medium to medium, gathering complexity as it goes."[24] By Jenkins's reckoning, there is one Batman. Fans summon all of his narratives when they encounter any one of these narratives.

Transmedia is, to this extent, Culturematic media. As the story escapes the creative control of a single artist, author, or studio, it is free to experiment. The story becomes a laboratory. And the reader or viewer become a cocreator and *bricoleur*, free to pick and choose which versions he or she wishes to treat as the favorite, interesting, credible Batman. Indeed, the reader or viewer is now free to mix and match the elements created by the experiments, choosing the atmosphere of the original comic book, some of the "pow" graphics of the TV show, Val Kilmer's version of Batman, Michael Caine's version of Alfred, Christopher Nolan's vision of the bat cave, and so on. In sum, a transmedia version of Batman releases a great crowd of possibilities into the public domain to be variously mashed and remastered by a broad public.

As stories leave old media and take up residence in new media, the possibilities multiply. Lance Weiler has argued for stories that are told in the world with the aid of the new technologies:

> As storytelling moves into the 21st century, it is now possible to tell stories not only across devices but also with connected elements in the real world. Thanks to technologies like RFID, augmented reality and geolocation, the physical world becomes a new storytelling playground for those interested in extending the stories they wish to tell.[25]

Kati London at Zynga created a game called Plundr. It uses Wi-Fi positioning to locate a user in the city and then uses this location as part of the game. In this pirate adventure, players move from one "island" in the city to another, to meet and "fight" with other players, er, pirates.[26]

With or without the technology, stories are now ubiquitous, no longer confined to a book or a theater but playing out in the life of the city, springing up in the most unlikely places. Punchdrunk staged *Macbeth* throughout the McKittrick Hotel in New York City. In all of these instances, the story is given its liberty. It is released from the control of any one storyteller, story, or medium. And it is turned over to the creativity of every viewer. And it is opened up to a great flood of cocreation and happenstance. Thus does narrative become a Culturematic.

In order to write his second novel, *The Magician King*, Lev Grossman made a machine that is a little like a Culturematic. He began the writing process by setting up two bins. And then filling them.

> One bin had to do with mood. I threw into it everything that *felt* the way I wanted *The Magician King to feel*. It didn't matter if it all fit together, I just threw it in . . . So in went: *The Voyage of the Dawn Treader*. *The Big Sleep*, by Raymond Chandler. *Ronin*. *The Bourne Identity*. *Cryptonomicon*. *Ubik*. Fafhrd and/or the Grey Mouser. Neil Gaiman's run on *Miracleman*. The Polanski movie *Frantic*. Beckett's *Endgame*. *Watership Down*. *Total Recall*. *Dangerous Liaisons*. *The Corrections*. Joe Abercrombie. Iain Banks. *The Venture Brothers*. Daniel Suarez's *Daemon*. Bits from Enid Blyton's *The Magic Faraway Tree*. Kazuo Ishiguro's *Never Let Me Go*. *Star Wars: The Force Unleashed*. (Look, it's my bin, I can put what I want in it.)[27]

Grossman didn't know at this point how he was going to use this material or even why he had chosen it. "It didn't matter if I could explain it, even to myself. If it felt right, it went in the bin."

The second bin contained elements for the plot of the book. Grossman wanted a descent to the underworld in the manner of Homer's *Odyssey*. He wanted swordfights, a magical boat, and a homeless dragon. And a quite a lot of other things, including wordless, silver gods and the end of the world.

> I can't tell you why I wanted these particular things, but when you're in a certain phase of novel-making, you're like a magpie: when something gleams at you funny, you swoop down and grab it and take it back to your nest, because you know, you just know, you're going to need it later . . .
>
> Once the bins were full, I had a pretty good idea of the kinds of feelings I wanted the book to create in its readers (Bin #1). The trick was to use the stuff in Bin #2 to build a machine that would make people feel the feeling in Bin #1. The machine would be the novel.

The bins are both opportunities, containing all the things you think you might want, and constraints. Once the bins are done, you have established a limit, though of course, wordless, silver gods and the end of the world probably didn't feel all that limiting. The author has given himself a little machine for generating the work.

Social Innovation

We talked about Culturematics of this kind when talking about the Pie Lab. John Bielenberg and his team had found a way into a community in Alabama. They were using pie to build connections and a platform from which to begin. The advantage of Pie Lab was that it did not presume to know what was good for Greensboro, or the best way to pursue this good. The idea of the Pie Lab was to find out what this community wanted.

This is the point of the Culturematic: to let us out of the gilded palace of our good intentions. We don't know what the world needs. Worse still, we don't know we don't know. Culture-matics allow us to probe the world and find out. To be sure, sometimes the need is perfectly clear. Only a quarter of the families in Hale County are connected to the water system. No need for a Pie Lab Culturematic here. Get those families running water! But even here, Culturematics turn out to be useful. Pam Dorr created a campaign to encourage people to buy a meter. Now the problem had Culturematic dimensions. Hooking people up to the water system one meter at a time—this made the problem easier and more interesting. Like DonorsChoose.org, the Buy a Meter campaign is literal, particular, and doable.[28]

UNICEF recently created a brilliant Culturematic in the form of a Manhattan vending machine that sells dirty, dangerous water. This makes the point forcefully and imaginatively: clean water is not available everywhere. And the Culturematic used an available technology in a new way. Vending machines are cheap, self-sufficient, and standalone. And they stand for a food system that is almost flawless when it comes to matters of quality control. What a wonderful way to make the point of our privilege and their need. Dirty water in a clean machine. Confronted by things "that don't go together," we are invited out of our complacent ideas about the Third World.[29]

Culturematics for social good can be little and personal. Matthew Stillman makes himself useful by setting up a little Culturematic in Union Square in New York City. This consists of two chairs, one table, and a sign that reads "Creative Approaches to What You Need to Be Thinking About."

> I sit out there with no computer, no cell phone, just waiting to talk with strangers about any subject at all that they are contending with and trying to offer a creative approach to it. No subject is off limit.[30]

The field of social innovation is growing at an extraordinary clip. We are better and better at problem solving in this area.[31] But it seems that the role of a deep, Culturematic exploration of problems and solutions has not been considered. It may be that some of the problems are so painfully obvious, that exploration seems unnecessary. On the other hand, the history of philanthropy and intervention by nongovernmental organizations tells us that the best solutions are not always or even often the most obvious ones. A broad outlook, in places that do not guarantee results, is called for even here.

The arts organization Noisivelvet created a pop-up park in Chicago. Almost the whole of a Logan Square street block was covered in grass and offered as a public play area . . . for four hours. Your Culturematic objective could be to create your own pop-up park and see what happens in four hours, how people use this space, and what happens to this little community's sense of community in the process. (Document everything. And share it with the rest of us.[32])

Actors

Acting that's fresh and interesting is a challenge. The moment we, the audience, get a whiff of formula, we're gone. What's an actor to do? If he's Scott Caan in the CBS hit series *Hawaii Five-O*, there's not one problem, but four.

First, Caan has a part in a police procedural. Police procedurals are the great workhorse of American television, as formulaic as it gets. (Between them, the *Law and Order* and *CSI* series produce a great chunk of prime time.) We know this formula inside out. Second, Caan is part of a familiar show (*Hawaii Five-O*). Third, Caan is playing a familiar role (sidekick). Fourth, he is playing a familiar character (Danno). Caan was quadruply bound: familiar genre, familiar show, familiar role, familiar character. He was virtually *obliged* to phone it in.

Caan found a way out of this artistic captivity. As he told *Entertainment Weekly*, "The last thing I wanted to end up being was a cliché. I wanted to be fresh and different, so I actually based my character on a criminal."[33]

Hey, presto. Caan plays *criminal*, and when this gets strained through *cop*, something interesting happens. We, the audience, can't actually see *criminal*. But somehow, it's bleeding through. As a result, this cop looks like something we haven't seen before, a character who seems to zig when we expect him to zag.

It's clever. Is this something Caan devised or a traditional tactic in the actor's skill set? In any case, it's a way to make popular culture that does not feel like predictable culture.

Artists

Francis Alÿs is a Belgian performance artist now living in Mexico City. New York's Museum of Modern Art recently exhibited his work. Peter Schjeldahl noted several works documented in the show. These include

> pushing a block of ice around Mexico City until it melted; walking around the same town with a large pistol to see what would happen (he was arrested after eleven excruciatingly long minutes); enlisting five hundred people, in Peru, with as many shovels, to move part of a mountainous sand dune; getting sixty-four Coldstream Guards to enter the City of London singly and fall into step as they found one another, until, fully assembled, they marched to the nearest bridge and dispersed.[34]

A lot of art is a shot in the dark. There is no certainty of meaning. The point is to see what meaning, what culture, will come from breaking the rules that govern the rest of cultural discourse. Much art is, to this extent, Culturematic-ish. But Alÿs goes further. He engages with the rules of Culturematic. Moving Coldstream Guards around a city so that they take on order and then surrender order—this is very Culturematic. It takes soldiers famous for their precision marching and treats them as a Rube Goldberg device. It's very "order out of accident," a study in the manner of mattering.

Schjeldahl notes a problem that haunts all Culturematics. He sees in Alÿs's art "pranks and caprices" and a certain "self-congratulatory presumption." And this is apt. Culturematics can look like stunts or pranks, like exercises in rule breaking undertaken purely for the fun (or mischief) of it. We can decide whether something is a prank or a Culturematic by asking a simple question. Is there an open curiosity, a certain literalness, at work here? Or is it self-conscious, perhaps even coy? If the art in question is looking for effect, it is not a Culturematic. It must be sincere in the what-if. If it knows what's going to happen, because it is looking to make an impression or create an effect, then it isn't a Culturematic. Culturematics that are coy or calculated aren't Culturematics.

Elevator Repair Service is an experimental theater company in New York City. With the help of installation artist Ben Rubin and UCLA statistician Mark Hansen, ERS recently performed *Shuffle*.

> [The performance is] a site-specific mash-up where the company attempts to read "The Great Gatsby", "The Sound and the Fury" and "The Sun Also Rises" simultaneously. The rearranged and overlapping texts produce compelling visual displays designed by Rubin and surprising, often absurd, micro-theater featuring

many veteran ERS performers. Audience is encouraged
to wander among the performers as they improvise.
With scripts generated in real time by digital algorithms,
phrases from the iconic novels of F. Scott Fitzgerald,
William Faulkner and Ernest Hemingway merge to
create a look back at some of America's favorite texts
that is at once disorienting and enlightening.[35]

Natsumi Hayashi is a teenager who lives in Japan. She takes photos of herself jumping in Tokyo. I know. Really? Jumping? She
takes these photos until she has one that makes it look as though
she's levitating.[36] In one way, Hayashi is an ordinary illusionist. She
wants to trick the eye and create an impression. And she knows
exactly the illusion she is trying to create: levitation. But if we look
at these photos for a moment, we are taken beyond the illusion,
beyond the sense of "oh, look" and beyond the sense of "interesting
trick, well played." We get a little mesmerized. And we begin to
think about cities, Tokyo, and train stations, for instance, a little
differently. It's like evaporation. Some cultural meaning comes up
off this exercise. We can't quite see it, but that doesn't mean it is
entirely undetectable. We can't quite tell what it is, but that doesn't
mean it is entirely unintelligible. We just go, "Hmm."

Web Sites

Getty Images has 24.7 million images. The problem: how to
introduce people to its images without overwhelming the viewer.
The answer was the Getty Moodstream on the Web site
moodstream.gettyimages.com. We set our preferences by mood
(a sliding scale for each mood: happy–sad, calm–lively, humorous–
serious, nostalgia–contemporary) and press Go. This begins a series

of images that pour through our computers. We can't say which photos are going to appear. We can't say in which order they are going to appear. We can't say which music will play or how it will interact with the image stream. As the stream pours, we pluck. By clicking "+" we can remove an image from the stream and add it to our light table.

Monoface (www.mono-1.com/monoface/main.html) is another wonder. This Web site opens with a face. If we click on any part of the face, it is replaced by a feature from a database of features. The result is an amazing Mr. Potato Head experience and a face that streams with features. In the language of linguistics, this treats the face as a set of paradigmatic classes out of which any number of combinations can be drawn. The result is not an utterance but a face that is grotesque, charming, and odd by turns. And a wonderful way to get to know the people at Mono, a branding company in Minneapolis and the 2010 Small Agency of the Year. ("I feel I've seen your nose somewhere before.")

To celebrate the release of the album *Suburbs*, Arcade Fire asked Chris Milk to create a Culturematic. Go to the Web site www.thewildernessdowntown.com/. You will be asked to enter the street address of the home you grew up in. The Web site then shows your address in a Google maps view. The image of a person running in a hoody is inserted into your neighborhood. You are invited to send a message to yourself.

Publishing

Take a look at this book ad:

> In the great tradition of Jorge Luis Borge's *Cronicas de Bustos Domecq*, *Army Man*, and *Might Magazine*, Matt Werner teamed up with the brilliant, though embattled,

yet-to-be-tenured Dr. Shaka Freeman to write one of the fake books referenced in *Pierre Menard, Author of the Quixote*. Excoriated by Borges scholars for its pseudo-historicism, anachronisms, and substandard grammar, *Papers for the Suppression of Reality* has been called "The worst book ever written on Jorge Luis Borges."[37]

Wait, what? This ad for *Papers for the Suppression of Reality* tells us two things about the book. First, that Werner and Freeman took the title of a fictional book as the pretext for a real book. Second, the book they wrote is very bad, indeed. It is in fact the very worst book ever written about Borges.

This breaks several conventions. In the usual scheme of things, books are supposed to be original. Second, books are not supposed to engage in literary in-fill, making fake books real. Third, ads for books are not supposed to be candid about the character flaws of their authors or the perilousness of their personal circumstances (the "embattled, yet-to-be-tenured" Dr. Shaka Freeman). Finally, ads are not supposed to trumpet the limitations of the book in question.

But this project breaks all these rules and manages in the process to arrest our attention. There is a good chance the whole thing is a literary stunt of some kind. But what kind? That question captures us, too. We are given a Web site, and perhaps there we will get to the bottom of things. In any case, we are invited to think new things or in new ways.

The history of publishing is a chronicle of imaginative undertakings. Authors are nothing if not ingenious. Kurt Vonnegut did a series of interviews with famous dead people, including Jesus, Hitler, and Isaac Asimov. Vonnegut partnered with Jack Kevorkian to create a new death experience and, through it, access to heaven and hell. Wait, what?

> During my most recently controlled near-death experience,
> I got to interview William Shakespeare. We did not hit it
> off. He said the dialect I spoke was the ugliest English he
> had ever heard, "fit to split the ears of groundlings." He
> asked if it had a name, and I said "Indianapolis."[38]

We have seen a series of what-if exercises that ask what if relatives of famous figures had written a book. Sena Naslund wrote a novel in the voice of Ahab's wife. Sandy Eisenberg wrote a children's book in the voice of Noah's wife.[39]

Start-Ups

The Summit Café in San Francisco is three things. It's a café on Valencia Street in the Mission District, where it sits next door to McSweeney's, the publishing experiment that Dave Eggers created. But it's also a tech incubator. Every four months, i/o Ventures, the creator of Summit Café, selects and funds a handful of small tech ventures. These start-ups meet at the Summit Café upstairs. Finally, it's an office space where independent contractors and entrepreneurs can rent desk space. "We're trying to gather together freethinkers, artisans, foodies, digital entrepreneurs," says Desi Danganan, Summit's managing director.[40]

The trouble with most start-ups is that they are about one thing. This would be fine if we could see where the opportunities are and how to get to them. But if the future is inscrutable, placing all our hopes on a single bet is dangerous. So the Summit Café has made sure it has three rivers running through it: people who just happen by, those who rent a desk, and those little ventures funded by i/o Ventures. Bring on the serendipity, as one piece of the café learns to stimulate, inspire, or incite another.

This means the Summit Café has quite a lot in common with McSweeney's, its next-door neighbor. McSweeney's was founded in 1998 as a literary journal. The journal began by publishing only works rejected by other magazines, but now it is large enough to reject its own. McSweeney's also has what Eggers calls "many, very smallish divisions," and these include a quarterly; a publishing house with several imprints; a monthly magazine called *The Believer* (my personal favorite); a quarterly DVD magazine with short films, documentaries, and instructional videos, including the work of Spike Jonze and Errol Morris; Voice of Witness, a book series dedicated to human rights crises; the Zeitoun Foundation, dedicated to aid in the rebuilding of New Orleans; and, finally, an Internet arm called McSweeney's Internet Tendency. In addition, Eggers founded a tutoring experiment called 826 Valencia. Oh, and a pirate supply store.[41] In all of this, Eggers has managed to publish many books, including his own best-selling *A Heartbreaking Work of Staggering Genius*.

Only a couple of years ago, the versatility of the Summit Café and McSweeney's would be treated as evidence of confusion, whimsy, or a certain refusal to get serious. But these days, when things are so very dynamic, the café's versatility looks like an excellent idea. And now that no one is quite sure what fiction is, and whether print is dead or just resting, McSweeney's is looking less self-indulgent and increasingly sage.

Every start-up wants to seed the world with several possibilities. This is what Snapple did in the early days. It would send out many flavors, stocking the shelf with an opportunity for the consumer to choose.[42] It was inviting the world to vote. This will not work if we are trying to discover the operation of radically different assumptions. In this event, we will have to send in the anthropologists. When cultural meaning is the quarry, the Culturematic may not serve us.

In all of this, the entrepreneur has to work at some point with capital suppliers. Even the most patient venture capitalists (VCs) will sometimes ask for clarity when all the Culturematic engineer can do is talk instincts and hunches. There is a simple fix. The VC can fund not the project but the entrepreneur and his or her project stream. Even here, the relationship is an unhappy one, and some entrepreneurs have decided to swear off VCs altogether. When Jared Cosulich and Adam Abrons founded their tech company, Irrational Design, they decided to refuse venture capital altogether. Cosulich says it's harder for an entrepreneur to "try crazy things" with VCs involved. His partner concurs: "They prefer that you double down on what's working."[43]

The Street

When Tony Blair, former British prime minister, published his memoirs, *A Journey,* a group of people wanted a way to protest the book and its contents. How to make a point publicly and cheaply? Someone had the good idea of quietly moving the book off the must-read tables to the crime section of the bookstore. Very cheap, quite public, and surprisingly effective. Media attention following, and eventually, a Facebook group sprung up. Now people began moving Blair's book to fantasy, dark fantasy, or horror sections, while others put it in children's literature and fairy tales. In supermarkets, the memoir was nestled amid rolls of toilet paper. One photograph posted on Facebook showed the book sitting beside Vanish, a stain remover.[44]

Speaking of urban spaces, what about graffiti? Is it a Culturematic? The answer is yes and no. When the graffitist is the English artist Banksy, the answer is yes.[45] Banksy's graffiti is Culturematic because it intervenes in the city with images that captivate us and move us to . . . something. As when Banksy created an image of a figure who looks like Charlie Brown on the outside of a burned-out building. The figure is holding a gas tank and smoking a cigarette. This is a side of Charlie Brown we have never seen before. The innocent is not so innocent. Contemplation ensues. So this graffiti qualifies. On the other hand, there is nothing imaginative about some guy writing his initials on the side of a bus over and over again. The motive here is obvious: self-advertisement. No culture, outside the graffiti world, is created or enhanced.

Tony Tempt1 is a graffiti pioneer who has been working in California since the 1980s. Diagnosed with amyotrophic lateral sclerosis in 2003 and now almost entirely paralyzed, he creates his work using technology and a team organized by the Graffiti Research Lab and the openFrameworks community. Tempt1 takes on the issue of self-advertisement directly. "THAT'S why I always paint TEMPT. Not to say 'hey, look at me, I'm a bad ass, I'm number one,' but rather, 'hey, look what's possible.'"[46] The spirit of the Culturematic says, "Investigate the world for what you don't know, instead of trying to brand it with what you do."

7 Culturematic Me

How should we live? In an inscrutable world, it's especially hard to say. In the old days, we explored our options, fixed on a career choice, got the right education, pursued the perfect job, and signed on with a powerful corporation. This strategy is now doubtful. We know our career will change several times, education will be continual, and a perfect job is unlikely at least in the early days. Most of all, we can no longer consider the corporation safe haven. Thomas Stewart puts it this way:

> We, your employer, no longer offer or even imply a
> guarantee of employment—you're here only as long as
> we need you. Instead, we offer you employability—stick
> with us, kid, and we'll reward you well, and when we
> dissolve the bonds, no hard feelings, no stigma, no
> problem. Plenty of people will want you because you
> picked up valuable skills here. Two birds in the bush are
> worth one in the hand.[1]

How should we live? Consider a Culturematic approach. Try lots of things. Try imaginative things. Cast the net wide. See what's out there. Canvass every "me" we might need to be the "me" we want eventually to be. Culturematics can be a device for self-invention, a way to investigate and fashion who we are.

Margaret Mitchell wrote *Gone with the Wind*, a blockbuster novel that was to become a blockbuster film, the two engraving themselves on American culture in the 1930s. But *Gone with the Wind* is not Mitchell's only work. A trip to the Margaret Mitchell House in Atlanta shows that Mitchell had been writing constantly since she was a young girl and that she produced many "books." Many are charmingly amateurish, binding out of ribbon, cover out of cardboard, but they *are* books, stories fully formed. Which means that when Mitchell sat down to write *Gone with the Wind*, she was, in a sense, an old hand at the writing game.

Compare Margaret Mitchell to Ruby Karelia. Ruby is eleven years old and lives in the Pacific Northwest. She does her own fashion. She also conducts fashion shows, gives fashion awards, and, with some frequency, wins these fashion awards. She takes photos and writes stories. She also keeps up a lively blog as well as a constant Facebook and Twitter stream. Here's a passage from a recent blog post:

> I really am sad right now . . . You know why? My stupid camera broke it's autofocus . . . and now the pictures I take are sick with blurriness. Poop . . .
>
> So me friends, I hope your having a cool February. To the max~!
>
> I'm not . . . Cause my POOPY CAMERA BROKE. Agh. I was enjoying capturing moments.[2]

In a way, Mitchell and Ruby are perfect opposites. Where Mitchell concentrated on her writing with what now looks like a single-minded focus, Ruby is broadcasting on all frequencies.

There is a chance that Ruby's is the better approach. Burying ourselves in the cultivation of a single talent is now ill advised. What we need are lots of little projects, sent out into different parts of the world, by means of many media. Thus do we carry on that irreplaceably useful conversation between now and next.

Of course, many of us have but a single passion. And in this event, the strategy must be to broadcast this message on every frequency in every modality available to us. Thus did Scott Schuman eventually invent a fashion blog called *The Sartorialist*. After two thousand posts, documenting photos of everyday people from the streets of New York City, the project turned into a monthly column in *GQ*, a six-figure book deal with Penguin, and a robust photography business.[3] We have extraordinary opportunities open to us. In addition to social media, blogs, and Twitter accounts, we can build community with www.mightybell, www.ning.com, and www.kickstarter.com. (Come join the Ning site for this book at www.culturematic.ning.com.)

As we have seen, the storefront in San Francisco called 826 Valencia contains a publishing house, a tutoring center, and a pirate supply store. To be fair, the pirate shop was a piece of the purest pragmatism. Dave Eggers's landlord told him that the building was zoned as retail space. So he *had* to have retail. Not everyone would have come up with pirate supply as the retail effort. Jolly Roger flags, glass eyes, scurvy prevention kits (limes), and seasickness pills were not guaranteed to find an audience. (This was well before *Pirates of the Caribbean*, when pirates were not yet dipped in Depp.) But as it turned out, the store ended up doing well enough to pay everyone's rent. An implausible experiment paid off.

The moral of the story: be alert to possibilities even if they are not especially plausible. Stewart Brand has made this a life principle. When *Reason* magazine asked him, "What do you think has placed you at so many interesting early stages of American cultural movements?" he had this reply:

> A mixture of curiosity, boredom, and absence of being dedicated to one big organization or one big ideology. I guess I agree with [science fiction writer] Bill Gibson's line that the future is already here; it's just not evenly distributed. I look for places where the future is turning up and look for a sense of "if this plays out, it'll change the world." And I go hang out when it's still taking shape. That led me to hang out with psychedelic drug people, then personal computer people, then MIT's Media Lab.[4]

These days, Brand keeps the company of bioengineers at Stanford, attends the iGEM (International Genetically Engineered Machine) Jamboree, and follows developments in microbial biology, synthetic biology, and geoengineering. In this case, the Culturematic strategy is to monitor the experiments undertaken by other people.

We might say that Brand is looking for the future at the far end of the Kauffman continuum.[5] This is where things are so new it is hard to say whether they are something or perhaps nothing at all. In the early days, the personal computer was for many people nothing at all. Who was going to need a computer of his or her own? Computers were for corporations and governments, not for desktops.

Brand can see the future before it has taken shape and form. All of us want to detect the future as soon as we are able. And this means putting some of our experiments way out there on the continuum.

When Mike Rowe took a job as host of a reality TV show called *Dirty Jobs*, it must have felt like the beginning of the end of his career. He was committing to shoveling excrement, crawling into small spaces, and putting himself in harm's way. It would have been one thing if there were something heroic about these undertakings. But this show threatened to make Rowe a permanent resident of the low-rent part of the entertainment universe. Was this the path of stardom? Would this make him admired? Who would sign him up as a celebrity spokesman? The Ford Motor Company did, paying Rowe a small fortune to appear in ads for the F-150 truck. There is no evidence Rowe chose *Dirty Jobs* as a path to stardom, but there is now evidence he should have done. The "experiment" paid off.

Celebrities are fluorescing in strange ways. In the old model, the star would move from an early career to stardom and never look back. (Jason Lee started as a pro skateboarder, Mickey Rourke as a boxer, Harrison Ford as a carpenter.) But now, celebs go looking for new careers *after* stardom. Ashton Kutcher achieved stardom with *That 70s Show* and *Dude, Where's My Car?* and then he decided to produce TV and social media projects that explored new domains (*Punk'd, Beauty and the Geek, Opportunity Knocks*). Tom Hanks and Stephen King write for *Entertainment Weekly*. Zach Galifianakis has his own talk show.[6] And these days, celebrities are now hiring themselves out as creative directors: Victoria Beckham for Land Rover, Lady Gaga for Polaroid, will.i.am for Intel, and Maria Sharapova for Cole Haan. We may think of these side projects as these celebrities' Culturematics, as explorations of the world to discover the options that exist after their red-hot stardom cools.

As we have seen, James Franco achieved stardom and then decided to explore simultaneous careers as a conceptual artist, fiction writer, and graduate student. Graduate student? When you are a Hollywood star, you don't pull all-nighters. And you certainly don't abase yourself before some schmo with tenure and an increasingly shaky grasp of the sixteenth-century sonnet. This is

Franco in full exploration mode. He is prepared to dismantle stardom for self-discovery. To be sure, this will serve him as an actor. (We know what happens when actors become the captives of their celebrity. All their acting starts to look like a cameo appearance. Robert Wagner is perhaps the best case in point.) But the larger point for Franco may be that this exploration will also serve him once his career begins to change.

To be sure, some of this is an attempt to leverage stardom and extend it. Some of it is merely the expression of the celebrity ego (as in, "I am so wonderful I should be doing everything!") But some of it is a Culturematic effort to cast the self wide and find out what's out there.

Make a Meme

Mel Gibson left rude and threatening messages on his wife's answering machine. She in turn released them to the press. Maureen O'Connor pounced. She turned three of the rants into Wordles, those word clouds discussed in chapter 3. Twenty minutes of work became a sensational meme and thirty-two thousand page views for *Gawker*. O'Connor had made a meme.[7]

Ian Spector dreamed up what he called "Chuck Norris facts." These included "Chuck Norris can sneeze without closing his eyes," and "Chuck Norris can believe it's not butter." These facts found their way into T-shirts and coffee mugs and eventually a best-selling book. Spector had made a meme.[8]

Drew Grant discovered an image that showed Eric Stoltz trying out for *Back to the Future*, and her Culturematic inserted Stolz in other Hollywood projects, including *Inception*, *Being John Malkovich*, and *Twilight*. Grant, too.[9]

Noticing that Charlie Sheen's outbursts in early 2011 sounded like those of the fictional character Ron Burgundy, Dan Gurewitch decided to ask people if they could tell the difference. Was it Sheen or Burgundy who said, "I am not Thomas Jefferson. He was a pussy." Give up? It was Charlie Sheen.[10]

Dream up a what-if, and you're on your way. You could use a what-if from this book, as in "What if you ate all your meals at Denny's (or somewhere else) this weekend?" Or install yourself in an airport to live (as Tom Hanks's character did in the 2004 film *The Terminal*) or merely to blog (as Alain de Botton did from Heathrow). Or go to an island called Robinson Crusoe to read the novel called *Robinson Crusoe* (as Jonathan Franzen did).[11] Or see how many *Law and Order* episodes you can watch in forty-eight hours. Tape your reactions, and create a two-minute clip that shows you gradually deteriorating on the couch, spouting plot lines and character clichés. Upload to YouTube. Await greatness.

Making memes takes a deft hand. There is no simple formula. In fact, we're not sure why rants from Gibson, facts from Norris, and recasting Stolz work so well. Many memes appear to work because they're odd. (See chapter 4 for some of the cultural properties of the Culturematic.) Our job as a meme maker is to keep trying. Keep pouring stuff into Wordle or onto T-shirts, and see what works. Spector's treatment of Chuck Norris seems to make Norris a mythic character. And that can't be right, can it? It's the tension between the ordinary and the odd that works here.

Celebrity turns out to be a rich vein, but it is not the only source of Culturematic materials. Noah Kalina took a picture of himself every day for around six years. He then put the pictures, all 2,356 of them, in sequence on YouTube in a clip that runs five minutes and forty-six seconds. It's Noah over and over and over again. For some reason, this is completely successful. This video has been viewed over 16 million times. Tron Guy posted pictures of himself dressed in a custom-made costume inspired by the 1980s sci-fi movie *Tron*. Minor celebrity ensued for both Noah and Tron Guy.[12]

The thing is to make lots of memes. As Brian Rafferty puts it, "Most Internet meme makers just release an idea into the wild, often with little expectation that it will get much attention. If it suddenly gains traction, the creator might wake up to find a crashed server and a lengthy Google Alerts update."[13]

Make a Metaphor (or Become One)

Here is *The Onion* passage that we noted in chapter 5. It is a splendid Culturematic and worth repeating.

> Monday's arrest is only the latest in a long string of legal troubles for the controversial [Alan] Greenspan [then chairman of the Federal Reserve Board], who has had 22 court dates since becoming Fed chief in 1987. Economists recall his drunken 1994 appearance on CNN's *Moneyline*, during which he unleashed a profanity-laden tirade against Bureau of Engraving & Printing director Larry Rolufs and punched host Lou Dobbs when he challenged Greenspan's reluctance to lower interest rates. In November 1993, he was arrested after running shirtless through D.C. traffic while waving a gun. And some world-market watchers believe the international gold standard has still not recovered from a May 1998 incident in which he allegedly exposed his genitals on the floor of the Tokyo Stock Exchange. The Tokyo case is still pending.[14]

This Culturematic uses simple metaphor. And metaphor is a little device for giving one thing the properties of another thing.[15] Here, Alan Greenspan and the Fed are turned into a rock band on a rampage. Culturematics work well when you combine things that stand well apart in our culture. It's hard to think of two things as far apart as rock bands and senior members of the government.

We are mad scientists mixing unstable cultural materials. The more disparate these materials, the more likely we are to get a chemical reaction. So if we take the TV show *The Real Housewives of Atlanta* and mix in Arianna Huffington, we get one thing. But if we mix in Hillary Clinton, we get something more explosive. And this is because Clinton is farther (in cultural space) from *Housewives of Atlanta* than Huffington is. We could mix in Katie Couric or Courtney Love. Each produces a different effect, and Love works strangely well. It may not be as stark a contrast as Clinton-Housewives, but it's fun to think about. Play with the formula.

Details matter. When *The Onion* writers put Greenspan in a rock-star lifestyle, they get the details exactly right. "Running shirtless through D.C. traffic while waving a gun" is superb. "The Tokyo case is still pending" is exactly the way a journalist would report this story.

Another option is to put *ourselves* in new identities. Bud Caddell, as noted earlier in the book, gave himself the identity of someone tweeting from a mailroom at the Sterling Cooper ad agency, as portrayed in the TV show *Mad Men*. Chris Poole, the founder of 4chan, briefly put himself into the identity of Jimmy Wales, the better to scorn Mr. Wales's fundraising efforts for *Wikipedia*.[16]

A guy who calls himself Dr. Claw sells lobster rolls from a van. The problem: this is illegal without a license. Dr. Claw decided that if he was going to live outside the law, he might as well style himself a "Lobstah pushah." He dresses in the manner of Sacha Baron Cohen's character Ali G (track suit, gold chains, baseball cap) and pretend his sales are a drug transaction. Customers call a phone number and when the roll is ready, the hand-off is made in a plain paper bag, with both parties looking nonchalantly away.[17]

Someone, we don't know who, decided to create an identity by combining former *Gourmet* editor Ruth Reichl with celebrity chef Anthony Bourdain. And presto, Ruth Bourdain. This new creature goes online and imitates the real Ruth Reichl.

So when Ruth Reichl tweets: "Good night. Hot kimchi, slicked with chilies. Smoky, sweet grilled beef in crisp lettuce. Sake. Slow stroll home down electric streets," Ruth Bourdain replies: "Bad night. Hot kimchi slicked w/chilies = spicarrhea. Smoking beef in lettuce ZigZags laced w/Sake didn't help. Streets electrified by ConEd."

The secret is mixing unstable elements. Lee Schrager loves Ruth Bourdain because, he says, "Tony and Ruth are . . . so unique and well-known. Merging them into one is so clever, [so] absurd."[18]

A Culturematic should make a small buzzer sound in our brain. It forces us to say "Wait, what? Greenspan can't be a rock star. Hillary Clinton can't be a Housewife of Atlanta." The mad scientist strikes again. Disparate parts of our culture are brought together. A lovely little what-if has been played out. Apparently, we quite like it when culture is reworked in this way. Well, not stupid people. Stupid people get confused, and then they blame the rest of us for their confusion. But the rest of the world, and that's most of the world, is delighted.

I suggest that when you create your Culturematic laboratory, you set aside a metaphor bench.

Make a Spectacle of Yourself

The first order of business for Canadian parents is to persuade their children never to make a spectacle of themselves. Sometime in the 1960s, I came across a newspaper photo of a man shouting at the prime minister. It happened in Vancouver, my hometown. The guy was even wearing a shirt I owned. I showed my father the picture and, with a look of deep shame, said, "Dad, I am not sure how to tell you this, but . . ." He believed me at first (and he took it amazingly well, considering), but I could hear him thinking, "It's happened. My son's finally gone and made a spectacle of himself."

In an era of Lady Gaga, Charlie Sheen, and Lindsay Lohan, spectacle is a part of our daily lives. But most of us remain bound by hundreds of small but powerful rules. How we speak, dress, move, interact—all of these are codified by soft law, the shared conventions of the social world. I recently wore a pair of red Air Jordans to a family gathering, and an in-law said, "Are you losing it?" It turns out red shoes are against the law at Connecticut picnics.

Some people dare break these laws. They put their individuality ahead of the group.[19] They invent their own code. The spectacular self has many precedents: the dandy crafted by Beau Brummell, and the decadent crafted by Huysmans. Noel Coward, Andy Warhol, and Quentin Crisp were spectacular. Despite modest origins and his youth, Brummell ruled matters of taste and society in London for nearly two decades. His authority came from nothing more than a spectacular self and his exquisite taste, said literary critic Ellen Moers: "Brummell had only to look upon or speak to or walk with a man to make him fashionable, and only to cut another to make him a pariah." Brummell dared even challenge the power of the prince regent. As Brummell put it, "I made him what he is and I can unmake him." Shocking. Spectacular. Courageous. (I will never wear my red Air Jordans to a family event again.)[20]

One reigning mistress of the spectacular is Lady Gaga, for whom art is all. She is theater. No gesture is too grand. No outfit too exaggerated. No song theme or video treatment too hyperbolic. Just when you think she's gone too far, that she must now tip into the ridiculous, she manages to redeem herself. For the rest of us, the secret to the spectacular is to find a balance.

Departing from the rules a little bit, turning up our collar, say—this isn't a violation that interests. We have only broken one rule, and it's not a rule anyone really cares about. Departing from the rules a lot, in the manner of Charlie Sheen in the winter of 2010, goes much farther, and much too far. Sheen broke many rules we do care about, and some of us now dismiss him as a kook.

Gregory was until recently my wife's colleague at work. He would sometimes show up wearing custom-made jodhpurs, Chesterfield jackets, and antique cufflinks. This drew attention and sometimes comment. Gregory dressed sumptuously, but he was always this side of "too much." The office was impressed, not put off. To be sure, the price for being even a little spectacular is sometimes exclusion. For the Brummels among us, this is a small price to pay.

Spectacle has to feel like an act of generosity on the part of the wearer. My wife and I were recently at a design event. We were introduced to a man who was dressed spectacularly well. But he seemed a little grand, strutting about, as if presenting himself for our admiration. This proved annoying, and we quietly ignored him until he went away. Spectacle must say, "This is what I give to you," not "This is what I take from you."

Being spectacular belongs to everyone. We don't need to be part of a subculture or a celebrity to take part. Take the case of the eleven-year-old called Ruby, whom we noted at the beginning of this chapter. Ruby manages to produce a self-created, self-contained spectacularness. No audience required.

I had a friend in Toronto who was pretty conventional in most respects, except that she used a metal lunch box as her purse. It might have been a Roy Rogers lunch box; I can't remember. The effect was impressive. It proved to be an icebreaker. Some people loved it and said things like, "Love your purse!" But other people were put off and would move away from her at cocktail parties as if she might be combustible.

Make an Exhibit of Yourself

Making an exhibit of yourself means capturing some part of your life in an enduring medium. It means making yourself persistent, so that your great, great grandchildren can consult the record and see who you were and how you lived.

Samuel Pepys, an Englishman, kept a diary for ten years, from 1660 to 1669. Through Pepys's eyes, we see the great fire of London, some of the plague years, the aftermath of the English civil war, and the rise of the English navy. Equally important, we see what life was like in the seventeenth century. We hear Pepys kicking himself for "carrying my watch in my hand in the coach all this afternoon, and seeing what o'clock it is one hundred times."[21] For the price of keeping a diary, Pepys won a measure of immortality. This can be your reward for making an exhibit of yourself.

You won't be the first in on this one. Steve Rubel, a maven of PR and the new media, is committing his life to digital memory, as have Gordon Bell at Microsoft and Steve Mann at MIT. It's called *lifelogging*. The new technology makes for recording possibilities Pepys would not have dreamed of.[22]

Creating the exhibit is harder than it looks. It is not enough to take a photograph. Or even a rich stream of photographs. Photos are not stable. Information begins to evaporate almost immediately. Within a couple of weeks, we can't always name every person in the photo. Within a couple of years, the what and the where are unclear. And with a couple of decades, the very point of the photo is mysterious. "I think that's my uncle or something," we say plaintively. "In Montreal, possibly?"

The point of the exhibit is to capture everything as soon as possible in as much detail as possible. The historians will still have a lot of reconstructing to do. The more you do for them, the more likely you are to achieve Pepys's immortality.[23] And remember, the future is interested in the minutia of daily life. In a couple of hundred years, every detail of our existence, however insignificant it is now, will be a matter of fascination. This is why we love watching Pepys watch his watch. Was it the novelty of the watch? Was it the cost? Was it the prestige or the workmanship? Was the pace of life increasing?

There is a second tier to Pepys, and that's context: the life of London that swirls around him. This means we have to get out of the house, out of our domestic circumstances, into the life of the city. Morgan Friedman has done a brilliant job documenting the life of New York City with a Web site called Overheard in New York City. Vivian Maier was a nanny in the Chicago suburbs and a secret shutterbug. She left behind 100,000 negatives and photographs that give us a breathtaking record of city life. Maier died in obscurity, but she will live in Pepysian memory.[24]

Another way to engage with the city is to play the flaneur. The flaneur is a person walking, watching, and otherwise engaging with the city as it presents itself to someone in motion and on foot. It's an idea discussed by gifted observers of contemporary life: Baudelaire, Simmel, Benjamin, and Sontag. Indeed, it has become so fashionable that it has become a kind of pose (Baudelaire's great fear realized). Read one of these masters, and give it a whirl.[25]

Beyond Pepys's life, beyond London, there is a third tier, and this is culture. What are the emotions, ideas, assumptions, and beliefs that we bring to the document? Capture these, too. And again, there is no such thing as too much detail. We have several records of the Great Fire of London, but it is when we see it through Pepys's eyes that the thing begins to live. Report what you are thinking. Bear witness. Use that video camera you have set up in the corner of the Culturematic laboratory, and capture culture.

Be an Anthropologist

Kate Fox is an English anthropologist. She collects some of her data by getting in the way. At the post office, for instance, Fox will cut into line. Then she watches to see what happens. People will communicate their unhappiness with this outrage in a variety of ways, sniffing, harrumphing, staring daggers. When Kate does something that provokes a reaction, she knows she has broken a rule. And she begins to investigate what the rule is, and how it helps define English life. (Oh, you think everyone queues? Have fun in parts of China.)[26]

Another way to be an anthropologist is to study the forms of social life. And these are everywhere. Kids started skating abandoned swimming pools in California in the 1970s. They were called Z-Boys. This is a perfect topic for study. Get a camera. Do some interviews. Find out everything someone will need to know in a hundred years to grasp what was going on here. Topics are everywhere. Recently, people in the suburbs were ripping out their kitchens, living rooms, and dining rooms and installing "great rooms." We do not have a good study of this social form. It's up to you. Contemporary culture is a lot of waterfront, but you can take a single topic of this kind and make it a bounded study. I call this *square-inch anthropology*.[27]

Anthropology begins with noticing. Someone went to the Boston Book Festival.[28] Here's what they saw: a literary tattoo, a Moleskine, cat jewelry, a *Chicago Manual of Style* tote bag, quirky hats, and a drunken author. These are telling details, but what do they tell us? What do these tell us about the Boston Book Festival? That's your job, to get inside what it feels like to be a participant. Why Moleskines and not Filofaxes? Why *quirky* hats?

Few people study American culture. Some of the exceptions are brilliantly interesting: Lloyd Warner's study of "Yankee City" (Newburyport, Massachusetts, I think) and Evon Vogt on a tiny town in Texas. There is opportunity everywhere. We can do what Flaubert did. Keep track of the things people say and the opinions that everyone seems to agree upon. (In Flaubert's day, everyone seemed to agree that actresses were the ruin of young men of good family.) Keep your eyes and ears open. I came back from a Saturday morning walk with an observation I hadn't made before: that American parents, at least in my part of the world, are now calling their children "buddy." Or do what *SNL*'s Fred Armisen and Sleater-Kinney's Carrie Brownstein did: an anthropology of your hometown. And very finely observed it is, too, right down to the facial expressions and turns of phrase.[29] If you are inclined to music, follow the example of the bard of the suburb, Ben Folds. Some of his work is great ethnography (e.g., "Steven's Last Night in Town").

Being an anthropologist gives you useful data. You have discovered one of the levers or the meanings of social life that will serve you in the construction of Culturematics. (A knowledge of the power of pie was essential for the Pie Lab in Hale County.) You have discovered the invisible meanings of American culture, and this gives you the ability to look for things like reality TV or fantasy football. Gather knowledge. Apply knowledge.

Be a Typifier

BusinessWeek sent observers to airports in Paris, Montreal, and New York City.[30] Their assignment: to study the business traveler.

Of course, travelers come in all shapes and sizes. If we look at them carefully, they are endlessly various. But "endlessly various" doesn't clarify the world for us. We can't act on "endlessly various."

Even in a postmodern world, we must generalize. We look for patterns. All those various travelers, do they exhibit shared properties? If we squint our eyes, we begin to see patterns. A typology begins to emerge.[31]

Here's what *BusinessWeek* came up with for an airport.

Luggage riflers

CNN segment chortlers

Twitchers and touchers

Fortress builders

Food stuffers

The wired neurotic

Tabloid readers

Chair hoarders

Is it perfect? I don't think it's meant to be perfect. But it's interesting. We can see airport life with new clarity. The typology gives us something to work with.

There's a guy who spends a lot of time in Union Square in New York City. He calls himself Normal Bob. (He is also known as Bob Hain). Normal Bob has created a typology that consists of "skaters," "scensters," "models," and "junkies." He also has documented Ramblin' Bill, The DJ, and Quarter Guy.[32]

The typifier asks, "What can I notice about people in the world, and can I create categories that capture some of what I notice?" How much of this world can we stuff into these categories? It's tough now that the world is so very various.[33] It might be impossible now to write the book Mitchell wrote twenty-five years ago on American lifestyles.[34] Typologies are out of fashion. But in the right hands, they can be useful. But if you were redesigning the airport, a good typology would be essential.

Typifying is illuminating. It helps us see something we knew but hadn't quite fully grasped. Take Woo girls as a case in point. Chances are, we have seen these women at the bar. More to the point, we have heard them there. But we didn't quite grasp that this was a *type* of person engaged in a *type* of behavior. And we didn't quite grasp the type until popular culture came to the rescue. An episode of *How I Met Your Mother* did a lovely little piece on the Woo girl. An entire culture is put on notice.[35]

Spotting and sorting culture in this manner is a way of creating culture. It gives us glasses with which to see the world. It makes things visible that were not clear before. Typologies are never perfect. And sometimes, they're wrong. But even when they are wrong, they make us smarter. Because we can fix a typology. We can't fix confusion.

Be a Cartographer

A couple of years ago, Rick Meyerowitz was on the A train in New York City. He was staring at the subway map, and he was thinking about lunch. Suddenly, station names began to look like food. Rick asked himself, "What if I redid the subway map [as] a food map?" He brought in his friend Maira Kalman, and the two of them renamed 468 stations. Avenue H became Mulligan Stew, Avenue J became Can of Soda, and Brighton Beach became Beach Stroganoff. *The New Yorker* published their map in 2004.[36]

We don't have to work with something as grand as a subway system. Over the course of many walks, I have remapped my little town in Connecticut. At least in my head. I live pretty close to "the old woman who listens to her TV really loudly. She's one hundred." I am up the street from the "the house built by that Swedish guy who eventually returned to Europe and died in a pauper's hospital." About a mile from my house is "smuggler's cove." Down the street is the "Chinese pavilion," and it's an easy walk from there to the "fortress of mystery," "where the roller coaster once stood," and "house of the trapped Brazilians." It's not a perfect map, but it captures parts of the town that seem to have escaped Rand McNally.

Maps used to belong to faceless bureaucracies and the state. They were literal. They gave up everything beautiful and imaginative to be accurate and clear. (By some miracle, even the most sober map around manages to turn into a thing of beauty in about twenty years. We don't know why. The New York Public Library has maps to take your breath away.) The Apache create maps rich in cultural meanings. Our official maps are literal. What you see is what we get. Until now. With the rise of a technologically empowered everyman, remapping is inevitable. One precedent was Saul Steinberg's *View of the World from 9th Avenue*, a cover drawing for *The New Yorker* in 1976. *The New Yorker* is a hot bed of the remapping movement. See the work of Roz Chast there.[37]

Another possibility is mapping the world from someone else's point of view. What does a big city look like to a newly arrived runaway? What does Rowayton look like to the hundred-year-old woman who lives down the street?[38]

Be a Curator

Piers Fawkes, Jason Kottke, Pip Coburn, Polly Labarre, Andrew Zolli, Arianna Huffington, Michael Hebb, Jerry Michalski, Sara Winge, Tim O'Reilly, Russell Davies, Mark Frauenfelder, Leora Kornfeld, Richard Saul Wurman, Cory Doctorow, David Pescovitz, Xeni Jardin, Tim Hwang, Christina Xu, Chris Anderson, Tom Guarriello, Michael Arrington, Craig Newmark, Billy Chasen, Louis Black, Mark Zuckerberg, Chris Hughes, Maria Popova, Chris Poole, Jimmy Wales, Julian Assange, and Matt Mullenwes. These people run conferences, magazines, aggregators, or networks where people, ideas, or events convene. (This paragraph makes me the greatest name-dropper in the history of the digital world.)

We can call them *curators*.[39] They are people who can examine the vast bodies of data and people and discover the ones that matter. But this is the first act of curation. The second is connecting. Once curators identify data and people, they connect them to other data and people. Thus does our world become still more feverish in its creativity.

Curation can be done by hand. Pip Coburn stages great lunches in New York City. I was coming out of one of them and found myself thinking, "I know there are a great many interesting people in New York City, but for some reason, I only meet them at Pip's events." Pip doesn't manage discussion. He relies on smart people to find their own way. Michael Hebb has made the Sorrento Hotel in Seattle a meeting ground for his Night School, Scotch and Soup, and One Pot. And then there are the larger venues like Piers Fawkes's PSFK and Tim Hwang's ROFLCon.

Curation can be done digitally. Here's how Maria Popova describes her Culturematic, Brain Pickings:

> Brain Pickings is about curating interestingness— picking culture's collective brain for tidbits of stuff that inspires, revolutionizes, or simply makes us think. It's about innovation and authenticity and all those other things that have become fluff phrases but don't have to be. Mostly, Brain Pickings is about ideas—revolutionary new ideas that no one has seen or thought of before, and old ideas that most have seen, but no one has thought of in this way before. Because creativity, after all, is simply our ability to tap into the mental pool of ideas we've accumulated over the years just by being present and alive and awake to the world, and to combine them in extraordinary new ways. We believe that creativity is a combinatorial force.[40]

Ideas and people tend to travel in packs. People in Silicon Valley tend to know other people in their industry or profession (Silicon Valley, say, or animatronics) and not to know people in even proximate industries (music, say, or anime). As Mark Granovetter and Ronald Burt tell us, something extraordinary sometimes happens when these worlds are brought together.[41]

This is where the curator comes in. By filling what Burt calls "structural holes" between communities, the curator can introduce parties that would otherwise find one another only through serendipity. The curator is effectively "shorting out" the world, crossing streams normally kept separate. In the immortal words of John Stuart Mill, "it is hardly possible to overrate the value . . . of placing human begins in contact with persons dissimilar to themselves, and with modes of thought and action unlike those with which they are familiar."[42]

There is another Culturematic angle here. It is to "recurate" the world. Jonathan Salem Baskin has gently hijacked museums by creating unauthorized audio tours that invite us to think about exhibits in new ways. For visitors to the Art Institute of Chicago, Baskin offers a new look at key paintings in the "American Art Before 1900" exhibit. He conspires to show where and how vampires were the inspiration for portraiture and abstract art. His what-if: what if artists were the only people who could see vampires in the nineteenth century? All institutions can be "recurated" in this way. But why stop there? The story of any corporation, neighborhood, or family could be retold on an audio tour suitable for delivery by smartphone.[43]

Be a Storyteller

A well-told story is a wonderful thing. I got to hear one in a tiny pub outside St. Andrews, Scotland. My Scottish brother-in-law was holding forth. As the story took hold, we ceased to be twenty people huddled against a fireplace with a North Sea gale outside. At his bidding, we stepped out of the pub into the story. Truth be told, I didn't like David very much, but he had me.

This oral tradition has moved from the fireside into the world, and it continues in new guises: the Hollywood film, stand-up comedy, improv theater, and spoken-word poetry. And of course, new media make stories open-ended, nonlinear, interactive, and absorbing in new ways. *World of Warcraft* is a kind of story engine. So are *Second Life* and *Call of Duty*.

Stories become Culturematics when they engage with the world. Ken Eklund has created a scenario game called *World Without Oil*, what he calls a massively collaborative, online "historical pre-enactment" of a global oil crisis. As Jane McGonigal says, games are becoming less a respite from the real world and increasingly a model for what we want the real world to feel like.[44] To play in the game is to act on the world. As we contemplate a great "gamification" of the world, we see games performing the triple play of the Culturematic: provoking the world, discovering meaning, and unleashing value.

One afternoon in 1849, George Parkman, a physician and one of the richest men in Boston, went missing. A manhunt uncovered pieces of a body buried under the Harvard Medical College. John Webster, a Harvard professor, was arrested for the murder, and there ensued what was possibly the most famous trial of the nineteenth century. One hundred and fifty years later, someone had the idea of retelling the Parkman murder story and did so with social media that tells this story in and around Boston, in the buildings and neighborhoods where it took place. Boston now has a little bit of its history written into the city, as it were, there for retrieval by anyone with a smartphone.[45]

David Bausola has built story engines that make narratives out of bits and pieces he discovers online. In his program Weavrs, he has invented nothing less than an identity engine. These are wonderful what-if devices. A San Francisco Web developer named Eric Eberhardt launched *You Are Listening to Los Angeles*. He took the live police feed and set it to ambient music. He has since created *You Are Listening To* Web sites for San Francisco, Chicago, and Montreal.[46] Making stories (and identities) out of found materials is a field with rich possibilities.

The mashable world of new media gives us many options. On a trip to Brazil, I was watching a Sherlock Holmes movie in my hotel room. The dialogue was in Portuguese and therefore lost on me. Culture hates a vacuum, and I found that bits of dialogue began to come spontaneously to mind. Presto! I had a little mash-up. We can add new dialogue to *any* movie. We may use Mystery Science Theatre 3000 as one model for this intervention.[47] Assuming that fair use of copyrighted materials can be evoked for this exercise, the possibilities are endless. The holy grail challenge: could you rewrite the dialogue of an entire film, giving a translation that matched and engaged the visual story line of the film in the construction of an entirely new narrative? It would take an astounding act of ingenuity.

In a digital age, we have several story vehicles, including the visuals that can be extracted from a game like *Halo* (as in the case of *Red and Blue*) or an immersive reality engine like *Second Life*.[48] We can also use comic engines like xtranormal.com and goanimate.com. A good deal of brilliant work has been created by adding new subtitles to a scene taken from the German film *Downfall*. People take a clip from the movie and then make up their own "translations." These give us Hitler flying into a rage over Windows Vista, the signing of Mats Sundin by the Vancouver Canucks, and *Wrestlemania XXV*. Robert Seizlak gave us a very funny "Hitler reacts to news about the iPhone prototype leak."[49]

We can also take some existing artifact and find the story within. Consider the famous photo taken during the construction of the Empire State Building. *New York Construction Workers Lunching on a Crossbeam* was taken by Charles C. Ebbets on September 29, 1932. It appeared in the *New York Herald Tribune*, and it shows eleven men eating lunch, seated on a girder with their feet dangling nonchalantly sixty-nine stories above the streets of New York City. No harnesses. No netting. Who *were* these guys? Could we reconstruct their stories? What events brought them to that beam? What events took them away from it? It would take a heroic act of digging, but what a piece of story-telling this would give us.

Be a Time Traveler

Here's what I want to do next spring. I want to return to 1955 and listen to every game played by the Brooklyn Dodgers, in real time, several games a week through to the end of the season.

I don't know what happened to the Dodgers that year. I have no idea whether Brooklyn did well or badly. So if someone can contrive to play the radio broadcasts over the week and send me newspaper clippings at the appropriate intervals, I can live the entire season with each inning, each game, and the season out-come as a complete surprise. Within certain limits, I can experi-ence the Brooklyn Dodgers of 1955 as if I had found a seam in time, stolen back in history, and managed to come upon these boys of summer as they played a season completely unaware that there was a time traveler in their midst.

Thank god for the death of "living memory." None of this makes any sense unless the knowledge of the season is completely extinguished for the participant. But happily it is. Unless some-one blurts out details or, horrors, the season's outcome, I will be listening to the 1955 season as innocent of its outcome as the fans of 1955. How many historical events could be replayed in con-temporary time?

Once we get the hang of this kind of time travel, we could cre-ate it for others. Coombe End Court, a retirement center in Marl-borough, Wiltshire, England, has a time-warp room. It's outfitted with a gramophone, manual typewriters, pictures of Elvis Presley and Marilyn Monroe, a telephone made of Bakelite, and furniture from the 1950s. The residents call this their reminiscence room. What surprised gerontologists was that those who use it need less Alzheimer's medication. As Leora Kornfeld observes, "apparently, parquet floors and rotary dial phones [can] accomplish what neuroleptic drugs can't."[50]

Time traveler can also be forward motion. Consider doing a Stewart Brand and William Gibson experiment, in which you go looking for the future. As we will see in the last chapter, Stewart Brand has spent much of his life searching for the future:

> I guess I agree with [science fiction writer] Bill Gibson's line that the future is already here; it's just not evenly distributed. I look for places where the future is turning up and look for a sense of "if this plays out, it'll change the world." And I go hang out when it's still taking shape.[51]

Find and visit the future somewhere near you. Or create a consultancy that advises others who wish to become time travelers. One inspiration: the Historical Consultancy 30–45, which gives advice in particular on life in Holland in the period 1930 to 1945.[52] Another inspiration: the invention of the Frank Reade laboratory by Paul Guinan and Anina Bennett.[53]

Where to Stage Your Culturematics

Running everything off one laptop in one place is possible. It's the model for most of us. It's how I made this book, sitting at a table in my kitchen. And it gives us extraordinary resources. (What is YouTube, if not the raw feed of contemporary culture?) But the configuration is far from ideal. In a perfect world, we would have several stations or desks. A little separation goes a long way.

The well-stocked laboratory would have a station that contains a video camera at the ready. No set-up. Instantaneous access. Any time we want to record a comment or interview someone on camera, we can get right to it. At another station, we might have the map we are making of our hometown. Decorate this with various images in the manner of a designer's inspiration board.[54] At another, we might have our time traveler project. At a fourth, the memes, stories, and ethnographies we are working on. At a fifth, notes and images (and an inspiration board) for the spectacle we are making of ourselves. Our computer might move between the stations. The point of many stations is to collapse the time needed to engage with each project.

As we build our laboratory, there are lots of inspirations to choose from: mad scientist, Victorian inventor, museum curator, medieval alchemist, Elizabethan secretary of the navy (aka Samuel Pepys). When Nike made it possible for us to customize shoes, he asked Nike to print "sweatshop" on his. Of course, they refused, and of course grad student Jonah Peretti took this refusal to the press, to the Net, and eventually to *The Today Show*. Hey presto, a political meme and celebrity for Peretti. He also created BlackPeopleLoveUs.com, the New York City Rejection Line, and FundRace.org. Later he helped found the Huffingtonpost.com. These Culturematics are personal, but that doesn't mean they can't find a large audience. In a new media world, any of us can create culture for all of us. As Guy Kawasaki puts it, "the nobodies are the new somebodies."[55]

Culturematics may start as matters of private enthusiasm. Some will produce a public piece of our culture. And all of them eventually become a vast basin of creativity, a shared laboratory, our product development zone, our collective off Broadway—the places we look to for new kinds of entertainment, education, politics, and commerce. The corporation continues to think of innovation as

R&D, as something that comes out of a lab. This is apt, as long as we remember that the lab is the world.

The Library Laboratory

The library in my little town in Connecticut buzzes with activity. So does the one next door in Darien. I fell to wondering whether libraries might be good places for people to gather to Culturematic. (Yes, now it's a verb.)

We can take any of the personal Culturematics above and make them a shared activity. We could create a meme-making station on one of the library computers. This would do random searches of the press (*Daily Beast* and *BusinessWeek*, say), clip thirty to sixty words, and insert them into Wordle for display on the computer in question. Wordles can also be made for the neighborhood or city, noting the names of teams, parks, businesses, and, of course, the library (figure 7-1). The trick is to get a group working on the best-word lists, and the best Wordle settings.

There should be a culture mixing station. Take Lance Armstrong, and put him in a new context. How about the Westminster Kennel Club dog show? They don't really go together. And this tells us something about both Armstrong and the dog show. Look for combinations that are robust in this way.

Have a look at figure 7-2. Keep trying combinations. The only person on the left-hand side I can imagine taking *every* job on the right-hand side is Jackie Chan. This says something interesting about Jackie Chan. (But what, exactly?)

Anthony Bourdain is the host of a food show called *No Reservations*. He is quirky and insouciant. These are excellent qualities for someone who runs what the Travel Channel calls a "culinary and cultural adventure show." But these are somewhat less appro-

FIGURE 7-1

Wordle for my hometown

priate for the unflappable voice of government. So consider making him a White House spokesperson. That's the idea. Find the combination that feels like a collision, then give an account of what creates the collision. Your turn.

Your library laboratory should have a couple of standing Culturematics that can be played and replayed, as a stimulus for debate. Consider "Recasting *NCIS*" (figure 6-1). Lab "techs" should be prepared to discuss whether, how, and why each candidate would or wouldn't be a good addition to the show. In a culture of growing variety, television shows remain relatively common knowledge. Almost everyone has seen *The View*, and almost everyone could play the Culturematic that contemplates recasting the show (Sarah Silverman? Katy Perry? Kim Kardashian?). Now construct your own Culturematics.

One project for the library laboratory is an anthropology of the local neighborhood or town. A couple of years ago, I wrote a blog post titled "How We Say Hello in New England."[56] It attempted

FIGURE 7-2

Culturematic reassignment machine

Anthony Bourdain	Noir detective
Jackie Chan	White House spokesperson
Mickey Drexler J. Crew CEO	USA Networks head of programming
Diane Keaton	Meth dealer
Arianna Huffington	High school principal
Phil Jackson	Cruise ship entertainment director
Bruce Willis	Karaoke master of ceremonies
Helen Mirren	Charlie Sheen replacement

to describe and explain the local ritual for greetings. Mostly I was complaining about how stingy my neighbors were with their hellos. A lively discussion followed, with a dozen people leaving comments on how greetings work in their part of the world (Buffalo, Vancouver, Scotland, Spain). One reader offered this charming comment: "I was raised in New England, and I can often tell when I'm doing this [i.e., giving a stingy hello]—and sometimes go so far as to wonder, 'Would it kill me to smile and say hello?' Then my next thought is 'Yes.'"

Every community has its characteristic pattern of thought and behavior. The laboratory anthropologists can document things they've noticed on Main Street or at the mall. Could the laboratory be the first to notice a new species of social life? Could it have been the first to notice and report something like the Woo girls we discussed above? Consider the IFC show *Portlandia* as one model for the form your work could take.

Library laboratories needn't make their own communities the sole focus of their ethnographic observations. There is the great vastness of popular culture to occupy us. Why not a hip-hop watch, where people gather to talk about what they are noticing as this musical form continues to evolve? There can be one for the Hollywood blockbuster. There could be a culture critic's corner, where the work of the best culture observers is identified and debated. (This would be a good place to discuss the work of cultural critics Brian Eno or Greil Marcus. There could be a corner for the discussion of cultural trends. Where, for instance, did the comedy of Judd Apatow come from, and why did it flourish so? Why is Zach Galifianakis an "it" actor at the moment?) There can be another for new trends in social media and social networks. When some member of the library community has gone on to stardom, it makes sense to have the celebrity return home as a favorite son or daughter. Noah Brier is an expert in social media; we should have him come back to Rowayton to give us the latest.[57]

Local history is a great opportunity for collaboration. Interviews are time-consuming. Knowledge mapping is time-consuming. Andy, a friend of mine in Rowayton, has an astounding knowledge of the history of the town. Every town has someone with this depth of knowledge. Get it on tape, and get the data on a map. Consider mixing real stories with imaginative stories in the manner of Rick Meyerowitz and Maira Kalman and their food map for the New York City subway system. Use food, use music, use films. Use culture to make culture.[58]

Fan fiction (or fanfic) is imaginative work that takes an existing story and adds on to it. The most famous fanfic was done for *The X-Files*, a TV show popular in the 1990s. Fans of the show would observe how an episode had ended, pick up the narrative threads, and keep writing. If the show ended with Mulder and Scully leaving town, someone in the fanfic community would write, "As they passed their motel, Mulder noticed a light moving in the room he had just vacated." The possibilities are large. Someone can write the conversations that passed between *American Idol* contestants backstage. Someone else can describe the secret life of Kimball Cho (Tim Kang) on *The Mentalist*, giving the backstory that explains why he never changes expression. As I was suggesting in "Be a Storyteller," there are entire movies waiting to be redubbed and ridiculed.

If our community were going to stage a Pie Lab, what would we use to accomplish it? Could we do a kind of Olympic torch run, and what would we do it for? What about a smart mob? Tiny music and film festivals are becoming increasingly popular. Look for the local connection that gives you a mandate. Rowayton was once the home of the film actor Sterling Hayden. Clearly, we should stage a little film festival dedicated to his work (e.g., *Dr. Strangelove*). The library laboratory should be a staging ground for digital shorts, Burning Man festivals (minus the Burning Men, of course), smart-mob events, and perhaps a time machine or two, making the library a place of feverish innovation. One last thing: there has got to be a standing camera of the kind created by Noah Kalina, and everyone should add his or her own image everyday.

8 The Corporate Culturematic

Sometimes the path to cultural innovation is not through a little Culturematic. Sometimes it's from a more formal, systematic search. Now we are looking for a blue ocean, a white space, or a disruptive innovation.[1] These are new markets or old markets transformed. What will we call the blue-ocean-white-space-disruptive-innovation? BOWSDI is the acronym, and that's too horrible to contemplate. I prefer *Culturematic*.

The Culturematic is three things for the organization. First, it is a way to escape shrinking margins and commodification. Mature markets attract competition, and competition sends prices downward. (For example, IBM sold the ThinkPad brand to Lenovo because offshore players were flattening margins and making ThinkPad's premium position impossible.) Second, on the positive side, the Culturematic is the route to large profits. Because the corporation is, for a while, the only occupant on the market, margins are rich. (In its early days, the iPhone was a blue-ocean smartphone. The profit per phone was $250, fully half the purchase price.[2]) Third and most important, discovering and occupying a new market is the way for a corporation to regain control of its destiny. A Culturematic releases us from the furious game of catch-up that rules our lives. We are now every other corporation's future. We control our destiny because we are their destiny.

Advances come from several sources. Sometimes, it is new technology that creates the new market. Steam disrupted sail in the nineteenth century. The personal computer opened up a new market unanticipated by the mainframe computer of the first half of the twentieth century. Amazon.com reinvented the bookstore; eBay, the auction house.

But sometimes, it is culture that supplies the new market, and this is where the Culturematic comes in. Charlie Merrill was a member of the investment community when it was still a place of white-shoe self-regard, a clubby world created for insiders, by insiders. Merrill opened up a Culturematic by reworking the cultural assumptions that governed the industry. As Giovanni Gavetti of the Harvard Business School observes, "it was only when he reimagined the managed investment business as a supermarket business that a new way to compete became visible to him."[3] It was precisely thus that Merrill created his blue ocean, white space, disruptive innovation—his Culturematic.

Reimagining is the key to the corporate Culturematic. We change the cultural terms of reference. And we do this by noting how culture configures the market in its present manifestation, and then propose and construct a new configuration. Chapter 3 told the story of the Apple Genius Bar. Apple took a look at the traditional terms of the economic transaction and reinvented them. Reworking the nature of the interaction turned the Genius Bar from a cost center to a profit center, creating value for the relationship, the brand, and, eventually, the bottom line.

This kind of Culturematic is difficult (however easy it looks after the fact). It requires that we discover new configurations when our thinking is dominated, invisibly and powerfully, by old configurations. These old configurations are the lens through which we see the world. They edit out the new configuration. They get in the way. Merrill's revolution and the Apple Genius Bar look obvious enough, but they require a powerful and difficult act of imagination. No one would bother, were the rewards not so high.

The trick then is to identify old configurations and discover new ones.

Starbucks: Third Place

Take the case of Starbucks and its much-vaunted "third place."[4] Howard Schultz had a question: if home is our first place, and work our second place, then was there a third place in the world? There wasn't one, really. (Not in North America, in any case. Schultz had found one in Milan in 1983.) There were public places, certainly. You could meet someone at a library, but "No talking!" You could take a table at a restaurant or a diner, but "No loitering!" (And keep that laptop stowed.) Nowhere could you treat a public space as if it were a relatively private space, a place you could put your feet up and settle in.

In North America, people in public were objects of suspicion. A man standing around on a street raised a question, "What's he doing there?" There was, in effect, a no-idling rule, and the rule was powerful. So powerful that people hanging around in public were obliged look at their watches ostentatiously, as if to say, "Look, I'm waiting for someone." Or they would look in a store window: "Behold, I am shopping." It was as if people had to create a cover story, because, in our culture, loitering in public was not OK.[5]

So what was the Starbucks Culturematic? It was the creation of a third space where people could loiter without attracting suspicion. This third place had public properties like the work space and private properties like the home space. It admitted outsiders and it permitted intimacy. It allowed people to put their feet up in the presence of total strangers.

Starbucks found a way to operate on culture. Schultz spotted the existence of two categories and the opportunity for a third. In the early days, Starbucks was a place you went to buy a bag of coffee beans. It would have to be transformed. Furniture, lighting, configuration, staff attitude—all of these would have to help create the new private-public space. Starbucks was creating a new category of social life and, in the process, created a Culturematic from which a great torrent of value would pour (figure 8-1).

And the world has since flowered with many such places. Indeed, North Americans feel ever more relaxed in public places.

FIGURE 8-1

Starbucks invents a category

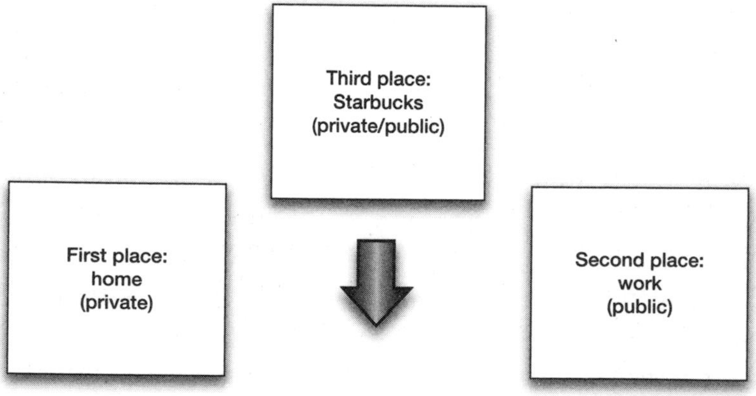

Microsoft Tries to Pull a Starbucks (and Almost Gets There)

When Google said its unofficial motto was "Don't be evil," everyone knew it was saying, "Don't be like Microsoft." By the first decade of the twenty-first century, Microsoft had dug itself a deep hole. It swamped smaller companies, treated business-to-business partners badly, and greeted consumer complaints with indifference. The software was bloated with features and inclined to crash. Microsoft didn't seem to care. Its arrogance went undiminished.[6]

Dramatic action was called for, so Microsoft hired one of the hot shops in the world of advertising, Crispin, Porter and Bogusky. Creative head Alex Bogusky was regarded as a miracle worker. Bogusky's idea was very corporate Culturematic. He created the "I am a PC" campaign. This featured ordinary people shot in an ordinary way, one cheerful soul after another saying, "I'm a PC." With a few seconds of handheld, low-resolution video, Microsoft was poised to tunnel out of its difficulty.[7]

Here's how it worked. Our culture has been predicated on a simple distinction between the mainstream and the avant-garde. The mainstream is supposed to be conventional, rule bound, and risk adverse. The avant-garde is supposed to be rebellious, creative, and risk taking. It's a crude distinction, but in our culture, it has proved a highly influential way of thinking about the world.[8] (So influential that during the postwar period, many ad men, embarrassed by their work in the mainstream, kept a secret, experimental novel manuscript in their desk drawer.)

Along comes Apple. Using cultural categories to construct its own Culturematic, Steve Jobs and the agency say, "Perfect! We'll play the avant-garde. PC can be mainstream." And so was born the "Mac vs. PC" campaign, starting in 2006 and crafted by the agency TBWA Media Arts Lab. "Mac vs. PC" showed Apple (as played by Justin Long) to be hip, gentle, and patient, and Microsoft (as played by John Hodgman) to be small-minded, smug, and annoying. It was a huge success. Microsoft was trapped.

What to do? Bogusky was alert to the changes taking place in his culture. And he noticed that the two-category system had exploded in the 1990s. In the addition to the mainstream and avant-garde categories, a large third space was opening up. This was driven by the great fragmentation of taste and preference and consisted of a large group of people who were creative and experimental but who didn't define themselves as hip.[9] They just were. "Creative but not cool" this was the banner of this new group of people and category in our culture.

Along comes Bogusky. He and Microsoft say, "Perfect! We'll play third space. Apple can be avant-garde." Thus did Microsoft find a way to tunnel under Apple's hipster image and out into the new world of the creatively unaligned (figure 8-2).[10]

Bogusky and Microsoft were not *creating* a third category as Starbucks had. They were taking advantage of one that had opened up on its own. The Culturematic challenge was noticing this third category and finding a way to get to it. The Bogusky ad

FIGURE 8-2

New category as escape vehicle

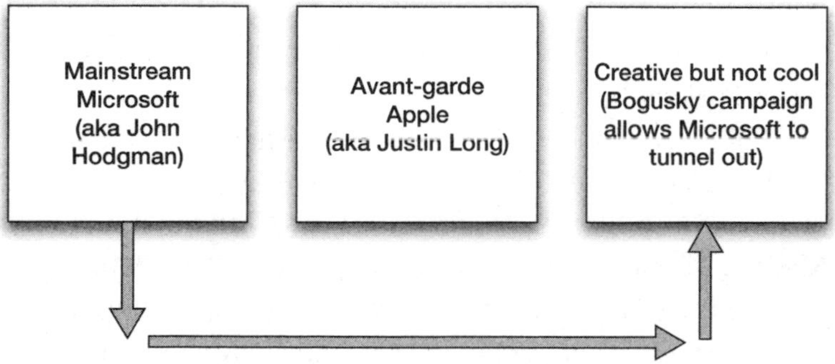

was a brilliant escape vehicle, but it's not clear if it worked. Microsoft is so marked by its bully-boy arrogance, that it was going to take more than an advertising campaign to save it. The jury is still out. This Culturematic is still in play.

Dove

Sometimes, the Culturematic is not a play upon cultural categories, but a play upon cultural conventions. According to the cultural conventions played out by the beauty industry, the image of beauty was mostly young, white, blond, and slim. So discovered Silvia Lagnado when she applied herself to the question on behalf of her employer, Unilever, and Dove, the beauty bar for which she was global brand director. What Lagnado discovered was a stunner. Only 2 percent of respondents in a worldwide study thought themselves beautiful. The closer Lagnado looked, the more she detected what Harvard Business School professor John Deighton calls a "current of deep discontent." The standard definition of beauty was being challenged. A cultural convention was breaking down.[11]

It turns out that a new idea of beauty had many friends. Feminists said our ideas of beauty should not come from fashion magazines. As America became more inclusive in matters of race and ethnicity, the old ideas of beauty were clearly too narrow. Parents were alarmed at the rising incidence of bulimia, anorexia, social anxiety, and teen bullying. Surely, new ideas of beauty could help here. Virtually everyone thought it was wrong that only 2 percent of women thought they were beautiful when evidently so many more women were so beautiful. (No one consulted men on the question, but it was pretty obvious where they stood on the issue. Clearly, they believe that vastly more than 2 percent of women were stunning and that almost all women were beautiful in some way.)

This change had momentum. And Dove had an opportunity. In the words of the mission statement, "Dove's mission is to make more women feel beautiful every day by broadening the narrow definition of beauty. Our notion of beauty is not elitist. It is celebratory, inclusive and democratic."[12]

In point of fact, corporations can't invent culture at will. Culture is a very large ocean liner. The corporation is the tiniest of tugboats. But Culturematic intercessions can happen under certain conditions. The cultural change must already be under way. And then the corporation must engage it perfectly. Push for new ideas of beauty too early, and Dove would find itself positioned as an outlier. Too late, and it would be seen as just another brand trying to get in on the action. But there it was, hidden in plain sight, a change in cultural conventions just at the moment of the tipping point, as millions of women began to repudiate these conventions en masse. By 2006, the results were in. Dove was named one of the ten brands with the greatest growth in the past three years.[13] The Campaign for Real Beauty Culturematic had worked.

Nike

In Martin Scorsese's film *GoodFellas*, we see Henry Hill (Ray Liotta) and Karen Friedman (Lorraine Bracco) entering the Copacabana through a side door and the kitchen.[14] We are swept into one of the defining institutions of the postwar period, the nightclub. With the benefit of hindsight, this looks like a toxic place. People were there to overdo it, consuming much too much alcohol, fat, sugar, salt, caffeine, and nicotine. Especially nicotine; the air is blue with smoke. The only place unhealthier than a nightclub was the resort where people added sun and chlorine to the list of dangerous substances to which they happily exposed themselves.

Cut to a track meet in Portland, Oregon. The time is the middle 1960s, almost exactly the moment Henry and Karen are visiting the Copacabana. But what a different world! Instead of seeing beefy guys in beautiful suits, we are looking at people who like to get up early and run fifteen miles before breakfast. They are lean. They are swift. And they suffer massive alcohol, fat, and sugar shortages. Nicotine? No nicotine. Standing beside his green Plymouth Valiant is Philip Knight. He is selling running shoes from the trunk. He has made the soles of these shoes himself with a waffle iron.[15]

This was America on the cusp of a massive change. People had been celebrating the prosperity of the postwar period with a riot of unhealthy behaviors. And out there on the West Coast, where so much of America was waiting to happen, was a new approach to the body, fitness, diet, and lifestyle. In the place of huge quantities of bad things consumed by sedentary people, Nike would encourage couch potatoes to embrace a complete repudiation of Copacabana excess. Over fifty years, the Nike revolution has been massively successful. Our bodies, our diets, our exercise regimes, have been transformed.

Here, too, we can see Knight spotting a change in the works. In the early days, Nike was really just for high-performance athletes, but Knight broadened the proposition until even people like Henry and Karen had their own running shoes and were now trying to work off all those flambé calories. Knight made himself a cause and a consequence of this deep cultural transformation. Like Lagnado, he had to choose his moment. Unlike Lagnado, he moved more than he followed the trend, pushing relentlessly, using the brilliant work of his agency, Wieden + Kennedy, to goad America out of its complacency and bad behaviors. "Just do it," he said impatiently. "Be like Mike," he dared us.

Knight opened up a vast Culturematic. He did so by capturing a new cultural configuration and riding it as if it were a thermal.

Again, the trick is spotting the change in culture and figuring out how to climb aboard. We can say that Target has ridden the design trend this way. Ralph Lauren and Tommy Hilfiger rode the preppie trend. Many great brands have tied their colors to the culture's mast in this way.

The Four Seasons

Hotels often have a problem. The first person to greet us, the man or woman at the front desk, sometimes makes us wish we had spent more on our suit and shoes. For some reason, they believe they are there to judge us. It turns out, this is an ancient responsibility:

> Throughout nineteenth-century American fiction, journalism, travel writing, cartoons, and folklore, [hotel clerks] were stock characters, their unhelpfulness and arrogance making them a constant source of grievances. [They were alleged to have] constantly ridiculed and intimidated guests. One commentator recalled that the hotel clerk was "feared by the general public," [someone] before whom the free-born American quailed."[16]

Professional snootiness can be even worse in the luxury hotel. It is not unusual for hotel staff to act if the status of the hotel was their own personal status. (The deeper problem may be that these employees are compensating for small salaries by paying themselves in arrogance.) Sniffing at the guests is no doubt fun for the hotel staff, but it is disastrous for the hotel. The hope of creating a good relationship with the customer has been diminished.

Isadore Sharp, founder of the Four Seasons, decided to take the problem in hand:

> At a meeting of all general managers, I told them, . . . "Customers seldom see or talk to you. They interact almost solely with our front line, three to seven junior employees. If that contact disappoints the customers we want as lifetime patrons, they become ex-patrons. But when our employees remember them, greet them, know what they want and provide it quickly, they create a loyal customer."[17]

The trouble, Sharp noted, was that it was not enough to turn employees into robots chirping happy greetings. To add real value, they actually had to respond to customers (and the moment) in all their individuality. It was necessary to encourage employees

> to act on their own, to see themselves, not as routine functionaries, but as company facilitators creating our customer base . . . to respond on their own to whatever comes up, [to] spot, solve, and even anticipate problems.

Sharp was taking on a deep-seated cultural convention, the one that allowed desk workers to get away with bad manners. And he was proposing a solution that would challenge yet another cultural convention, the one that said the hotel staff member was a functionary from whom initiative could not, should not, be expected. But when Sharp addressed his management, he realized there was a third, still deeper culture convention that stood in the way:

> I realized more clearly what I was facing: a giant management turnaround, one that would overthrow the century-old concept that a company is a machine: that

management is a profession based solely on logic sans emotion, that labor is a cost to be controlled, not an asset to be enhanced, and that an atmosphere of fear and anxiety is more productive than one of enjoyment. For most of our managers and supervisors, it was less a process of learning than unlearning, which is much more difficult.

To reform the hotel business and to build consumer loyalty, Sharp was going to have to take issue with the culture that informed the people on the front desk and those who made up management. A fundamental shift in idea and attitude was called for. This was nothing less than a reinvention of the luxury hotel industry. This was more difficult than securing finance or pouring concrete. It meant that he would have to see and shape practices that were so time honored they had disappeared from view.

Operating on Culture

The corporate Culturematic comes in several forms. It can come from finding a new cultural category. Starbucks did a kind of positioning exercise and said, "Look, there is room for a third place here." Sometimes the culture play has to do with a change in cultural conventions and the opportunity this opens up. Dove took advantage of a change in the idea of beauty. Nike took advantage of new food and fitness conventions. The Apple Genius Bar began playing on new approaches to the relationship with the consumer. And the Four Seasons was working with new ideas of the customer, the staff member, and the hotel. In each case, someone in the corporation had been climbing the scaffolding of culture and spotted a new opportunity.

Cirque du Soleil opened up its Culturematic by reinventing the circus. Charles Merrill opened up his Culturematic by reinventing the investment business. (And we must admire the sheer power of his act of imagination. Thinking about this business as if it were a supermarket, how extraordinary!) NFL Films reinvented football, actually helping it steal baseball's position as America's national game. The people who created Web 2.0 managed to put Silicon Valley's Humpty Dumpty back together again. One idea now prevailed in the face of diversity, confusion, and great faintness of heart.

All of these are the triumph of idea over reality. But none of them can happen by simple fiat, by declaring that football, the stock market, Silicon Valley, fitness, and cafés are now transformed. First, there has to be a cultural change in play. Second, there has to be a careful strategic and tactical undertaking to find out what is now culturally possible, what has momentum. Third, the innovation has to be made and presented with the same deft hand. In each case, a nuanced and well-crafted Culturematic is called for.

Culturematics are a management challenge. The corporation will need to send people out to map culture. As an anthropologist, I am inclined to think that this is a job for anthropologists. But in my better moments, I understand that designers and sociologists can probably do just as well. It will take still other people to analyze the results and propose action. Strategy departments are not yet experts at culture, but this can be put right quickly enough. And it will probably take a chief culture officer in the C-suite. (But considering I wrote a book titled *Chief Culture Officer*, this is exactly what you would expect me to say.) This much is clear. It will take a system and a team. But only thus can we hope to discover the blue oceans, the white spaces, and the disruptive innovations that culture makes available to us.

Culturematics for the CEO

There are six steps for managing Culturematics from the C-suite.

1. Bully the Bullies

Innovations are the new kids on the block. They are picked on and laughed at. The corporation already has a range of products and services that give the corporation its reason to be. The people who manage these incumbents scorn the newcomers or, worse, treat them as "threats to the firm's core identity and values."[18] It is the CEO's job to make everyone play nicely and to give the innovations a place to play and room to grow. Innovations, especially the radical ones, are at odds with the corporate culture and therefore hard to reckon with. It is much easier for the corporation to return to form and go with what it knows. So even when an innovation has a champion and a budget line, it needs a protector. That's the CEO.

2. Discover the Vectors Outside

There's no point sending Culturematics into the future randomly. There are too many formal possibilities, too many destinations, too many Culturematics. We need to know, roughly, the vectors in which the investment has hope of return. More plainly, the Culturematic engineers need to know where to fish, and this answer can only be supplied by the person with the broadest strategic vision, the CEO.

This vision was once shaped by Theodore Levitt's famous question: what business are you in?[19] The correct way to answer this question in Levitt's day was to generalize. Levitt originally asked his question of the people who ran railroads. They were *not* in the business of trains, he scolded them. They were in the business of transportation. The way to think strategically was to avoid the literal and think more abstractly.

This is now the wrong answer. Generalizing merely gives us a broader view of our existing industry, in Levitt's case, transportation. The correct answer now might be "to get out of transportation and get into computers." This response follows a logic that says, "In the future, people will become (more) stationary, and we will bring the office, entertainment, and conferences to them." In a turbulent world, generalizing may not fix the "myopia" Levitt so despised, but may exacerbate it.

In a world of real dynamism, the strategic thing to do is to entertain a radically different future with radically different structural properties. Post-Levitt, we are not looking merely for generalities or to avoid nearsightedness. We are looking for a variety of view corridors, let's call them, that give the corporation diverse ideas of what the corporation is and what it might become. And this means the CEO must entertain what Michael Tushman, Wendy Smith, and Andy Binns call "multiple and often conflicted strategy agendas."[20]

Once the CEO can see into many futures, he or she is in a position to say *where* the corporation should be firing its Culturematics. For Levitt's railroad clients, this might have meant trains, transportation, computers, and perhaps even digital conferencing hardware.[21]

3. Find the Assumptions Inside

Every corporation is predicated on a set of assumptions. They serve as the infrastructure of thought and action. Some of these assumptions are visible. (For example, many corporations are now using an "experience marketing" model from Pine and

Gilmore.[22]) Many assumptions are invisible. For most of the twentieth century, soft drink manufacturers believed, without thinking about it, that sugary sodas were a permanent fixture in the American diet. Americans would always want them. Water? That was what the tap was for. No one was ever going to pay for water. By the 1990s, both Coke and Pepsi had water brands. And it happened just in time: in the period from 1997 to 2005, per-capita consumption of bottled water increased by 90 percent.[23]

Invisible assumptions are treacherous. Levitt caught the Detroit automobile industry making assumptions about what the consumer wanted. Basic research was left undone. Indeed, Detroit was the captive of a circularity. The industry "only researched . . . [what] it had already decided to offer." This is in the nature of an assumption. It disappears from view. The deepest assumptions go without saying. When we do refer to them, often it is a single, unthinking buzzword. Our assumptions are built in or, as Richard Foster and Sarah Kaplan prefer, "locked in."[24]

In a perfect world, these assumptions would float to the surface when they expire. As fish do. But they don't. So we keep using them. After all, they are deeply implicated in the way we see the world, the stuff of our best hunches and most powerful intuitions. Breaking up is hard to do.

So it's up to the CEO to send in the assumption hunters.[25] They will act like ferrets, rooting around for the assumptions that invisibly shape the corporation. Some of these assumptions will come from MBA training. Some will come from the latest book on management. Some will come from the professional culture of the chief information officer or chief financial officer. The hunters must work comprehensively. We need to know where all the assumptions are buried, and then assess whether and how any of them can blind us to the future.

4. Create the Catalysts

Scott Cook, cofounder of Intuit, wanted a new approach to innovation. He turned to Kaaren Hanson, and the two of them created innovation catalysts who could help create prototypes, run experiments, and learn from customers. The new system had hothouse consequences. The Intuit tax group began by observing customers in the world:

> The team created multiple concepts and iterated with customers on a weekly basis. They brought customers in each Friday, distilled what they'd learned on Monday, brainstormed concepts on Tuesday, designed them on Wednesday, and coded them on Thursday, before the customers came in again.[26]

Building and launching a series of Culturematics, Intuit was now able to speed up the innovation cycle and to make it zero in on opportunity as never before. Catalysts such as these are excellent teams with which to build and refine Culturematics.

5. Measure Return on Investment

Culturematics may be cheap, but they are not free. One of the key management decisions is how much to invest in them and how to measure return on investment.

Here's how Procter & Gamble's A. G. Lafley and Wharton's Ram Charan advise us to think about the problem:

> Think about measuring innovation as you would an investment portfolio, where you are concerned with the total return rather than individual stocks, bonds, or mutual funds. The key is not to measure each project

individually and then declare victory or defeat, but to measure total investment over a period of time compared to total output. This pools high- and low-risk projects and encourages people to take canny chances.[27]

6. Cultivate a Deeper Field of Vision

Nimble corporations are learning to abandon their existing business model before someone rips it out from under them. The good CEO prepares the corporation by mapping out useful options and getting the corporation ready to make the transition if and when the moment comes.

In the old model, as we have seen, the CEO was called to answer the question posed by Levitt: what business are we (really) in? The post-Levitt approach, as we have also seen, insists on something broader. As it turns out, the real answer to Levitt's question is, "We are in business, plain and simple, and we go where opportunity takes us."

Blast. This means the CEO can no longer rely upon the corporation's deep familiarity with the industry or sector. The corporation must now teach itself about other parts of the world, even industries that are not adjacent to its part of the world. Actually, it's worse than that. The CEO has to cultivate something more than a general idea of, say, digital conference hardware. No, CEOs need a deep and exacting knowledge, good enough to allow them to identify the state of play, the competitive set, consumer taste and preference, and much more.

Blast again. Digital conference hardware is just one of the options that might work for this railway. The future may lie in another direction altogether. The well-prepared CEO will have four or five dramatically different scenarios. And for each of these scenarios, he or she needs a set of plans to allow the corporation to hit the ground running. We are approaching a world of such turbulence that only instantaneous response will give the corporation any hope of survival. If we wait till the change is upon us to begin our reaction, surely we must perish.

The CEO must be able to see further than anyone into a variety of futures.

Culturematics for Managers

Managers must have their own laboratories, ones in which they spend one day a week building and testing their own Culturematics. But it also makes sense to survey Culturematics being conducted "out there" in the world and to bring in for further development the ones that look promising. This casts the manager in the role of the A&R executive, as the music industry calls it. *A&R* stands for "artists and repertoire," that is, the people who scout talent and oversee development for a record label.[28]

This is also the way Hollywood executives make and manage bets in the script development process. Execs spend their time monitoring contemporary culture, reading *Variety*, listening to their colleagues and competitors, doing lunch with other players, and reading the shifting winds of consumer taste and preference. The good executive has lots of scripts in development. Some are complete and awaiting a production. Some are half written and awaiting completion. Some are still a concept in a writer's head. The big investment has not been made yet. The projects are still open to change. As the exec sees the world changing, he or she can rework the portfolio. It is hard to know exactly how this model would translate to the corporation's Culturematic investment, but I don't think it is too soon for managers there to buy the Porsche, get the sunglasses, and start investing in Italian shoes.

At the other end of the pipeline, the corporation wants a cheap and cheerful way of putting Culturematics before the consumer. The system created by Intuit serves this purpose. We might also work out a deal with retail. We need shelf space to serve as our deep space. We are going to put things there and invite the consumer to give it a try. In the early days, Snapple used its retail channel as a product innovation instrument.[29] When it sent product to its mom-and-pop outlets, they would try new flavors and see which ones worked.

We are going to have to be explicit. The label is going to have to say this is an experiment. But why not? Most consumers engage in variety seeking, in any case. Why not invite them to pursue it within a purchase instead of across purchases? Let us treat the Kellogg's variety pack as an exemplar here. Let's send out a flotilla of options and let the consumer contemplate our options. Experimental products are going to have to come with toll-free numbers and Web addresses so that consumers can comment.

Culturematics give the consumer a chance to say, "Well, yes, I see what you're doing here, but what I *really* want is . . ." This is what happens, in any case. The report comes back from a consultancy like IDEO. It reads: "Consumers like the product, but when we went into their homes, we discovered they had plugged it in upside down! Apparently, that's the way they want to use it!" The point of a Culturematic is to make this sort of thing work to our advantage, to make consumer ingenuity (and bloody-mindedness) not the cause of failure, but the beginning of wisdom.

A More Porous Corporation

Innovation demands a new kind of corporation, one that changes the boundary between the corporation and the world. We have to become more porous. We have to let the corporation out and the world in. This spells the end of the corporation as a tightly defined, carefully bounded, organization that has all but only the people it needs performing all but only the tasks it needs to perform.

Let me offer one example. IBM decided recently to rethink its alumni network. The old model said that the network should consist of anyone who had *retired* from IBM. Kevin Clark wondered if this wasn't a little shortsighted. He proposed that the network should include everyone who had quit IBM and anyone IBM had ever fired. ("Everyone had to get over the 'hurt feelings' problem," he said.) Now the alumni network included everyone who had ever *worked* for IBM. Then Clark said, "Listen, there's a good chance that everyone in the industry is someday going to work for IBM, so let's start building a connection now. Wherever you are in the industry, whoever you are, you have a connection to us." Now the alumni network was the whole of the industry. Clark had taken a tiny, well-defined category and blown it up. In the process, the network was no longer the retirees, but everyone in the industry. IBM was now a more porous corporation.[30]

Innovation will demand this order of porousness and still more. I keep picturing that image from a science fiction movie, the one that shows the starship with thousands of small craft coming and going (e.g., *The Fifth Element* or *Independence Day*). The corporation will be not only the products and services we have in production at the moment, but also all the things we have in play, all those tiny bets we have fired into deep space. In a sense, we are looking at the end of the headquarters view of the corporation, the one that says, "This is where the corporation is really resident. Right here." Now we are looking at a *spread* corporation, a *distributed* enterprise.

Crowdsourcing puts a vast tidal system at our disposal. A firm like Victors and Spoils can solicit opinion not as consumer response but as producer concept. This is one of the most potent ways to make people outside the corporation collaborators and cocreators. It is an excellent way to put the product development lab out in the world. The gaming activity created by the likes of Jane McGonigal should be useful here as well. People will throw off lots of useful data as they play games of the kind that McGonigal has created for Microsoft and PBS. These games could be considered Culturematics making Culturematics. P&G has created several ways of partnering with the world. Its Future Works business incubator is designed expressly to track discontinuous ideas into new categories or across existing ones. And the company's Connect + Develop program means to connect P&G with the best thinkers, wherever they are.[31]

At some point, we will learn to roll out the proposition in stages to create testing and proving grounds. Damian Kindler created a science fiction show called *Sanctuary* first as webisodes and then as a Syfy cable show, scaling up as bigger budgets and audiences became available. Journalists use occasional pieces to test for what their next book should be. The music and film industries have used the festival scene as a sorting device, waiting to see what makes it up the fish ladder. The trick is not to wait until something reaches us. We have to own the fish ladder.[32]

There are many new changes that will be required of us. The objective in all of them is to create a corporation that is porous enough to let new products out and intelligence in. In a sense, the corporation is turning into a Culturematic.

Conclusion

In the classical and medieval eras, the Mediterranean was the center of the world that mattered. North Africa, Egypt, Greece, Rome, everything turned on it. Spain was the western border of this world, and the motto of the Spanish royal family was emphatic: *Ne Plus Ultra*. "Nothing beyond us."

After Spain discovered the New World, it became clear that something was going to have to change. The world was much larger and more various than anyone had imagined. Richer, too, for all that South American gold and silver! Spain, it turned out, was less a border of the known world and more a gateway to the new. What to do? Someone consulted the humanist scholar Marliano, who suggested that the royal family drop the "Ne."

The motto now reads *Plus Ultra*. "More besides." Brilliant. Spain had found a way to acknowledge that there were worlds, geographical and intellectual, beyond the traditional one. And it had found a way to make a not-so-subtle claim to them. Marliano's new motto has a useful vagueness, allowing the royal family to say, "Um, we're not sure what's out there, but whatever it is, it belongs to us. Get used to it."[33]

In the twentieth century, the future was merely our margin, the edge of an otherwise comfortable world. It mattered from time to time, when some innovation (cars! computers! Tang!) appeared or when cataclysm broke out. But it didn't matter in an enduring, structural way. We responded as we had to, and once things were back to normal, we returned to normal. *Ne plus ultra*.

Then the world became more turbulent. Change is everywhere and inexorable. All of us began to respond more aggressively, and this made things go faster still. We haven't officially changed our motto, but perhaps we should. Now it's "plus ultra." The future is a more various and destabilizing thing than it has ever been before. Indeed, it is so turbulent it has outstripped our instruments of prognostication. Scenarios, strategy, projection, planning, are going dark. The more we think about the future, the more we realize it is "more besides." More besides, and we're not sure what. That's what our Culturematics are for. Fire when ready.

Acknowledgments

My devout thanks to Pamela, and to Molly, Vivienne, and especially Zsa Zsa, who give me every kind of inspiration, forgiving in the meantime the commotion that appears to be my "method." Thanks are due to my superb editor, Tim Sullivan. This guy is talent with a capital T. Thanks are due to Kate Lee, my agent, for patient council and sage advice. Special thanks to those who offered particular thoughts and advice on the project: Ed Batista, Tommy and Andrew Bergman, Ana Domb, Gareth Kay, Leora Kornfeld, Rick Liebling, Anne Moscicki, Eric Nehrlich, Jason Oke, Elana Rubinfeld, Parmesh Shashani, David Smith, Sara Winge, and Timothy Young.

Every writer draws inspiration from diverse sources, but these days, now that we are gifted with social media and expanding networks, this is especially true. Thank you to the following people: Collyn Ahart, George Anastopalo, Marcie Anthone, Paola Antonelli, Tom Asacker, Ivan Askwith, Laurie Baird, Toby Barlow, Andrew Barnett, Eren Beggs, Katherine Bell, Brad Berens, Russ Bernard, Hargurchet Bhabra, Rick Boyko, Alan Brewer, Noah Brier, Bud Caddell, Bryan Castaneda, Kevin Clark, Pip Coburn, Beth Coleman, Ian Condry, Tyler Cowen, Steve Crandall, John Cruickshank, Tony and Jo D'Amelio, Russell Davies, John Deighton, Jim and Lima Dingwall, Jonah Disend, Judith Donath, Zsa Zsa Donath, Mark Earls, Griffin Farley, Piers

Fawkes, Sam Ford, Gregg Fraley, Charles Frith, Nick Gillispie, Leah Goldman, Michele Goodman, DeeDee Gordon, Howard Goldkrandt, Dan Gould, Katarina Graffman, Ed Greenspon, Ric Grefé, Susan Griffin, Brad Grossman, Tom Guarriello, John Gundy, Kate Hammer, Emily Hare, Michael Hastings-Black, Jens Hilgenstock, Ryan Holiday, Christine Huang, Henry Jenkins, Liz and Jerry Kathman, Brian Kenney, Rob Kozinets, David Kuehler, Tom Laforge, Peter Laywine, Guy Lanoue, Heather LeFevre, Anne Lewison, Xiaochang Li, Gloria Loree, Todd Lowe, Ben Malbon, Beatriz Mallory, Roger Martin, Mary and Steve Mazur, Peter McBurney, Emmet McCusker, Joe and Christine Melchione, Nilofer Merchant, Jerry Michalsky, Alan Middleton, Mary Mills, Debbie Millman, Mauricio Mota, Mark Murray, Indy Neogy, Keith Newton, Bill O'Connor, Charlotte Oades, Jason Oke, Lisa Parrish, Loren and Jan Parsons, Martin Perelmuter, Daniel Pereira, Adriano Fromer Piazzi, Alejandro Piscitelli, Barbara Pomorska, Faith Popcorn, Virginia and Steve Postrel, Heather Reisman, Monica Ruffo, Sheila Sales, Lee Sankey, Ralph Santana, Lance Saunders, Richard and Pam Shear, Naunihal Singh, David Smith, Ruth Soenius, Peter Spear, Suzanne Stein, Rick Sterling, Paola Storchi, Cheryl and Craig Swanson, William Uricchio, Jean Vaughn, Ilya Vedrashko, Carlos Veraza, Lisa Verenko, Tony Vitale, Petar Vujosevic, Helen Walters, Alisa Weinstein, Martin Weigel, Bob Woodard, Khalil Younes, and Nora Young.

Notes

Introduction

1. Information on the Culture Lab at the Godrej Group is from Parmash Shahani, personal communication, August 23, 2010. For Gary Hamel's laboratory, see Alan Murray, "The End of Management," *Wall Street Journal*, August 21, 2010, http://online.wsj.com/article/SB100014240527487044761045754397236955796 64.html?mod=WSJ_business_LeftSecondHighlights. See also David Edwards, *The Lab: Creativity and Culture* (Boston: Harvard University Press, 2010); Chuck Salter, "Syyn Labs's League of Extraordinary Nerds," *Fast Company*, January 10, 2011, www.fastcompany.com/magazine/152/the-league-of-extraordinary-nerds.html.

2. *Wikipedia*, s.v. "*Saturday Night Live*: Production Process," http://en.wikipedia .org/wiki/Saturday_night_live#Production_process, last modified October 23, 2011; Joel Stein, "Straight Outta Narnia," *Time*, April 17, 2006, www.time.com/time /magazine/article/0,9171,1184075,00.html.

3. Mark Frauenfelder, *Made by Hand: Searching for Meaning in a Throwaway World* (New York: Portfolio, 2010); Matthew B. Crawford, *Shop Class as Soulcraft: An Inquiry into the Value of Work* (New York: Penguin Press, 2009).

4. Warren Berger, *Glimmer: How Design Can Transform Your Life, and Maybe Even the World* (New York: Penguin Press, 2009), is a terrific account of the world of design, but too often, it sounds like hagiography, a reverential treatment of the designer.

5. I admire the way this title acknowledges the paradox: Ravi Jain, Harry C. Triandis, and Cynthia W. Weick, *Managing Research, Development and Innovation: Managing the Unmanageable*, 3rd ed. (Hoboken, NJ: Wiley, 2010).

6. My inspiration is Paul Kemp-Robertson, ed., "The 5 Percent Club," Publicus + Contagious [magazine] Seminar, Cannes Lions International Advertising Festival, June 2011, which discussed the need to "devote a small but significant portion of . . . budgets and time to running creative experiments." For more on the 5 Percent Club, see

Contagious, "The 5 Percent Club: Risk and Reward as Change Continues," June 28, 2011, www.contagiousmagazine.com/2011/06/cannes.php. See also Gareth Kay, "How to Think and Make Small," *Brand New*, May 19, 2011, http://garethkay.typepad .com/brand_new/2011/05/how-to-think-and-make-small.html.

Chapter 1

1. Fantasy Sports Trade Association, "Fantasy Sports Participation Sets All-Time Record, Grows Past 32 Million Players," press release, June 10, www.fsta.org/blog /fsta-press-release; Stephen Dorman, "The Fantasy Football Phenomenon," *Acorn*, August 3, 2006, www.theacorn.com/news/2006-08-03/Sports/076.html.

2. For sales figures for *Julie and Julia*, see Joy Butler, "Are Recipes Copy-rightable? Rights Clearance Observations about Julie & Julia, Deceptively Delicious, and The Sneaky Chef," *Guide Through the Legal Jungle Blog*, January 29, 2008, www.guidethroughthelegaljungleblog.com/2008/01/are-recipes-cop.html. For the *Super Size Me* figures, see Nash Information Services, "Super Size Me," *The Numbers: Box Office Data, Movie Stars, Idle Speculation*, n.d., www.the-numbers .com/movies/2004/SIZEM.php. For sales figures for *Eat, Pray, Love*, see Motoko Rich, "Eat, Pray, Love. Then What? Get Married," *New York Times*, August 20, 2009, www.nytimes.com/2009/08/20/books/20book.html?_r=1. See also Julie Pow-ell, *Julie and Julia: My Year of Cooking Dangerously* (New York: Little, Brown and Company, 2009); Morgan Spurlock, *Super Size Me* (Sony Pictures, 2004); Elizabeth Gilbert, *Eat, Pray, Love: One Woman's Search for Everything Across Italy, India and Indonesia* (New York: Penguin Press, 2010).

3. *The Real World* is not the first reality TV program in the United States. This distinction belongs to a show that appeared on PBS in 1973, *An American Family*. The difference between *An American Family* and *The Real World* is that the former compressed seven months of filming into twelve hours of air time, giving the editors more control than *The Real World* editors would have. The *American Family* editors could pick and choose their footage, crafting stories as they went. *The Real World* editors, on the other hand, were obliged to use much of what was shot. Finally, the PBS show was about an extant family and not a collection of strangers. Story lines came built in. *The Real World* had more randomness in play. For more on reality TV, see Kelefa Sanneh, "The Reality Principle," *The New Yorker*, May 9, 2011, 72–77, www.newyorker.com/arts/critics/atlarge/2011/05/09/110509crat_atlarge_sanneh.

4. *Wikipedia*, s.v. "List of David Letterman sketches," http://en.wikipedia.org /wiki/List_of_David_Letterman_sketches, last modified August 21, 2011.

5. K. C. D'Alessandro, "Pilot Programs," Museum of Broadcast Communica-tions Page, n.d., www.museum.tv/eotvsection.php?entrycode=pilotprogram, accessed July 27, 2010.

6. *Wikipedia*, s.v. "The Real World: Pilot," http://en.wikipedia.org/wiki /The_Real_World:_Pilot, last modified October 16, 2011.

7. Robert Sullivan, "Reality Rules," *Vogue*, June 2001, http://web.archive.org /web/20080610170308/http://www.style.com/vogue/feature/052401/page2.html.

8. For a long list of reality TV programs, see *Wikipedia*, s.v. "List of reality television programs," last modified October 16, 2011, http://en.wikipedia .org/wiki/List_of_reality_television_programs. For reality TV statistics, see "'American Idol' Premiere Hits New Audience High," *USA Today*, January 18, 2006, www.usatoday.com/life/television/news/2006-01-18-idol-record-audience_x.htm; John Timpane, "Reality TV Saturating Life in the Real World," *Philadelphia Inquirer*, May 16, 2010, www.philly.com/inquirer/front_page/20100516_Reality _TV_saturating_life_in_the_real_world.html. According to Screen Actors Guild, "Report on Worldwide Television and Feature Film Production," press release, August 1, 2006, www.sag.org/content/report-on-worldwide-television-and-feature-film-production, the growth of reality programming, also called *unscripted programming*, has been explosive: "Scripted prime time one-hour and half-hour broadcast and cable television programs that aired in the U.S. grew from 123 in 2000 to 152 in 2005 (24%). From 2000 to 2005 reality programs jumped from 24 to 174 (625%)."

9. James Poniewozik, "Why Reality TV Is Good for Us," *Time*, February 12, 2003, www.time.com/time/magazine/article/0,9171,421047-1,00.html. See also Ed Batista, "Steven Johnson, Reality TV and Texas Ranch House," *Ed Batista Blog*, May 3, 2006, www.edbatista.com/2006/05/steven_johnson_.html.

10. DK Holland, "Helter Skelter: Can Thinking Wrong Be Absolutely Right?" n.d., *Communication Arts*, www.commarts.com/Columns.aspx?pub=4398&pageid=1442.

11. John L. Edge, "The Healing Powers of a Pie Shop," *New York Times*, October 10, 2010, www.nytimes.com/2010/10/10/magazine/10pielab-t.html.

12. The proposal that raised funds for Pie Lab can be found at Kickstarter, "Pie Lab: A Food Project in Greensboro, AL by John Bielenberg," Kickstarter Projects Page, n.d., www.kickstarter.com/projects/795396878/pielab. The phrase "pop-up experimental pie shop" is from that page.

13. Elizabeth Evitts Dickinson, "Project M: Thinking Wrong, Doing Right," *Metropolis Magazine*, January 30, 2009, www.metropolismag.com/story/20090130/ project-m-thinking-wrong-doing-right; Edge, "Healing Powers of a Pie Shop"; Alissa Walker, "PieLab in Rural Alabama Serves Up Community, Understanding, and, Yes, Pie," *Fast Company*, June 19, 2009, www.fastcompany.com/blog/alissa-walker /designerati/project-ms-pielab-rural-alabama-serves-community-understanding-and-ye. Colin McMullan, an artist living in Williamsburg, New York, has created a tiny "micro-library" that sits at the intersection of Leonard and Withers Streets. It is about four feet high and is stuffed with an odd assortment of books, zines, and cycling

maps. Compared with a conventional library, McMullan's corner library is small and unsystematic. But contents matter less than the library's social purpose. Like the Pie Lab, this experiment is designed, McMullan says, "to help neighbors meet, know, and help each other" (Ashlea Halpern, "Guerrilla Librarians Making Noise," *Wall Street Journal*, July 22, 2011, A17, http://online.wsj.com/article/SB100014240531119034 61104576458750406784300.html).

14. Alyson Shontell, "Fantasy Football Is an $800 Million Industry, but Who's Profiting?" *Business Insider*, September 2, 2010, www.businessinsider.com/fantasy-football-is-an-800-million-industry-but-whos-profiting-2010-9; Greg Bulmash, "Fantasy Sports: The Original Social Network," PowerPoint deck, *Slideshare*, August 19, 2010, www.slideshare.net/mobile/rtc123/fantasy-sports-the-original-social-network.

15. Jack Larsen and Tom Marks, *Hawaiian Pineapple Entrepreneurs* (McMinnville, OR: Creative Company, 2010).

16. Mike Florio, "Minimum Salaries Shoot Up Under New Deal," NBC Sports Talk, *Pro Football Talk*, July 25, 2011, http://profootballtalk.nbcsports.com/2011 /07/25/minimum-salaries-shoot-up-under-new-deal/.

17. Anne Bogart, *And Then, You Act: Making Art in an Unpredictable World* (New York: Routledge, 2007), 74.

18. Tim O'Reilly, "Hardware, Software, and Infoware," in *Open Sources: Voices from the Open Source Revolution*, ed. Chris DiBona, Sam Ockman, and Mark Stone (Sebastopol, CA: O'Reilly, 1999), http://oreilly.com/catalog/opensources/book /tim.html; Tim O'Reilly, "What Is Web 2.0: Design Patterns and Business Models for the Next Generation of Software," O'Reilly Page, September 30, 2005, http://oreilly.com/web2/archive/what-is-web-20.html; Tim O'Reilly and John Battalle, "Web Squared: Web 2.0 Five Years On," Web 2.0 Summit, San Francisco, October 20–22, 2009, www.web2summit.com/web2009/public/schedule/detail /10194. Tim O'Reilly is the founder and CEO of O'Reilly Media. Dale Dougherty is a cofounder of O'Reilly Media and the founder and publisher of *Make* magazine. I am grateful to Sara Winge for telling me about the origins of Web 2.0.

19. The very influential Esther Dyson had adopted the form for a newsletter *Release 1.0* and for Esther Dyson, *Release 2.0: A Design for Living in the Digital Age* (New York: Broadway Books, 1997).

20. *Wikipedia*, s.v. "Web 2.0 Summit," http://en.wikipedia.org/wiki/Web_2.0 _Summit, last modified October 23, 2011; Isaiah Berlin, *The Crooked Timber of Humanity: Chapters in the History of Ideas* (New York: Fontana Press, 1991). Among the differences of opinion at the 2004 Web 2.0 Conference were rival claims about who had created the term "Web 2.0" (*Wikipedia*, s.v. "Web 2.0 Summit").

21. Edward Sapir, "Communication," in *Encyclopedia of the Social Sciences* (1931), 4:78-81; J. L. Austin, *How to Do Things with Words* (New York: Oxford

University Press, 1965); Stanley Jeyaraja Tambiah, *Culture, Thought, and Social Action: An Anthropological Perspective* (Cambridge, MA: Harvard University Press, 1985).

22. Robert Kozinets, "Can Consumers Escape the Market? Emancipatory Illuminations from Burning Man," *Journal of Consumer Research* 29 (June 2002): 20–38.

23. Burning Man, "What Is Burning Man? 1986 to 1996," Burning Man Page, n.d. www.burningman.com/whatisburningman/1986_1996/, accessed November 29, 2010.

24. Grant McCracken, *Chief Culture Officer: How to Create a Living, Breathing Corporation* (New York: Basic Books, 2009), 19–20.

25. Daniel Bell, *The Cultural Contradictions of Capitalism* (New York: Basic Books, 1996).

26. John Kearon, "The Death of Innovation," *Market Leader*, September 21–24, 2010, 20–24, http://www.brainjuicer.com/xtra/BrainJuicer_Kearon_Innovation.pdf; W. Chan Kim and Renée Mauborgne, *Blue Ocean Strategy: How to Create Uncontested Market Space and Make Competition Irrelevant* (Boston: Harvard Business School Press, 2005). Unilever is not the only one have trouble with organized innovation; see "Bamboo Innovation," *The Economist, Schumpeter Blog*, May 5, 2011, www.economist.com/node/18648264?story_id=18648264.

Chapter 2

1. Michael E. Raynor, *The Strategy Paradox: Why Committing to Success Leads to Failure* (New York: Crown Business, 2007), Kindle location 84. Specifically, Raynor says, "No one can legitimately claim to have a meaningful ability to foresee the future in anything like the level of detail required to make consistently successful strategic commitments" (Kindle location 201). I have restricted myself to measures of turbulence in the economy, but as Andrew Gamble, professor of politics at Cambridge, says, this turbulence has also come to politics: "Politics everywhere is in a strange febrile state. There is a deep sense of unease about the future. The pace of change continues unrelentingly. Older ideological moorings have either dissolved or are no longer trusted. We face a range of complex challenges, some of them close at hand, others much more distant, and our politics is so obsessed with short-term calculations and the passing passions of the twenty-four-hour news cycle that it often seems quite inadequate at dealing with them. There is an angry resentful mood against politics and politicians in many countries" (Andrew Gamble, "Boomers and Bust," *Times Literary Supplement* 5628 [2011]: 28).

2. Andrew Grove, *Only the Paranoid Survive: How to Exploit the Crisis Points That Challenge Every Company* (New York: Crown Business, 1999), Kindle location 188.

3. James Champy and Nitin Nohria, *Fast Forward: The Best Ideas on Managing Business Change* (Boston: Harvard Business Press, 1996); Tyler Cowen, *Creative Destruction: How Globalization Is Changing the World's Cultures* (Princeton, NJ: Princeton University Press, 2004); Stan Davis and Christopher Meyer, *Blur: The Speed of Change in the Connected Economy* (New York: Grand Central Publishing, 1999); Philip Evans and Thomas S. Wurster, *Blown to Bits: How the New Economics of Information Transforms Strategy* (Boston: Harvard Business Press, 1999); Richard Foster and Sarah Kaplan, *Creative Destruction: Why Companies That Are Built to Last Underperform the Market—And How to Successfully Transform Them* (New York: Currency/Doubleday, 2001; New York: Crown Business, 2004); James Gleick, *Faster: The Acceleration of Just About Everything* (New York: Vintage, 2000); Grove, *Only the Paranoid Survive*; Charles Handy, *The Age of Paradox* (Boston: Harvard Business Press, 1995); Charles Handy, *The Age of Unreason* (Boston: Harvard Business Press, 1991); Kevin Kelly, *Out of Control: The New Biology of Machines, Social Systems, & the Economic World* (New York: Basic Books, 1995); Tom Peters, *Thriving on Chaos: Handbook for a Management Revolution* (New York: Harper Paperbacks, 1988).

4. Grant McCracken, *Transformations: Identity Construction in Contemporary Culture* (Bloomington: Indiana University Press, 2008).

5. Foster and Kaplan, *Creative Destruction*, 62.

6. Bret Easton Ellis, interview by Charlie Rose, *Charlie Rose*, PBS, August 17, 2010, www.charlierose.com/view/interview/11176. Remark appears around the 5:30 mark.

7. Horace Newcomb, ed., and Museum of Broadcast Communications, *Encyclopedia of Television*, 2nd ed. (New York: Fitzroy Dearborn, 2004), 1465.

8. Benjamin Svetkey, "War Games," *Entertainment Weekly*, December 21, 2007, 29–37; Alex Dobuzinskis, "Hollywood Rethinks Use of A-List Actors," *Reuters*, November 13, 2009, www.reuters.com/article/2009/11/13/us-alist-idUS-TRE5AC5AI20091113. This dark suspicion has haunted Hollywood since William Goldman's famous "Nobody knows anything" (William Goldman, *Adventures in the Screen Trade* [New York: Warner Books, 1983], 39).

9. *Wikipedia*, s.v. "*The Good Guys* (2010 TV Series)," http://en.wikipedia.org/wiki/The_Good_Guys_(2010_TV_series), last modified October 7, 2011.

10. Leslie Moonves, interview by Tina Brown, *Topic A*, CNBC, November 21, 2004, www.topicawithtinabrown.com/thisweek11212004.html.

11. Tim Harford, "Why Social Marketing Doesn't Work," *Undercover Economist*, July 16, 2011, http://timharford.com/2011/07/why-social-marketing-doesn%E2%80%99t-work/.

12. A. G. Lafley and Ram Charan, *The Game-Changer: How You Can Drive Revenue and Profit Growth with Innovation* (New York: Crown Business, 2008); Michael

Mandel, "This Way to the Future," *Business Week*, October 11, 2008; Scott Berkun, *The Myths of Innovation* (Sebastopol, CA: O'Reilly, 2010); John Hagel III, John Seely Brown, and Lang Davison, "Shaping Strategy in a World of Constant Disruption," *Harvard Business Review*, October 2008; Nassim Nicholas Taleb, *The Black Swan: The Impact of the Highly Improbable* (New York: Random House, 2007); Peter Schwartz, *The Art of the Long View: Planning for the Future in an Uncertain World* (New York: Currency/Doubleday, 1996); Clayton M. Christensen, *The Innovator's Dilemma: When New Technologies Cause Great Firms to Fail* (Boston: Harvard Business School Press, 1997); Polly LaBarre, "The Industrialized Revolution," *Fast Company*, November 1, 2003, www.fastcompany.com/magazine/76/revolution.html.

13. Joseph A. Schumpeter, *Can Capitalism Survive? Creative Destruction and the Future of the Global Economy* (New York: Harper Perennial Modern Classics, 2009); Jim Collins, "The Secret of Enduring Greatness," *Fortune Magazine*, November 25, 2008, http://money.cnn.com/2008/04/18/news/companies/enduring_greatness. fortune/index.htm; Harris Collingwood, "The Sink-or-Swim Economy," *New York Times*, June 8, 2003.

14. Both quotes from Debbie Millman, *Brand Thinking and Other Noble Pursuits* (New York: Allworth, 2011). Statistics on new-product failures from Carmen Nobel, "Clay Christensen's Milkshake Marketing," Harvard Business School Working Knowledge paper, February 14, 2011, http://hbswk.hbs.edu/item/6496.html? wknews=02142011.

15. W. Chan Kim and Renée Mauborgne, *Blue Ocean Strategy: How to Create Uncontested Market Space and Make Competition Irrelevant* (Boston: Harvard Business School Press, 2005); Mark W. Johnson, *Seizing the White Space: Business Model Innovation for Growth and Renewal* (Boston: Harvard Business Press, 2010).

16. Tim Brown, *Change by Design: How Design Thinking Transforms Organizations and Inspires Innovation* (New York: HarperBusiness, 2009), Kindle location 1340. On flatter, more egalitarian organizations, see Stephan H. Haeckel, *Adaptive Enterprise: Creating and Leading Sense-And-Respond Organizations* (Boston: Harvard Business Press, 1999); John Henry Clippinger, *The Biology of Business: Decoding the Natural Laws of Enterprise* (San Francisco: Jossey-Bass, 1999). Andrew S. Grove, *Only the Paranoid Survive: How to Exploit the Crisis Points That Challenge Every Company* (New York: Crown Business, 1999), Kindle location 188.

17. Remarks given by John McArthur during the October 1996 Symposium held in his honor, as quoted in Jeffrey Cruikshank, Linda Doyle, and Thomas McCraw, "The Intellectual Venture Capitalist," in *The Intellectual Venture Capitalist: John H. McArthur and the Work of the Harvard Business School, 1980-1995*, ed. Thomas K. McCraw and Jeffrey L. Cruikshank (Boston: Harvard Business Press. 1999), 34–35.

18. David Gray, "Wanted: Chief Ignorance Officer," *Harvard Business Review*, November 2003, http://hbr.org/2003/11/wanted-chief-ignorance-officer/ar/1.

19. Jim Collins and Jerry I. Porras, *Built to Last: Successful Habits of Visionary Companies* (New York: HarperBusiness, 2004), 141.

20. Sarah Jane Gilbert, "The Accidental Innovator: Q&A with Robert D. Austin," Harvard Business School Working Knowledge paper, July 5, 2006, http://hbswk.hbs.edu/item/5441.html.

21. Peter Sims, *Little Bets: How Big Ideas Emerge from Small Discoveries* (New York: Random House Business Books, 2011), Kindle location 217.

22. Andrew Stanton, quoted in ibid., Kindle location 701.

23. Peter Sims, "Daring to Stumble on the Road to Discovery," *New York Times*, August 6, 2011, www.nytimes.com/2011/08/07/jobs/07pre.html.

24. Tim Hartford, "Trial, Error and the God Complex," video, TED Talks, July 2011, www.ted.com/talks/tim_harford.html; Tim Harford, *Adapt: Why Success Always Starts with Failure* (New York: Farrar, Straus and Giroux, 2011); Kathryn Schulz, "Kathryn Schulz on Being Wrong," video, TED Talks, April 2011, www.ted.com/talks/kathryn_schulz_on_being_wrong.html. Schulz's talk is surely one of the best TED talks on record. See also Kathryn Schulz, *Being Wrong: Adventures in the Margin of Error* (New York: Ecco, 2010; reprint 2011).

25. Thomas J. Peters and Robert H. Waterman, *In Search of Excellence: Lessons from America's Best-Run Companies* (New York: Harper Paperbacks, 2004), 201; Ben R. Rich and Leo Janos, *Skunk Works: A Personal Memoir of My Years of Lockheed* (Boston: Back Bay Books, 1996).

26. On Whole Foods, see Brown, *Change by Design*, Kindle location 939. On Google, see Ben Elgin, "Managing Google's Idea Factory," *BusinessWeek*, October 3, 2005, www.businessweek.com/magazine/content/05_40/b3953093.htm. Many of the 22,800 patents held by 3M came from this program (Kaomi Goetz, "How 3M Gave Everyone Days Off and Created an Innovation Dynamo," *Fast Company Design*, February 1, 2011, www.fastcodesign.com/1663137/how-3m-gave-everyone-days-off-and-created-an-innovation-dynamo. For more on the Clay Street Project, see Clay Street Project Web page, https://theclaystreetproject.pg.com/claystreet/default.aspx. Brice Westring quote in Lafley and Charan, *The Game-Changer*, 200.

27. Henry William Chesbrough, *Open Business Models: How to Thrive in the New Innovation Landscape* (Boston: Harvard Business Press, 2006); Henry William Chesbrough, *Open Innovation: The New Imperative for Creating and Profiting from Technology* (Boston: Harvard Business Press, 2006); John Winsor, *Spark: Be More Innovative Through Co-Creation* (Chicago: Agate B2, 2010); Robert Berner, "P&G, New and Improved," *BusinessWeek*, July 7, 2003, www.businessweek.com/magazine/content/03_27/b3840001_mz001.htm; Michael Schrage, *Getting*

Beyond Ideas: The Future of Rapid Innovation (New York: Wiley, 2011); Eric von Hippel, *Democratizing Innovation* (Cambridge, MA: MIT Press, 2006).

28. Henry Jenkins, *Textual Poachers: Television Fans & Participatory Culture* (New York: Routledge, 1992); von Hippel, *Democratizing Innovation*; Clay Shirky, *Here Comes Everybody: The Power of Organizing Without Organizations* (New York: Penguin Press, 2008; reprint 2009).

29. Cory Doctorow, *Makers* (New York: Tor Books, 2010), Kindle location 81.

30. Leight Buchanan, "How Great Entrepreneurs Think," *Inc.com*, February 1, 2011, www.inc.com/magazine/20110201/how-great-entrepreneurs-think.html#. For more on what some are calling effectual reasoning, see Stuart Read et al., *Effectual Entrepreneurship* (New York: Routledge, 2011). Also see Saras D. Sarasvathy, *Effectuation: Elements of Entrepreneurial Expertise* (Northampton, MA: Edward Elgar Publishing, 2009).

31. Errol Morris, *Fast, Cheap and Out of Control* (United States: Sony, 1998), videocassette.

32. See John Kay's more elegant expression of this issue: *Obliquity: Why Our Goals Are Best Achieved Indirectly* (New York: Penguin Press, 2011).

33. Quoted in Lafley and Charan *The Game Changer*, 209–210.

34. Gareth Kay, "On Thinking Small," *Creative Review*, August 2011, www.creativereview.co.uk/back-issues/creative-review/2011/august/summer-reading-on-thinking-small (subscription required). See also Gareth Kay, "How to Think and Make Small," *Brand New*, May 19, 2011, http://garethkay.typepad.com /brand_new/2011/05/how-to-think-and-make-small.html.

35. Grant McCracken, "Your Faithful Correspondent at Conde Nast," *CultureBy: This Blog Sits at the Intersection of Anthropology and Economics*, January 8, 2007, http://cultureby.com/2007/01/from_your_faith.html.

36. Or to put this in the language of Michael Polanyi, "we can know more than we can tell" (*The Tacit Dimension* [Chicago: University of Chicago Press, 2011], 4).

37. Malcolm Gladwell, *Blink: The Power of Thinking Without Thinking* (Boston: Back Bay Books, 2007).

38. Robert K. Merton and Elinor Barber, *The Travels and Adventures of Serendipity: A Study in Sociological Semantics and the Sociology of Science* (Princeton, NJ: Princeton University Press, 2003).

39. Ronald S. Burt, *Brokerage and Closure: An Introduction to Social Capital* (New York: Oxford University Press, 2007), 59.

40. Steven Johnson, *Where Good Ideas Come From: The Natural History of Innovation* (New York: Riverhead, 2010), Kindle location 282.

41. Information on the Culture Lab at the Godrej Group is from Parmash Shahani, email communication, August 23, 2010. For Gary Hamel's laboratory, see

Alan Murray, "The End of Management," *Wall Street Journal*, August 21, 2010, http://online.wsj.com/article/SB10001424052748704476104575439723695579664.html?mod=WSJ_business_LeftSecondHighlights. David Edwards, *The Lab: Creativity and Culture* (Cambridge, MA: Harvard University Press, 2010); Chuck Salter, "Syyn Labs's League of Extraordinary Nerds," *Fast Company*, January 10, 2011, www.fastcompany.com/magazine/152/the-league-of-extraordinary-nerds.html.

42. Ed Cotton, "Why Agencies Need Ads," *Influx Insights*, November 5, 2010, www.influxinsights.com/blog/article/2636/why-agencies-need-labs.html.

43. BBH Labs Web page, "About BBH Labs," http://bbh-labs.com/about.

44. Ben Malbon, *Clubbing: Culture and Experience* (New York: Routledge, 1999).

45. Edwards, *The Lab*, Kindle location circa 120–144.

46. Ibid., Kindle location circa 93.

47. Ronald S. Burt, "Network Duality of Social Capital," in *Social Capital: Reaching Out, Reaching In*, ed. Viva Ona Bartkus and James H. Davis (Northampton, MA: Edward Elgar Publishing, 2010), 39–40.

48. For more on Steve Crandall, see "Steve Crandall," Coburn Ventures Web page, n.d., www.coburnventures.com/Research_Fellows/Research_Fellow_Steve_Crall.html.

49. *Wikipedia*, s.v. "Bell Labs," http://en.wikipedia.org/wiki/Bell_Labs, last modified October 26, 2011.

50. Katherine Rosman, "As Seen on TV: Brand Bethenny," *Wall Street Journal*, November 24, 2010, http://online.wsj.com/article/SB100014240527487043693045756326732636667274.html?KEYWORDS=bethenny.

51. Sam Anderson, "The James Franco Project," *New York Magazine*, July 25, 2010, http://nymag.com/print/?/movies/profiles/67284/.

52. I will not violate the law of nonvacuous contrast (*Wikipedia*, s.v. "Principle of nonvacuous contrast," http://en.wikipedia.org/wiki/Principle_of_nonvacuous_contrast, last modified November 19, 2010).

53. For more on seed bombs and guerrilla gardening, see Guerrilla Gardening home page, www.guerrillagardening.org/; *Wikipedia*, s.v. "Guerrilla gardening," http://en.wikipedia.org/wiki/Guerrilla_gardening, last modified August 29, 2011.

54. James Q. Wilson and George L. Kelling, "The Police and Neighborhood Safety," *The Atlantic*, March 1982, 29–38; Malcolm Gladwell, "The Tipping Point," *The New Yorker*, June 3, 1996, www.gladwell.com/1996/1996_06_03_a_tipping.htm.

55. Tom Peters, *The Circle of Innovation: You Can't Shrink Your Way to Greatness* (New York: Vintage, 1999), 460.

56. Ray Oldenburg, ed., *Celebrating the Third Place: Inspiring Stories About the "Great Good Places" at the Heart of Our Communities* (New York: Da Capo Press, 2002).

57. *Wikipedia*, s.v. "Dick Tuck," http://en.wikipedia.org/wiki/Dick_Tuck, last modified September 10, 2011.

58. T. F. Peterson, *Nightwork: A History of Hacks and Pranks at MIT* (Cambridge, MA: MIT Press, 2003); Neil Steinberg, *If at All Possible, Involve a Cow: The Book of College Pranks* (New York: St. Martin's Press, 1992); Charlie Todd and Alex Scordelis, *Causing a Scene: Extraordinary Pranks in Ordinary Places with Improv Everywhere* (New York: William Morrow, 2009).

59. Tony Attwood, *The Complete Guide to Asperger's Syndrome* (Philadelphia: Jessica Kingsley, 2008); Tyler Cowen, *Create Your Own Economy: The Path to Prosperity in a Disordered World* (New York: Dutton, 2009).

60. Heather Brooke, *The Revolution Will Be Digitised: Dispatches from the Information War* (London: William Heinemann, 2011).

61. Kyle Vanhemert, "Coffee-Powered 'Carpuccino' Infuriates Car Lovers, Coffee Lovers, Pun Lovers," *Gizmodo*, March 6, 2010, http://gizmodo.com/5487377/coffee+powered-carpuccino-infuriates-car-lovers-coffee-lovers-pun-lovers.

62. Mark Earls, *Herd: How to Change Mass Behaviour by Harnessing Our True Nature* (New York: Wiley, 2009); Alex Bentley, Mark Earls, and Michael J. O'Brien, *I'll Have What She's Having: Mapping Social Behavior* (Cambridge, MA: MIT Press, 2010).

63. For more on Asperger's syndrome, see Attwood, *Complete Guide to Asperger's Syndrome*. For a broader culture treatment of autism, see the excellent book Cowen, *Create Your Own Economy*.

64. Daniel Bell, *The Cultural Contradictions of Capitalism: 20th Anniversary Edition* (New York: Basic Books, 1996).

65. Peters, *Thriving on Chaos*; Seth Godin, *Small Is the New Big: And 183 Other Riffs, Rants, and Remarkable Business Ideas* (New York: Portfolio, 2006); William C. Taylor and Polly G. Labarre, *Mavericks at Work: Why the Most Original Minds in Business Win* (New York: Harper Paperbacks, 2008). People like these are called the "unacknowledged legislators" of the business world in John Micklethwait and Adrian Wooldridge, *The Witch Doctors: Making Sense of the Management Gurus* (New York: Three Rivers Press, 1998); Mihaly Csikszentmihalyi, *Flow: The Psychology of Optimal Experience* (New York: Harper & Row, 1990).

66. Peter Drucker, *The Age of Discontinuity* (New Brunswick, NJ: Transaction Publishers, 1992); Daniel Bell, *The Coming of Post-Industrial Society: A Venture in Social Forecasting* (New York: Basic Books, 1973); Thomas H. Davenport and John C. Beck, *The Attention Economy: Understanding the New Currency of Business* (Boston: Harvard Business Press, 2002); Thomas A. Stewart, *The Wealth of Knowledge: Intellectual Capital and the Twenty-First Century Organization* (New York: Doubleday Business, 2001); Richard Florida, *The Rise of the Creative Class: And How It's Transforming Work, Leisure, Community, and Everyday Life* (New York: Basic Books,

2003); Susan Crawford, "The Origin and Development of a Concept: The Information Society," *Bulletin of the Medical Library Association* 71, no. 4 (1983): 380–385; Tyler Cowen, *The Age of the Infovore: Succeeding in the Information Economy* (New York: Plume, 2010).

Chapter 3

1. *Wikipedia*, s.v. "Rube Goldberg," http://en.wikipedia.org/wiki/Rube _Goldberg, last modified October 27, 2011.

2. "Best Rube Goldberg Ever," video, YouTube, July 6, 2007, www.youtube .com/watch?v=RouXygRcRC4.

3. Cliff Kuang, "Eye Candy: OK Go's Insane Rube Goldberg Machine," *Fast Company*, March 2, 2010, www.fastcompany.com/1567383/eye-candy-ok-gos-insane-rube-goldberg-machine; "MythBusters Rube Goldberg Machine: www .HumorKick.com," video, YouTube, December 13, 2006, www.youtube.com /watch?v=lCYg_gz4fDo; Adam Frucci, "New Guinness Rube Goldberg Ad Directed by Bravia 'Bouncing Balls' Creator," Gizmodo, November 9, 2007, http://gizmodo.com/320849/new-guinness-rube-goldberg-ad-directed-by-bravia-bouncing-balls-creator.

4. For the run-out-of-gas mission, see "Ran over by Ford Fiesta__.flv," video, YouTube, May 18, 2010, http://www.youtube.com/watch?v=o56TYuVbrp0.

5. For the lost-keys mission, see Ford Motor Company, "Busk or Bust," Ford Fiesta Movement, 2009, http://chapter1.fiestamovement.com/missions/view/691.

6. For more of the Fiesta campaign, see Bud Caddell, interview with author, December 22, 2009, in Grant McCracken, "The Bud Caddell Interview," *CultureBy: This Blog Sits at the Intersection of Anthropology and Economics*, January 5, 2010, http://cultureby.com/2010/01/bud-caddell-interview.html; Grant McCracken, "How Ford Got Social Marketing Right," *Harvard Business Review Blog Network*, January 7, 2010, http://blogs.hbr.org/cs/2010/01/ford_recently _wrapped_the_firs.html.

7. Dan Harmon, interview with Toph Eggers, *The Believer* 9, no. 5 (2011): 69–73.

8. The SETI project was suspended briefly, but now with a successful fundraising campaign behind it, it is scheduled to go back online (Deborah Netburn, "SETI Institute's Telescopes to Go Back Online, Resuming Hunt for Alien Life," *Los Angeles Times*, August 9, 2011, http://latimesblogs.latimes.com/nationnow /2011/08/seti-institute-allen-telescope-array-to-go-back-online-in-september .html).

9. Brian McConnell, *Beyond Contact: A Guide to SETI and Communicating with Alien Civilizations* (Sebastopol, CA: O'Reilly, 2001), 5. According to "How

Does SETI@home Work?" *How Stuff Works*, April 1, 2000, http://computer.howstuffworks.com/question204.htm, "the antenna used for SETI@home records 35 gigabytes of data every day. According to the SETI@home site, the average home computer takes about 30 hours to process one 'work unit,' and the 35 gigabytes of daily data is broken into 140,000 work units. That's 4.2 million hours of computation time to process a single day of data."

10. I am grateful to Jason Oke and Gareth Kay for their presentation on this campaign: Jason Oke and Gareth Kay, "How to Do Connections Planning in 2009," conference proceeding, Planningness 2009, San Francisco, www.slideshare.net/jasonoke/connections-planningness.

11. The advertising agency responsible for this campaign was TWBA\Chiat\Day, USA. The creative team was large, and I list them here: Global Director of Media Arts: Lee Clow; Executive Creative Director: Rob Schwartz; Group Creative Director: Jimmy Smith; Writer/Co-Creator: Brent Anderson; Writer/Co-Creator: Steve Howard; Replay Project & Series, Head Producer: Brian O'Rourke; Assistant Producer: Tim Newfang; Director of Business Affairs: Linda Daubson; Business Affairs Manager: Anne Thomasson; Group Account Director: Brynn Bardacke; Management Supervisor: Jiah Choi; Account Supervisor: Amy Farias; Account Executive: Adam Bersin; Directors: Kris Belman and Scott Balcerek.

12. Noreen O'Leary, "Do Cannes Winners Translate to ROI?" *Brandweek*, July 12, 2010, 6. *Replay* was named one of CNN's top stories of 2009 and was picked up as a TV series for Fox Sports Net.

13. Joel Stein, "Straight Outta Narnia," *Time*, April 17, 2006, www.time.com/time/magazine/article/0,9171,1184075,00.html.

14. For more on *Saturday Night Live*, see *Wikipedia*, s.v. "Saturday Night Live: Production Process," http://en.wikipedia.org/wiki/Saturday_night_live#Production_process, last modified October 23, 2011. See also Stein, "Straight Outta Narnia."

15. Ethan Thompson, "Convergence Comedy: Andy Samberg vs. SNL," *Flow*, June 26, 2008 http://flowtv.org/2008/06/convergence-comedy-andy-samberg-vs-snlethan-thompson-texas-am-corpus-christi/; Jeff Pruett, "Saturday Night Live Debuts: This Day in History, 10/11/1975," *Slinking Toward Retirement*, October 11, 2010, http://slinkingtowardretirement.com/?p=9442; The Lonely Island, "Ras Trent," video, SNL Digital Short, NBC, n.d., www.hulu.com/watch/40968/saturday-night-live-snl-digital-short-ras-trent; The Lonely Island, "Dick in a Box," video, SNL Digital Short, NBC, first aired December 16, 2006, www.youtube.com/watch?v=WhwbxEfy7fg; The Lonely Island, "Jizz in My Pants," video, SNL Digital Short, December 8, 2008, www.youtube.com/watch?v=4pXfHLUlZf4&feature=relmfu; The Lonely Island, "Shy Ronnie 2: Ronnie and Clyde," video, The Lonely Island Web page, October 30, 2010, www.thelonelyisland.com/video/ronnie-and-clyde.

16. Grant McCracken, "Story Time 15: Emergency Ethnography for Coca-Cola Company in Japan," *CultureBy: This Blog Sits at the Intersection of Anthropology and Economics*, November 18, 2005, http://cultureby.com/2005/11/story_time_15_e.html.

17. David Weinberger, *Small Pieces Loosely Joined: A Unified Theory of the Web* (New York: Basic Books, 2003).

18. Alan Schwarz, "Giving Proper Gravestones to Negro Leagues Players," *New York Times*, June 30, 2010, www.nytimes.com/2010/07/01/sports/baseball/01tombstone.html?scp=1&sq=negro&st=cse, explains the three men's rationale for their mission: "In the words of Dr. Jeremy Krock, a 52-year-old anesthesiologist from Peoria, Ill., 'A lot of these guys, by the time Jackie Robinson made it, they were way past their prime. It was too late for them. And not having a marker on their grave for people to remember them only made it worse.'"

19. These stats are from Leena Rao, "New Twitter Stats: 140M Tweets Sent Per Day, 460K Accounts Created Per Day," *Techcrunch*, March 14, 2011, http://techcrunch.com/2011/03/14/new-twitter-stats-140m-tweets-sent-per-day-460k-accounts-created-per-day/. The remainder of this essay and all the quotes that follow in this section are from Terry Gross, "Twitter's Biz Stone on Starting a Revolution," *Fresh Air*, NPR, February 16, 2011, www.wbur.org/npr/133775340/twitters-biz-stone-on-starting-a-revolution. For more on "phatic data," see Grant McCracken, "Now Social Networks Work: The Puzzle of Exhaust Data," *CultureBy: This Blog Sits at the Intersection of Anthropology and Economics*, July 2007, http://cultureby.com/2007/07/how-social-netw.html.

20. Rebecca Leung, "NFL Films, Inc. Father-Son Team Establishes Gold Standard for Sports Photography," *CBSnews.com*, January 6, 2004, http://www.cbsnews.com/stories/2004/01/26/60II/main595946.shtml.

21. Greg Eno, "Pro Football Hall of Fame: Ed Sabol's NFL Took on a Life of Its Own," *Bleacher Report*, February 12, 2011, http://bleacherreport.com/articles/606368-pro-football-hall-of-fame-ed-sabols-nfl-took-on-a-life-of-its-own.

22. Leung, "NFL Films, Inc. Father-Son Team."

23. Frank Rose, *The Art of Immersion: How the Digital Generation Is Remaking Hollywood, Madison Avenue, and the Way We Tell Stories* (New York: W. W. Norton, 2011), Kindle location 235. Thanks to Howie Goldkrand for the reference here. David Shields, *Reality Hunger: A Manifesto* (New York: Vintage, 2011).

24. For more on the transmedia notion, see the defining statement in Henry Jenkins, *Convergence Culture: Where Old and New Media Collide* (New York: New York University Press, 2006; revised 2008).

25. The Super Bowl version of the ad can be found at "Old Spice: The Man Your Man Could Smell Like," video, YouTube, February 4, 2010, www.youtube.com

/watch?v=owGykVbfgUE. For commentary on the opening "Bruce Campbell" moment of the campaign, see Grant McCracken, "Brand Triage: Tale of Two Perfumes," *CultureBy: This Blog Sits at the Intersection of Anthropology and Economics*, August 15, 2008, http://cultureby.com/2008/08/brand-triage-a.html.

26. Teressa Iezzi, "Agency of the Year: Wieden + Kennedy Portland," *Creativity*, January 23, 2011, http://creativity-online.com/news/wieden-kennedy-portland-is-agency-of-the-year/148395.

27. Marshall Kirkpatrick, "How the Old Spice Videos Are Being Made," *ReadWriteWeb*, July 14, 2010, www.readwriteweb.com/archives/how_old_spice _won_the_internet.php.

28. Advertising Federation of Central Oregon, "Lessons I Learned from the Man Your Man Could Smell Like," *AdFedCO Blog*, September 30, 2010, www.adfedco.org/blog/2010/09/lessons-i-learned-from-the-man-your-man-could-smell-like/.

29. Data for the Response campaign was from Wieden + Kennedy, "Old Spice: Digital Response," Wieden + Kennedy Web site, July 14, 2010, www.wk.com /campaign/digital_response/from/old_spice.

30. I am indebted to Michael Hastings-Black for pointing this out to me. See Rich Whittle, "Two Dollar Holler," *Dane Carlson's Business Opportunities Weblog*, April 29, 2009, www.business-opportunities.biz/2009/04/21/two-dollar-holler/; Helen A. Cooper et al., *Life, Liberty, and the Pursuit of Happiness: American Art from the Yale University Art Gallery* (New Haven, CT: Yale University Press, 2008).

31. Thomas McNamee, *Alice Waters and Chez Panisse* (New York: Penguin, 2008), Kindle location 253.

32. Jack Shelton, quoted in ibid., Kindle location 1215.

33. Alice Waters, quoted in ibid., Kindle location 1572.

34. McNamee does a great job teasing out the many forces and people who helped make Chez Panisse. See also Paul Aratow, "A Chez Panisse Birthday Remembrance," *Los Angeles Times*, September 1, 2011, www.latimes.com/features/food /la-fo-chez-panisse-20110901,0,2165032.story.

35. Evelyn Rodriguez, "The Unconference," post on Google+, August 9, 2011, https://plus.google.com/110308609618542819697/posts/5PqHt1kby4t. Used by permission. Thank you, Ms. Rodriguez.

36. For information on urban games, see Ed Grabianowski, "How Urban Gaming Works," *How Stuff Works*, n.d., http://adventure.howstuffworks.com/outdoor-activities/urban-sports/urban-gaming1.htm; Hubbub, "Koppelkiek," Hubbub Web page, n.d., http://whatsthehubbub.nl/projects/koppelkiek/.

37. Yukari Iwatani Kane and Ian Sherr, "Secrets from Apple's Genius Bar: Full Loyalty, No Negativity," *Wall Street Journal*, June 16, 2011, http://online.wsj.com

/article/SB10001424052702304563104576364071955678908.html?mod=WSJ
_hp_mostpop_read.

38. Many Eyes Home page, www-958.ibm.com/software/data/cognos/manyeyes/.

39. Jonathan Feinberg, "Wordle," in *Beautiful Visualization: Looking at Data Through the Eyes of Experts*, ed. Julie Steele and Noah Iliinsky (Sebastopol, CA: O'Reilly, 2010), 37–58.

40. Max Weber, "Science As Vocation," in *From Max Weber: Essays in Sociology*, ed H. H. Gerth and C. Wright Mills (New York, Oxford University Press, 1946), 129–156.

41. Howard Rheingold, *Smart Mobs: The Next Social Revolution* (New York: Basic Books, 2003); Improv Everywhere home page, www.improveverywhere.com. See, for example, an event at a Manchester, England, market: "Supermarket Flashmob," video, YouTube, June 13, 2007, www.youtube.com/watch?v=X4GMXavfKPY.

42. Grant McCracken, *Chief Culture Officer: How to Create a Living, Breathing Corporation* (New York: Basic Books, 2009), 17–21; "The T-Mobile Dance," video, YouTube, January 16, 2009, www.youtube.com/watch?v=VQ3d3KigPQM.

43. Rodney Graham, quoted in Hamza Walker, "Exhibit Essay: Rodney Graham, School of Velocity, Parsifal, October 1–November 12, 1995," n.d., Renaissance Society at the University of Chicago, www.renaissancesociety.org/site/Exhibitions/Essay.Rodney-Graham-School-of-Velocity-Parsifal.87.html.

44. James Hibberd, "Why This Man Has 40,000,000 Viewers," *Hollywood Reporter*, December 1, 2010.

45. Dick Wolf is the creator of *Law & Order, Law & Order: Special Victims Unit, Law & Order: Criminal Intent, Law & Order: UK, Law & Order: Los Angeles*, and *Law & Order: Trial by Jury*.

46. For the production logo for Bad Hat Harry Productions, see "Bad Hat Harry Productions & NBC Universal Television (2004)," video, YouTube, September 22, 2009, www.youtube.com/watch?v=rT5TAy7hJ_8.

47. Chuck Lorre, "The Official Vanity Card Archives," Chuck Lorre Productions, card 1, n.d., www.chucklorre.com/index.php?p=1.

48. In vanity card 345, which appeared at the end of an episode of *The Big Bang Theory*, Lorre sent us this message, a reference apparently to the difficulty that Charlie Sheen has created in his professional life: "And finally, when your life takes a path you could never have foreseen, it's humbling. In a good way. It's kind of like a friendly reminder from the universe that while you may think you have the starring role in the movie of your life, you're actually just a bit player trying to grab a quesadilla off the craft services table when no one's looking" (ibid., card 345, http://www.chucklorre.com/index.php?p=345).

49. Carrie Fisher, *Postcards from the Edge* (New York: Simon & Schuster, 1987), is an account of a hyperbolic Hollywood.

Chapter 4

1. F. R. Cloak, "Is a Cultural Ethology Possible?" *Human Ecology* 3 (1975): 161–182; Douglas Rushkoff, *Media Virus! Hidden Agendas in Popular Culture* (New York: Ballantine Books, 1994); Richard Brodie, *Virus of the Mind: The New Science of the Meme* (Carlsbad, CA: Hay House, 2011); Henry Jenkins et al., "If It Doesn't Spread, It's Dead (Part One): Media Viruses and Memes," *Confessions of an Aca/fan*, February 11, 2009, www.henryjenkins.org/2009/02/if_it_doesnt_spread_its_ dead_p .html; Grant McCracken, *Plenitude* (Toronto: Periph.: Fluide, 1997).

2. Brian Raftery, "So, Tron Guy, Gem Sweater Lady, and the Firefox Walk into a Bar . . . ," *Wired Magazine*, June 23, 2008, www.wired.com/entertainment /theweb/magazine/16-07/mf_roflcon.

3. Frank O'Hara, *Lunch Poems* (San Francisco: City Lights Publishers, 2001); Gus Powell, *The Company of Strangers* (Atlanta/New York: J&L Books, 2007).

4. Grant McCracken, "Square Inch Anthropology," *CultureBy: This Blog Sits at the Intersection of Anthropology and Economics*, December 17, 2010, http://cultureby.com/2010/12/square-inch-anthropology.html.

5. If we need a grander term, call it our *expansionary individualism* (Grant McCracken, *Transformations: Identity Construction in Contemporary Culture* [Bloomington: Indiana University Press, 2008]).

6. Stuart Kauffman, *At Home in the Universe: The Search for the Laws of Self-Organization and Complexity* (New York: Oxford University Press, 1996).

7. Kenny Loggins quote from Mo Rocca, "Celebrities in Their Own Words, Others' Voices," transcript, *Sunday Morning*, CBS, May 16, 2010, www.cbsnews .com/stories/2010/05/16/sunday/main6489596.shtml.

8. Jerry Saltz, "Sincerity and Irony Hug It Out," *New York Magazine*, June 7, 2010, 57.

9. Lawrence Weschler, "An Interview with Margaret and Christine Wertheim," *The Believer*, February 9, 2011, 58–66. See David Edwards's approach to this blurring of science and art: David Edwards, *Artscience: Creativity in the Post-Google Generation* (Cambridge, MA.: Harvard University Press, 2010).

10. John Wilder Tukey, *Exploratory Data Analysis* (Reading, MA: Addison-Wesley, 1977), vi.

11. Steve Jobs, "You've Got to Find a Job You Love," *Stanford News Services*, June 15, 2005, http://news-service.stanford.edu/news/2005/june15/jobs-061505.html.

12. James Lovelock, *Gaia: A New Look at Life on Earth* (New York: Oxford University Press, 2000). The point about not being able to throw things away, because we no longer have an "away," is from Allan Chochinov, editor-in-chief at Core 77.com. I heard him speak at a PSFK gathering in New York City, February 1, 2011.

13. Miguel Nelson, quoted in Linda Immediato, "Social Chemists: Miguel Nelson and Sherry Walsh," *LA Weekly*, April 23, 2009, www.laweekly.com/2009-04-23/la-life/social-chemists/.

14. Wikipedia, s.v. "*The Blair Witch Project*," http://en.wikipedia.org/wiki/The_Blair_Witch_Project, last modified November 2, 2011.

Chapter 5

1. This process was brilliantly examined by Michael Arlen in his study of an AT&T ad (Michael Arlen, *Thirty Seconds* [New York: Penguin Press, 1981]).

2. Josh Rottenberg, "The Piracy Debate: The Rough Seas of the Upcoming 'Pirates of the Caribbean' Films," *Entertainment Weekly*, July 7, 2006.

3. Maureen Ryan, "The Subversive Delights of 'Ugly Betty,'" *Chicago Tribune*, November 16, 2006, http://featuresblogs.chicagotribune.com/entertainment_tv/2006/11/ugly_betty_laun.html.

4. William Blake, *The Complete Poetry and Prose of William Blake*, 2nd ed. (Berkeley: University of California Press, 2008).

5. "Greenspan, Entourage, Demolish Hotel Room," *The Onion*, February 17, 1999, http://origin.theonion.com/content/node/29329.

6. M. Foucault, *The Order of Things: An Archaeology of the Human Sciences* (New York: Vintage Books, 1973).

7. Lou Pearlman was the producer of boy bands in the 1990s. He was responsible for the Backstreet Boys. Ron Popeil is an American inventor and infomercial personality. He is responsible for the Showtime Rotisserie ("Set it and forget it!") and the immortal words "But wait, there's more!" (Malcolm Gladwell, "The Pitchman: Ron Popeil and the Conquest of the American Kitchen," *The New Yorker*, October 30, 2000, www.gladwell.com/2000/2000_10_30_a_pitchman.html).

8. My friend Rick Liebling believes that *Miami Vice* would have been more interesting if, for instance, Kid Rock had played the Colin Farrell role. I agree with him.

9. Ingrid Sischy, "Calvin to the Core," *Vanity Fair*, April 2008, http://www.vanityfair.com/culture/features/2008/04/calvin200804.

10. Jon Pareles, "Idealism and Bawdiness Under Many Guises," *New York Times*, May 12, 2008, www.nytimes.com/2008/05/12/arts/music/12badu.html?_r=1&th&emc=th.

11. Compare Fussell's position to the one taken by Dave Hickey, who argues, "Good taste is the residue of someone else's privilege" (Dave Hickey, *Air Guitar: Essays on Art & Democracy* [Los Angeles: Art Issues Press, 1997], 54). Thanks to Ed Batista for this reference.

12. Russell Lynes, *The Tastemakers: The Shaping of American Popular Taste* (New York: Dover, 1980); Dwight MacDonald, *Against the American Grain* (New York: Random House, 1962); George W. S. Trow, *Within the Context of No Context* (New York: Atlantic Monthly Press, 1997); Northrop Frye, *The Modern Century* (New York: Oxford University Press, 1969).

13. Pew Research Center, *A Portrait of Generation Next: How Young People View Their Lives, Futures and Politics* (Washington, DC: Pew Research Center Reports, January 9, 2007), 21, http://people-press.org/reports/pdf/300.pdf.

14. Crawford Brough Macpherson, *The Political Theory of Possessive Individualism: Hobbes to Locke* (New York: Oxford University Press, 1964).

15. William Burroughs, quoted in Steven Watson, *The Birth of the Beat Generation: Visionaries, Rebels and Hipsters, 1944–1960* (New York: Pantheon Books, 1995), 246.

16. Donald R. Katz, *Home Fires: An Intimate Portrait of One Middle-Class Family in Postwar America.* (New York: Perennial, 1993).

17. Edmond Burke, *A Philosophical Enquiry into the Origin of Our Ideas of the Sublime and Beautiful,* edited with an introduction and notes by J. T. Boulton (London: Routledge & Kegan Paul, 1958), 57.

18. Susan Sontag, "Notes on Camp," in *Against Interpretation and Other Essays* (New York: Farrar, Straus and Giroux, 1966), 275–292, especially 290.

19. David Samuels, "The Rap on Rap," *The New Republic*, November 11, 1991.

20. "Jay-Z," VH1.com, n.d., http://www.vh1.com/artists/az/jay_z/artist.jhtml; Johnny Black, "The Greatest Songs Ever: Hard Knock Life," *Blender Magazine*, November 2002, www.blender.com/guide/articles.asxpx?id=827; Henry A. Rhodes, "The Evolution of Rap Music in the United States," curriculum unit 93.04.04, Yale–New Haven Teachers Institute, New Haven, CT, 1993, www.yale.edu/ynhti/curriculum/units/1993/4/93.04.04.x.html; David Samuels, "The Rap on Rap: The 'Black Music' That Isn't Either," *The New Republic*, November 11, 1991.

21. For an interesting development of this theme, see Faris Yakob, "Talent Imitates, Genius Steals: A Brief History of Recombinant Culture," *Convergence Culture Consortium*, October 15, 2008, http://farisyakob.typepad.com/weeklyupdate_100808_final2.html. I believe that it's possible to take this argument too far, as I argue here: Grant McCracken, "Who and What Is an Entrepreneur?" *Harvard Business Review Blog*, July 25, 2011, http://blogs.hbr.org/cs/2011/07/who_and_what_is_an_entrepreneu.html.

22. Jon Pareles, "That Blob of Multiplying Genres? It's Music," *New York Times*, February 23, 2003.

23. Matthew McKinnon, "Grime Wave: Grime Is the Sound Track of East London," *CBC.ca*, May 5, 2005, www.cbc.ca/arts/music/grimewave.html.

24. Kevin Flanagan, "Surreal 'Sunshine' Astounds," *The Flat Hat*, March 26, 2004, http://flathat.wm.edu/2004-03-26/story.php?type=4&aid=1" (accessed August 1, 2011).

25. David Kamp, *The United States of Arugula: How We Became a Gourmet Nation* (New York: Broadway Books, 2006), 331.

26. Ibid., 333.

27. Daniel Day-Lewis, quoted in Lynn Hirschberg, "The New Frontier's Man," *New York Times*, November 11, 2007, www.nytimes.com/2007/11/11 /magazine/11daylewis-t2.html?_r=1&ref=magazine&oref=slogin.

28. Kathy Griffin, talking about Barbara Walters in her stand-up routine *Allegedly*, www.youtube.com/watch?v=KuBfdxlmHF0, YouTube, June 29, 2009; Barbara Walters and Kathy Griffin, talking about Paris Hilton, *The View*, www.youtube.com/watch?v=kQfxghF1iGY.

29. Ibid.

30. Grant McCracken, "Kathy Griffin," *CultureBy: This Blog Sits at the Intersection of Anthropology and Economics*, June 7, 2007, http://cultureby.com/2007 /06/kathy_griffin.html.

31. Leora Kornfeld, "The Teletrickster's Way: Transcending the Rational and Reconstituting Media Discourse," *Trickster's Way* 1, no. 1 (2002), www.trinity.edu /org/tricksters/trixway/current/Vol%201/Vol%201_1/cornfeld.html. For more on the trickster theme, see K. L. Nichols, "Introduction to Native American Tricksters," Native American Trickster Tales Web site, n.d., http://members.cox.net/academia/coyote.html.

Chapter 6

1. Grant McCracken, "The Hammer Grammer (How to Make Culture)," *CultureBy: This Blog Sits at the Intersection of Anthropology and Economics*, August 31, 2009, http://cultureby.com/2009/08/the-hammer-grammer-how-to-make-culture.html); Grant McCracken, "The Secret Script at USA Networks (aka the 'Enmeshed Male')," *CultureBy: This Blog Sits at the Intersection of Anthropology and Economics*, February 5, 2010, http://cultureby.com/2010/02/the-secret-script-at-usa-networks-aka-the-enmeshed-male.html.

2. Grant McCracken, "Calling All CCOs: How Good Is Your Gut?" *CultureBy: This Blog Sits at the Intersection of Anthropology and Economics*, May 13, 2010, http://cultureby.com/2010/05/calling-all-ccos-how-good-is-your-gut.html; Grant McCracken, "The Good Guys," *CultureBy: This Blog Sits at the Intersection of Anthropology and Economics*, June 15, 2010, http://cultureby.com/2010/06/the-good-guys.html.

3. Kim Masters, "NBC Chairman Robert Greenblatt Shares His Plan to Rebuild the Network," *Hollywood Reporter*, June 15, 2011, www.hollywoodreporter .com/news/nbc-chairman-robert-greenblatt-shares-201962?.

4. Steve Neale, *Genre and Hollywood* (London: Routledge, 2000).

5. Roger Ebert, *Roger Ebert's Movie Yearbook 2009* (Kansas City, MO: Andrews McMeel Pub., 2008), 824.

6. Matt Mullenweg, "How 'The Fighter' Shot 35 Days [sic] Worth of Fight Scenes in Only Three Days," *Signal vs. Noise*, April 4, 2011, http://37signals.com /svn/posts/2840-how-the-fighter-shot-35-days-worth-of-fight-scenes-in-only-three-days. My thanks to Tim Sullivan for this reference.

7. See my discussion of the filmmaker Leslie Dektor in Grant McCracken, *Chief Culture Officer: How to Create a Living, Breathing Corporation* (New York: Basic Books, 2009), 79–82.

8. Grant McCracken, "Ida Blankenship R.I.P.," *CultureBy: This Blog Sits at the Intersection of Anthropology and Economics*, September 22, 2010, http://cultureby .com/2010/09/ida-blankenship-r-i-p.html.

9. Stephen L. Vaughn, ed., *Encyclopedia of American Journalism* (Boca Raton, FL: CRC Press, 2008), 286.

10. J. C., "N.B.: Den of Antiquity," *Times Literary Supplement*, October 23, 2009, 36.

11. Yes I Am Precious Web site, http://ycsiamprecious.com/.

12. Breakfast, "We Break Stuff, Quickly," Breakfast Web page, March 2010, http://breakfastny.com/2010/03/we-break-stuff-quickly/.

13. Gareth Kay, "Release Your Inner Salvador," *Brand New*, November 4, 2010, http://garethkay.typepad.com/brand_new/2010/11/release-your-inner-salvador.html.

14. For more on the ad in question, see *Wikipedia*, s.v., http://en.wikipedia.org /wiki/Gorilla_(advertisement), last modified November 5, 2011.

15. Linda Tischler, "Clan of the Caveman," *Fast Company*, June 1, 2007, 104, www.fastcompany.com/magazine/116/features-clan-of-the-caveman.html.

16. Steve Casimiro, "Hollywood Stands on Top of Kilimanjaro, Jimmy Chin Does Climb in Flipflops," *Adventure Journal*, January 12, 2010, www.adventure-journal.com/2010/01/hollywood-stands-on-top-of-kilimanjaro-jimmy-chin-does-climb-in-flipflops/.

17. Derek Thompson, "Burger King's Horrible, Creepy Ad Campaign Isn't Working," *The Atlantic*, June 22, 2009, www.theatlantic.com/business/archive /2009/06/burger-kings-horrible-creepy-ad-campaign-isnt-working/19870/.

18. For more on Stephen Gordon and Restoration Hardware, see Funding Universe, "Company Histories & Profiles: Restoration Hardware, Inc.," n.d., www.fundinguniverse.com/company-histories/Restoration-Hardware-Inc-Company-History.html.

19. B. Joseph Pine II and James H. Gilmore, *The Experience Economy: Work Is Theater & Every Business a Stage* (Boston: Harvard Business Press, 1999). For more on the Hershey's storefront, see Hershey's, "Hershey's Times Square," Hershey's

Web page, n.d., www.thehersheycompany.com/about-hershey/visit-hershey/retail-stores/times-square.aspx.

20. Grant McCracken, "The Artisanal Trend and 10 Things That Define It," *CultureBy: This Blog Sits at the Intersection of Anthropology and Economics*, November 9, 2006, http://cultureby.com/2006/11/the_artisanal_m.html; Michael Idov, "Bitter Brew: I Opened a Charming Neighborhood Coffee Shop; Then It Destroyed My Life," *Slate Magazine*, December 29, 2005, www.slate.com/id/2132576.

21. Jessica Gelt, "Kogi Korean BBQ, a Taco Truck Brought to You by Twitter," *Los Angeles Times*, February 11, 2009, www.latimes.com/features/food/la-fo-kogi11-2009feb11,0,159741.story.

22. "Virtual Grocery Store in South Korea Subway via Tesco Home Plus," TrendsHQ, n.d., http://trendshq.com/virtual-grocery-store-in-south-korea-subway-via-tesco-home-plus/.

23. Jonathan Miller, "Plays and Players," in *Nonverbal Communication*, ed. R. A. Hinde (Cambridge: Cambridge University Press, 1972).

24. I am paraphrasing here. For the full and graceful statement of the argument, see Henry Jenkins, *Convergence Culture: Where Old and New Media Collide*, rev. ed. (New York: New York University Press, 2008).

25. Lance Weiler, "Culture Hacker: A Storytelling Pandemic," *Filmmaker*, January 18, 2011, www.filmmakermagazine.com/news/2011/01/culture-hacker-a-storytelling-pandemic/; Lance Weiler, "Lance Weiler's Transmedia Project 'Pandemic 1.0' Premieres at Sundance (and Online)," *No Film School*, January 25, 2011, http://nofilmschool.com/2011/01/lance-weilers-transmedia-pandemic-1-0/.

26. For more on Plundr, see Area/Code, "Plundr," Area/Code Web page, n.d., http://areacodeinc.com/projects/plundr/.

27. Lev Grossman, "Writing the Magician King," *Fantasy Matters*, n.d., http://fantasy-matters.com/node/158.

28. Alissa Walker, "PieLab in Rural Alabama Serves Up Community, Understanding, and, Yes, Pie," *Fast Company*, June 19, 2009, www.fastcompany.com/blog/alissa-walker/designerati/project-ms-pielab-rural-alabama-serves-community-understanding-and-ye; Buy a Meter Web site, www.buyameter.org/.

29. Yofred Moik, "UNICEF Installs Dirty Water Vending Machine in Manhattan," PSFK Web page, July 16, 2010, www.psfk.com/2010/07/unicef-installs-dirty-water-vending-machine-in-manhattan.html. There are many uses for vending machines. See, for example, Will Wlizlo, "Vending Machines That Quit Cold Turkey," *Utne*, June 23, 2010, www.utne.com/Arts/Vending-Machines-that-Quit-Cold-Turkey.aspx.

30. Matthew Stillman, "When the Homeless Dream of Dragons," Stillman Says Web page, n.d., http://stillmansays.com/2011/03/when-homeless-dream-of-dragons/.

31. Dave Tait, "Innovation in Africa," *Design in Africa*, October 23, 2008, http://designinafrica.wordpress.com/2008/10/23/innovation-in-africa-tips/.

32. Jake Malooley, "How to Make a Pop-up Park," *Time Out Chicago*, June 21, 2011, http://timeoutchicago.com/things-to-do/this-week-in-chicago/14821919 /how-to-make-a-pop-up-park. For more on Noisivelvet, see Noisivelvet Web page, www.noisivelvet.com.

33. Lynette Rice, "Scott Caan: Fall TV's New Action Star," *Entertainment Weekly*, November 5, 2010, www.ew.com/ew/article/0,,20437665,00.html.

34. Peter Schjeldahl, "For Laughs: Things That Francis Alÿs Does," *The New Yorker*, May 23, 2011, 84.

35. For more on Elevator Repair Service and Shuffle, see www.elevator.org.

36. Natsumi Hayashi, "Yowayowa Camera Woman Diary," Web page, http://yowayowacamera.com/; Martin Bryant, "Japanese Girl's Incredible 'Levitation' Photos," *The Next Web*, August 12, 2011, http://thenextweb.com/shareables /2011/08/12/japanese-girls-incredible-levitation-photos/.

37. Advertisement for *Papers for the Suppression of Reality*, in *The Believer*, May 2011, back cover.

38. Maria Popov, "Kurt Vonnegut's Fictional Interviews with Luminaries," *Brain Pickings*, May 15, 2011, www.brainpickings.org/index.php/2011/05/11/god bless-you-dr-kevorkian/.

39. Sena Jeter Naslund, *Ahab's Wife: Or, The Star-Gazer: A Novel* (New York: Harper, 2009); Sandy Eisenberg Sasso, *Noah's Wife: The Story of Naamah* (Woodstock, VT: Jewish Lights Publishing, 2002).

40. Matt Haber, "The Summit Café: Coffeehouse and Tech Incubator," *BusinessWeek: Online Magazine*, February 11, 2011, www.businessweek.com /magazine/content/11_08/b4216076334973.htm.

41. Dave Eggers, "Dave Eggers' Wish: Once Upon a School," talk given at TED Conference, February 2008, Monterey, CA, www.ted.com/talks/dave_eggers makes_his_ted_prize_wish_once_upon_a_school.html.

42. John Deighton, "How Snapple Got Its Juice Back," *Harvard Business Review*, January 2002, 47–53; John Deighton, "Snapple," Case N9-599-126 (Boston: Harvard Business School, July 8, 1999), 1–17.

43. Adriana Gardella, "Irrational Design, a Start-Up, Shuns Venture Capital," *New York Times*, February 16, 2011, www.nytimes.com/2011/02/17/business /smallbusiness/17sbiz-irrational-design.html.

44. David Enrich and Paul Sonne, "Bicycle Mischief Targets Barclays," *Wall Street Journal*, September 18, 2010, http://online.wsj.com/article/SB10001424052748704 858304575498031387359768.html?KEYWORDS=barclays.

45. See Banksy's Web site at www.banksy.co.uk/.

46. This quote is from a postcard used to promote the Tempt1 Kickstarter page, www.kickstarter.com/projects/571943958/tempt1-and-eyewriter-art-by-eyes. For more on the Graffiti Research Lab, see *Wikipedia*, s.v. "Graffiti Research Lab," http://en.wikipedia.org/wiki/Graffiti_Research_Lab, last modified June 27, 2011. For more on the openFrameworks community, see *Wikipedia*, s.v. "openFrameworks," http://en.wikipedia.org/wiki/OpenFrameworks, last modified November 3, 2011.

Chapter 7

1. Thomas Stewart, "The Great Conundrum: You vs. the Team," *Fortune*, November 25, 1996, http://money.cnn.com/magazines/fortune/fortune_archive /1996/11/25/218717/index.htm.

2. Ruby Karelia, "I like pie," February 7, 2011, http://rubykarelia .blogspot.com/2011/02/i-like-pie.html.

3. For more on Scott Schuman and his projects, see *The Sartorialist* Web site, www.thesartorialist.blogspot.com/.

4. Brian Doherty, "The Visionary," *Reason Magazine*, September 10, 2010, http://reason.com/archives/2010/09/10/the-visionary.

5. Grant McCracken, *Flock and Flow: Predicting and Managing Change in a Dynamic Marketplace* (Bloomington: Indiana University Press, 2006).

6. *Wikipedia*, s.v. "Between Two Ferns with Zach Galifianakis," http://en .wikipedia.org/wiki/Between_Two_Ferns_with_Zach_Galifianakis, last modified November 3, 2011.

7. Maureen O'Connor, "Mel Gibson's Rants, Visualized," July 13, 2010, *Gawker.com*, http://gawker.com/5585971/mel-gibsons-rants-visualized.

8. Brian Raftery, "So, Tron Guy, Gem Sweater Lady, and the Firefox Walk into a Bar . . . ," *Wired Magazine*, June 23, 2008, www.wired.com/entertainment / theweb/magazine/16-07/mf_roflcon.

9. Drew Grant, "5 Pop Culture Moments That Could Have Used More Eric Stoltz," *Crushable*, October 13, 2010, http://crushable.com/entertainment/5-films-that-could-have-used-eric-stoltz/.

10. Dan Gurewitch, "Charlie Sheen vs. Ron Burgundy: Who Said It?" *College Humor*, March 1, 2011, www.collegehumor.com/article:1814021.

11. Jonathan Franzen, "Farther Away," *The New Yorker*, April 18, 2011, 80–94.

12. Noah Kalina, "Noah Takes a Photo of Himself Every Day for 6 Years," video, YouTube, uploaded August 27, 2006, www.youtube.com/watch?v= 6B26asyGKDo; Raftery, "Tron Guy, Gem Sweater Lady"; Mark Borden, "The New Influentials," *Fast Company*, October 25, 2010, www.fastcompany.com/magazine /150/the-new-influentials.html; Rob Walker, "When Funny Goes Viral," *New York Times*, July 16, 2010, www.nytimes.com/2010/07/18/magazine/18ROFL-t.html?

_r=2&pagewanted=all; Diana Kimball, "ROFLcon: Origins," *Diana Kimball: Regular Expressions Blog*, March 8, 2011, www.dianakimball.com/2011/03/roflcon-origins.html.

13. Raftery, "Tron Guy, Gem Sweater Lady."

14. "Greenspan, Entourage, Demolish Hotel Room," *The Onion*, February 17, 1999, http://origin.theonion.com/content/node/29329.

15. J. David Sapir and Jon Christopher Crocker, eds., *The Social Use of Metaphor: Essays on the Anthropology of Rhetoric* (Philadelphia: University of Pennsylvania Press, 1977).

16. For more on Bud Caddell, see Grant McCracken, *Chief Culture Officer* (New York: Basic Books, 2010).

17. Baylen Linnekin, "The Lobster Underground: Food Vendors vs. the State," *Reason Magazine*, April 2011, 48–53, http://reason.com/archives/2011/03/10/the-lobster-underground/singlepage.

18. Lee Schrager is the director of the New York City Wine and Food Festival (Sumathi Reddy, "Ruth Bourdain: A Delicious Mystery," *Wall Street Journal*, June 7, 2010, http://online.wsj.com/article/SB10001424052748704002104575290840191496332.html?KEYWORDS=bourdain).

19. This is perhaps what Oscar Wilde meant when he said, "Classicism is the subordination of the parts to the whole; decadence is the subordination of the whole to the parts" (J. Edward Chamberlin, *Ripe Was the Drowsy Hour: The Age of Oscar Wilde* [New York: Seabury Press,1977], 95).

20. Ellen Moers, *The Dandy: Brummell to Beerbohm* (New York: Viking, 1960), 26, 28; Susan Sontag, "Notes on Camp," in *Against Interpretation and Other Essays* (New York: Farrar, Straus and Giroux, 1966), 275–292; Martin Burgess Green, *Children of the Sun: A Narrative of "Decadence" in England after 1918* (New York: Basic Books, 1976); Joris-Karl Huysmans, *Against Nature* (New York: Penguin Books, 1971); Donna C. Stanton, *The Aristocrat as Art: A Study of the Honnête Homme and the Dandy in Seventeenth- and Nineteenth-Century French Literature* (New York: Columbia University Press, 1980).

21. Samuel Pepys, "The Dairy of Samuel Pepys," entry for May 13, 1665, www.pepysdiary.com/archive/1665/05/13/. See also the wonderful Web site created for Pepys's diary: Duncan Grey, "Samuel Pepys Diary," Duncan Grey Web page, 2002–2011, Cambridge, UK, www.pepys.info/.

22. Clive Thompson, "What If You Never Forgot Anything: How Microsoft's Gordon Bell Is Reengineering Human Memory," *Fast Company*, November 1, 2006, www.fastcompany.com/magazine/110/head-for-detail.html; *Wikipedia*, s.v. "Lifelog," http://en.wikipedia.org/wiki/Lifelog, last modified October 20, 2011; Keith Kleiner, "The Vicon Life Recorder: Lifelogging Takes Another Step Forward," *Singularity Hub*, October 28, 2009, http://singularityhub.com/tag/life-recording/.

23. For a superb piece of reconstruction, see Bill Kluver, *A Day with Picasso: Twenty-Four Photographs by Jean Cocteau* (Cambridge, MA: MIT Press, 1997).

24. McCracken, *Chief Culture Officer*, Paul Laster, "Daily Dose Pick: Vivian Maier," *Flavorwire*, February 17, 2011, http://flavorwire.com/152720/daily-dose-pick-vivian-maier.

25. *Wikipedia*, s.v. "Flâneur," http://en.wikipedia.org/wiki/Fl%C3%A2neur, last modified November 6, 2011.

26. Kate Fox, *Watching the English: The Hidden Rules of English Behaviour* (Boston: Nicholas Brealey Pub., 2008).

27. *Wikipedia*, s.v. "Z-Boys," http://en.wikipedia.org/wiki/Z-Boys, last modified October 24, 2011; Grant McCracken, "Square Inch Anthropology," *CultureBy: This Blog Sits at the Intersection of Anthropology and Economics*, December 17, 2010, http://cultureby.com/2010/12/square-inch-anthropology.html. I asked a blog reader to do a "square inch" on Steampunk (Grant McCracken, "Steam Punk: A Square Inch of Contemporary Culture by Carlen Lea Lesser," *CultureBy: This Blog Sits at the Intersection of Anthropology and Economics*, December 21, 2010, http://cultureby.com/2010/12/square-inch-anthropology.html). Thank you, Carlen.

28. Grant McCracken, "Making Culture, Categorizing Culture," *CultureBy: This Blog Sits at the Intersection of Anthropology and Economics*, January 10, 2011, http://cultureby.com/2011/01/making-culture-categorizing-culture.html.

29. Evon Zartman Vogt, *Modern Homesteaders: The Life of a Twentieth Century Frontier Community* (Cambridge, Mass.: Belknap Press of Harvard University Press, 1955); W. Lloyd Warner et al., *Yankee City*, abridged (New Haven, CT: Yale University Press, 1963); Grant McCracken, "Why Do American Parents Call Their Kids Buddy?" *CultureBy: This Blog Sits at the Intersection of Anthropology and Economics*, November 16, 2010, http://cultureby.com/2010/11/why-do-american-parents-call-their-kids-buddy.html; Gustavo Flaubert, *Dictionary of Accepted Ideas*, revised (New York: New Directions, 1968); Grant McCracken, "The Genius of Portlandia," *HBR Blog Network*, January 27, 2011, http://blogs.hbr.org/cs/2011/01/the_genius_of _ portlandia.html.

30. Tim Murphy, "Airport Gate Semiotics," *BusinessWeek*, January 5, 2011, 76–77, http://images.businessweek.com/slideshows/20110105/airport-semiotics/.

31. Mary Douglas, David L. Hull, and Nelson Goodman, *How Classification Works: Nelson Goodman Among the Social Sciences* (Edinburgh: Edinburgh University Press, 1993).

32. Grant McCracken, "Normal Bob, Extranormal Anthropologist," *CultureBy: This Blog Sits at the Intersection of Anthropology and Economics*, December 3, 2010, http://cultureby.com/2010/12/normal-bob-extranormal-anthropologist.html.

33. Grant McCracken, *Plenitude* (Toronto: Periph.: Fluide, 1997).

34. Arnold Mitchell, *Nine American Lifestyles: Who We Are and Where We're Going* (New York: Warner Books, 1984).

35. *Urban Dictionary*, s.v. "Woo girl," November 17, 2008, www.urbandictionary .com/define.php?term=woo+girl. See "Woo Girl" segment, *How I Met Your Mother*, CBS, on YouTube, www.youtube.com/watch?v=vodPodgWh8E&NR=1, uploaded December 29, 2010.

36. For more on the map by Meyerowitz and Kalman, see Rick Meyerowitz, "The New York City Sub Culinary Map," n.d., www.rickmeyerowitz.com /New%20subculinary.html. Robin Richards created an infographic of Microsoft's acquisitions and investments rendered in the form of the London subway system (Robin Richards, "Microsoft Acquisitions and Investments," October 11, 2010, Ripetungi Web page, http://ripetungi.com/microsoft-acquisitions-and-investments/).

37. Keith H. Basso, "'Stalking With Stories': Names, Places and Moral Narratives Among the Western Apache," in *Text, Play and Story: The Construction and Reconstruction of Self and Society* (Washington, DC: American Ethnological Society), 19–55; Roz Chast, *Theories of Everything: Selected, Collected, and Health-Inspected Cartoons, 1978–2006* (New York: Bloomsbury, 2006).

38. For technology to help you build maps, see the map builder at www.mapbuilder.net/. See also Bartlett Centre for Advanced Spatial Analysis, Web page, www.casa.ucl.ac.uk/software/gmapcreator.asp.

39. I hate this term. Grant McCracken, "Curator: Meme in Motion," *CultureBy: This Blog Sits at the Intersection of Anthropology and Economics*, March 28, 2008, http://cultureby.com/2008/03/curator-birth-o.html.

40. Maria Popova, "Brain Pickings: About," Brain Pickings Web page, n.d., www.brainpickings.org/index.php/about/.

41. Ronald S. Burt, *Brokerage and Closure: An Introduction to Social Capital* (New York: Oxford University Press, 2007); Mark Granovetter, "The Strength of Weak Ties: A Network Theory Revisited," *Sociological Theory* 1 (1983): 201–233.

42. John Stuart Mill, *The Principles of Political Economy* (Classics-Unbound, 2009), Kindle location 11639.

43. For more on Baskin's venture, see AmuseumGuides, "Curiously Entertaining Audio Tours," www.amuseumguides.com.

44. Jane McGonigal, *Reality Is Broken: Why Games Make Us Better and How They Can Change the World* (New York: Penguin Press, 2011).

45. "Walking Cinema: Murder on Beacon Hill," November 17, 2009, www.parkmanmurder.com/Parkman_Murder_Application.html. See also Rama, Crimson Bamboo, "Do You Hear Voices? The Giskin Anomaly Survey: Balboa Park," augmented-reality application for iPhone and other cell-phones, presented by the Balboa Park Online Collaborative, Balboa Park, San Diego, www.giskin.org.

46. For more on David Bausola's work, see "An API for Your Alter Egos," April 19, 2011, http://philterphactory.com/. For more on the amazing *You Are Listening* project, see "You Are Listening to Montréal," n.d., http://youarelistening.to/montreal.

47. For more on Mystery Science Theater 3000, see *Wikipedia*, s.v. "*Mystery Science Theater 3000*," http://en.wikipedia.org/wiki/Mystery_Science_Theater _3000, last modified November 4, 2011. Mapping on one feed on another creates interesting artifacts. Recently, pretty much by accident, I combined a song ("Your Ex-Lover Is Dead" from the album *Set Yourself on Fire*, by Stars) with a movie, *Nanny McPhee Returns*. (Combine the scene that starts at 6:30 with music that starts at the 30-second mark.) For some reason the combination works well.

48. David Kazzie, "So You Want to Write a Novel," video, YouTube, November 24, 2010, www.youtube.com/watch?v=c9fc-crEFDw; Ellen Gamerman, "Animation Nation," *Wall Street Journal*, February 11, 2011, http://online.wsj.com/article /SB10001424052748704858404576134203647487090.html?KEYWORDS=ellen+ gamerman.

49. For the clip in question, see "Hitler Reacts Clip with No Subtitles," video, YouTube, uploaded December 25, 2009, www.youtube.com/watch?v=W _hjicxtx80. See also *Wikipedia*, s.v. "Adolph Hitler in popular culture," http://en.wikipedia.org/wiki/Hitler_Reacts_(Internet_meme)#Hitler_as_internet _meme, last modified November 6, 2011; Robert Seizlak, "Hitler Reacts to News of the iPhone 4 Prototype Leak," Vimeo Web page, April 21, 2010, http://vimeo .com/11111267.

50. Chris Wild, "Retronautic Rest Home," *How to Be a Retronaut: If the Past Is a Foreign Country, This Is Your Passport*, December 1, 2010, www.howtobearetronaut .com/2010/12/retronautic-rest-home/.

51. Brian Doherty, "The Visionary," *Reason Magazine*, October 2010, http://reason.com/archives/2010/09/10/the-visionary.

52. For more on the Historical Consultancy, see Historisch Adviesbureau (Historical Consultancy) 30–45 home page, www.hab3045.nl/uk/index.htm.

53. Frank Reade was the fictional hero of nickel weeklies published in the nineteenth century. He created robots and flying vehicles. Guinan and Bennett have mocked-up photos, artifacts, and historical documents to make Reade appear real (Paul Guinan, "Frank Reade," n.d., www.bigredhair.com/frankreade/index.html). See also Paul Guinan and Anina Bennett, *Boilerplate: History's Mechanical Marvel* (New York: Abrams Image, 2009).

54. For examples of designer's inspiration boards, see the Flickr group dedicated to them: www.flickr.com/groups/inspirationboards/.

55. Kawasaki started at Apple and then made himself an arbiter of content online. He has more than 42,000 Facebook fans and 280,000 Twitter followers, and he runs news-aggregator site Alltop (Borden, "The New Influentials").

56. Grant McCracken, "How We Say Hello in New England," *CultureBy: This Blog Sits at the Intersection of Anthropology and Economics*, July 31, 2007, http://cultureby.com/2007/07/how-we-say-hell.html.

57. Brian Eno, Oblique Strategies: Over One Hundred Worthwhile Dilemmas, http://rtqe.net/ObliqueStrategies/; Greil Marcus, *The Dustbin of History* (Cambridge, MA: Harvard University Press, 1997); *Wikipedia*, s.v. "Judd Apatow." *Wikipedia*, http://en.wikipedia.org/wiki/Judd_Apatow, last modified November 11, 2011; "Noah Brier," *Fast Company*, n.d., http://www.fastcompany.com/user/noah-brier.

58. Once complete, weave your local history into projects that are capturing stories internationally. See the project at History Pin, "History Pin: Pin Your History to the World," home page, www.historypin.com.

Chapter 8

1. W. Chan Kim and Renée Mauborgne, *Blue Ocean Strategy: How to Create Uncontested Market Space and Make Competition Irrelevant* (Boston: Harvard Business School Press, 2005); Mark W. Johnson, *Seizing the White Space: Business Model Innovation for Growth and Renewal* (Boston: Harvard Business Press, 2010); Clayton M. Christensen, *The Innovator's Dilemma: When New Technologies Cause Great Firms to Fail* (Boston: Harvard Business School Press, 1997).

2. Darren Murph, "50-percent of Your iPhone Purchase to Pad Apple's Wallet?" *Engadget*, January 18, 2007, www.engadget.com/2007/01/18/50-percent-of-your-iphone-purchase-to-pad-apples-wallet/.

3. Giovanni Gavetti, "The New Psychology of Strategic Leadership," *Harvard Business Review*, July–August, 2011, 122; Joseph Nocera, "Charles Merrill: Main Street Broker," *Time*, December 7, 1998, www.time.com/time/magazine/article/0,9171,989774,00.html.

4. Howard Schultz and Joanne Gordon, *Onward: How Starbucks Fought for Its Life Without Losing Its Soul* (Emmaus, PA: Rodale Books, 2011), 13.

5. Erving Goffman, *The Presentation of Self in Everyday Life* (New York: Doubleday/Anchor Books, 1959).

6. Macworld Staff, "'I'll Kill Google,' Threatens Ballmer: Microsoft Bruiser on the Warpath," *PC Advisor*, September 5, 2005, www.pcadvisor.co.uk/news/desktop-pc/5030/ill-kill-google-threatens-ballmer/. For more on Microsoft's reputation, see Debora Spar, "Trusting Microsoft," chapter 6 in *Ruling the Waves* (New York: Harcourt, 2001).

7. Danielle Sacks, "Alex Bogusky Help Microsoft Beat Apple?" *Fast Company*, June 1, 2008, www.fastcompany.com/magazine/126/believe-it-or-not-hes-a-pc.html. Bogusky has since left Crispin Porter (Danielle Sacks, "Alex Bogusky Tells All: He

Left the World's Hottest Agency to Find His Soul," *Fast Company*, August 9, 2010, www.fastcompany.com/alex-bogusky-tells-all. "I am a PC"—the egalitarian response to Apple that Microsoft has settled on for its ongoing campaign—has worked well to lift PC users' perception of the brand as technologically and environmentally advanced (Brad Stone, "In Campaign Wars, Apple Still Has Microsoft's Number," *New York Times*, February 3, 2009, www.nytimes.com/2009/02/04/business/media/04adco.html).

   8. Lionel Trilling, *Beyond Culture: Essays on Literature and Learning* (New York: Penguin, 1965), preface.

   9. Grant McCracken, *Plenitude* (Toronto: Periph.: Fluide, 1997).

   10. Of course, advertising can merely change the terms of reference. It cannot change the history or the reputation of the brand. This is up to Microsoft. Bogusky had made a start. The rest was up to Microsoft. At least now it had movement, where before, it had stasis.

   11. John Deighton, "Dove: Evolution of a Brand," Case 9-508-047 (Boston: Harvard Business School, March 24, 2008), 3.

   12. As quoted in ibid., 4.

   13. Research results from Landor Associates, as reported in ibid., 7.

   14. For the scene with commentary, see "GoodFellas (1990): The Copacabana Shot," video, YouTube, uploaded February 11, 2010, www.youtube.com/watch?v=IBMKyNJvNV8.

   15. Donald Katz, *Just Do It: The Nike Spirit in the Corporate World* (Holbrook, MA: Adams Media Corporation, 1995).

   16. Andrew K. Sandoval-Strausz, *Hotel: An American History* (New Haven, CT: Yale University Press, 2008), 180, 181.

   17. Isadore Sharp, *Four Seasons: The Story of a Business Philosophy* (New York: Portfolio, 2009), Kindle edition, 98–99. All the Sharp quotes are from this book.

   18. Michael L. Tushman, Wendy K. Smith, and Andy Binns, "The Ambidextrous CEO," *Harvard Business Review*, June 2011, 75, http://hbr.org/2011/06/the-ambidextrous-ceo/ar/1.

   19. Theodore Levitt, "Marketing Myopia," *Harvard Business Review*, July–August 1960, 45–56.

   20. Tushman, Smith, and Binns, "The Ambidextrous CEO." For Roger Martin's version of this intellectual challenge, see Roger L. Martin, *Opposable Mind: Winning Through Integrative Thinking* (Boston: Harvard Business Press, 2009).

   21. According to these assumptions, (1) commuting to work digitally will become a reality in the next ten years, and (2) the world of higher education is about to be disintermediated as newspapers recently were. As a result, great chunks of rail and air traffic will be eliminated.

22. B. Joseph Pine II and James H. Gilmore, *The Experience Economy: Work Is Theater & Every Business a Stage* (Boston: Harvard Business Press, 1999).

23. Steven Martinez, "Soft Drink Companies Make Splash in Bottled Water," *Amber Waves*, June 7, 2007, www.ers.usda.gov/AmberWaves/June07/Findings /SoftDrink.htm.

24. Theodore Levitt, "Marketing Myopia," in *The Marketing Imagination* (New York: The Free Press, 1960; new, expanded ed., 1986), 154; Gregory Bateson, *Steps to an Ecology of Mind: Collected Essays in Anthropology, Psychiatry, Evolution, and Epistemology* (San Francisco: Chandler Publishing Company, 1972); Richard Foster and Sarah Kaplan, *Creative Destruction: Why Companies That Are Built to Last Underperform the Market—And How to Successfully Transform Them* (New York: Crown Business, 2011; reprint 2004).

25. Grant McCracken, "Assumption Hunters," *Research Memo: MIT Convergence Culture Consortium*, August 2011, www.convergenceculture.org/research/c3-assumptionhunters-full-public.pdf.

26. Roger L. Martin, "The Innovation Catalysts," *Harvard Business Review*, June 2011, 86, http://hbr.org/2011/06/the-innovation-catalysts/ar/1.

27. A. G. Lafley and Ram Charan, *The Game-Changer: How You Can Drive Revenue and Profit Growth with Innovation* (New York: Crown Business, 2008), 212.

28. *This Is Spinal Tap*, a "mockumentary" about the music business, is about a band so out of touch with current taste and preference the label has decided to pull the plug. The boys are too stupid to grasp what is happening to them, but the label is about to give them a lesson in what the world is like without industry support (Rob Reiner, director, *This Is Spinal Tap* [MGM Studios, 1984]).

29. John Deighton, "How Snapple Got Its Juice Back," *Harvard Business Review*, January 2002, 47–53.

30. This account of the IBM Alumni Network is from Kevin Clark, telephone interview with author, July 2011. My thanks for his willingness to share.

31. John Winsor, *Spark: Be More Innovative Through Co-Creation* (Evanston, IL: Agate, 2011); Jane McGonigal, *Reality Is Broken: Why Games Make Us Better and How They Can Change the World* (New York: Penguin Press, 2011); Lafley and Charan, *The Game-Changer*, 125.

32. Grant McCracken, *Flock and Flow: Predicting and Managing Change in a Dynamic Marketplace* (Bloomington: Indiana University Press, 2006).

33. Margery Corbett and R. W. Lightbown, *The Comely Frontispiece: The Emblematic Title-Page in England, 1550–1660* (London: Routledge and K. Paul, 1979).

Index

About the Author

Trained as an anthropologist at the University of Chicago, Grant McCracken has studied American culture and business for twenty-five years. He has been featured on the *Oprah Winfrey Show* and has worked for many corporate clients, including Coca-Cola, Intel, IBM, IKEA, Chrysler, Nike, and Kimberly-Clark. He started the Institute of Contemporary Culture at the Royal Ontario Museum and has taught anthropology at the University of Cambridge, ethnography at MIT, and marketing at the Harvard Business School. He is the author of several books, most recently, *Chief Culture Officer*.